Ethnographies of Archaeological Practice

Worlds of Archaeology Series

Series Editors:
Heather Burke (Flinders University, Australia) and
Alejandro Haber (Universidad Nacional de Catamarca, Argentina)

Sponsored by the World Archaeological Congress, this series of original edited and authored books seeks to access and promote contemporary developments in world archaeology. It will draw upon work conducted in both the Northern and Southern Hemispheres and open a channel for people from non-Western countries to challenge the existing preconceptions about the role of archaeology in contemporary societies. The series editors seek to consciously structure the series to facilitate dialogue and critical exchange both within and between countries. Volume editors and authors will be encouraged to structure their books so that they reflect the global diversity of archaeology, not only in content but also in style and format. The goal is to link a decolonized archaeology to current political issues, as well as to archaeological theory and practice in all parts of the world.

Ethnographies of Archaeological Practice: Cultural Encounters, Material Tranformations, edited by Matt Edgeworth

Ethnographies of Archaeological Practice

Cultural Encounters, Material Transformations

Edited By
Matt Edgeworth

A Division of
ROWMAN & LITTLEFIELD PUBLISHERS, INC.
Lanham • *New York* • *Toronto* • *Oxford*

AltaMira Press
A division of Rowman & Littlefield Publishers, Inc.
A wholly owned subsidiary of The Rowman & Littlefield Publishing Group, Inc.
4501 Forbes Boulevard, Suite 200
Lanham, MD 20706
www.altamirapress.com

PO Box 317
Oxford
OX2 9RU, UK

British Library Cataloguing in Publication Information Available

Library of Congress Cataloging-in-Publication Data

Ethnographies of archaeological practice : cultural encounters, material transformations /
   edited by Matt Edgeworth
      p. cm. — (Worlds of archaeology series)
   Includes bibliographical references and index.
   ISBN-10: 0-7591-0844-7 (cloth : alk. paper)
   ISBN-10: 0-7591-0845-5 (pbk. : alk. paper)
   ISBN-13: 978-0-7591-0844-8 (cloth : alk. paper)
   ISBN-13: 978-0-7591-0845-5 (pbk. : alk. paper)
   1. Archaeology—Methodology—Congresses. 2. Archaeology—Field work—
Congresses. 3. Ethnoarchaeology—Congresses. I. Edgeworth, Matt. II. Series.
CC75.O27 2006
930.101—dc22   2005031723

Printed in the United States of America

∞™ The paper used in this publication meets the minimum requirements of
American National Standard for Information Sciences—Permanence of Paper
for Printed Library Materials, ANSI/NISO Z39.48-1992.

Contents

Illustrations

Foreword

As the first volume to be published in the *Worlds of Archaeology* series, *Ethnographies of Archaeological Practice: Cultural Encounters, Material Transformations* represents far more than the vision of Matt Edgeworth and Denise Gomes for a challenging session at the Fifth World Archaeological Congress. It also embodies our vision for a new WAC series that foregrounds the many regional strengths of archaeology as it is practiced around the world. Why publish a new WAC series? Partly the intent is to expand WAC's publication sphere, but it is also our aim to develop the creative potential of WAC beyond the current streams of archaeological practice. The regional diversity regularly highlighted during World Archaeological Congresses is linked to different conceptual ways of imagining the past and the many social roles that are fulfilled by the practice of archaeology in different parts of the world. These social, cultural, and political kaleidoscopes are ultimately personal, producing ever-changing patterns of interaction and interpretation. As a result, not only are there many different geographical and political worlds but also as many different ways of imagining archaeology as there are cultural experiences of it. One of the main aims of the *Worlds of Archaeology* series is to communicate some of these lived experiences and, in so doing, to use the global diversity of archaeology to access new, disparate, and challenging ways of imagining the past.

Another key aim of the WOA series is to recognize that sometimes what claims to be "world archaeology" is really a remapping of colonial ties, interpreting material through the lens of British or American academic eyes, rather than through the eyes of the archaeologists from the countries being studied, who live directly with the social consequences of their work. A comparable process occurs within countries, as internal colonialism, when archaeologists return to the cities after conducting fieldwork in remote areas. Thus, one major focus of this series is the context within which knowledge is produced. The concern is not only who is speaking but also how the author's perspectives are constructed through colonialism and the author's particular cultural experience of being an archaeologist in that place at that time.

It is precisely this analysis of the cultural experience of being an archaeologist, and the consequent assumptions this entails about how the past should be imagined, that *Ethnographies of Archaeological Practice* centralizes. If archaeology is inadvertently caught in a process of looking at its own image as reflected in a mirror (a kind of self-referential, theoretical autism), then this cycle can only be broken by considering our own practice as a matter of ethnographic objectification. To see oneself as the Other brings several invisible issues to the fore, particularly the implicit practice of archaeological objectification. Archaeologists look at objects and talk about people. An ethnography of archaeological practice implies looking at archaeologists' material engagements and talking about archaeologists. It questions the taken-for-granted assumption of being able to speak for another through observing the materiality of their practice. At the same time, archaeology is seen as a lived-in practice (a cultural experience) rather than an untouchable academic expert knowledge. Social relationships, practicalities, and cultural rules become the framework for understanding, just as they do when we, as archaeologists, study other people. By stepping outside of a privileged panoramic view, *Ethnographies of Archaeological Practice* sets out to question the ways in which the discipline is constructed, and to what ends, and asks each one of us to consider not only what we do but also why and how we do it.

Our hope for the *Worlds of Archaeology* series is that it will facilitate dialogue and critical exchange both within and between countries. Royalties from all volumes are donated to the World Archaeological Congress to support the travel of people from economically disadvantaged communities or countries to WAC conferences. The pricing structure of this series has also been designed to enable a substantial quantity of the print run to be distributed free of charge to libraries and other public institutions in low-income countries.

Alejandro Haber and Heather Burke, series editors

Preface

What happens when the unusual step is taken of turning the ethnographic method back onto archaeological practice itself? That was the question asked at an all-day conference session at the Fifth World Archaeological Congress in Washington, D.C., in 2003, and is the central challenge posed by this book. The chapters collected here meet the challenge in different ways. Most are based on actual ethnographies carried out on archaeological sites, yet the reader should not expect to find a single answer or even a single question in these pages. Running through the book is a spirit of experimentation, the trying out of alternative approaches. In putting the book together, we intend to show the range and variety of work recently or currently being conducted and thereby to provoke readers into imagining how the archaeological activities they are familiar with might be interpreted from an ethnographic perspective, or even to experiment with taking up an ethnographic stance on archaeological practices themselves. For there is something about the idea of such work that goes right to the heart of the relationship between anthropology and archaeology, challenging basic tenets of both disciplines, unsettling conventional values, and inviting new perspectives on established practices.

To look at archaeological practice from the standpoint of an ethnographer can be to experience it afresh, to encounter it as if for the first time—literally to re-encounter it. There are many encounters and re-encounters with the cultural practices of archaeology represented here. Archaeologists, sociologists, and ethnographers cross the boundaries of their respective disciplines. They situate their papers in many different areas of intellectual discourse and come from places as far apart as Turkey and Australia, Belgium and Brazil, Sweden and

Mexico, the United Kingdom and the United States. They write on subjects as wide-ranging as heritage management practices on the Orkney Isles; a multinational research dig in Sicily; the finding of traces of previous archaeological interventions on a Late Paleolithic site in Germany; interactions between archaeologists and local Maya farmers in relation to ancient sites in the Yucatán Peninsula; the experience of excavating in Amazonia in the company of hired workers and a local shaman; and much more. Famous sites like Çatalhöyük and Leskernick make an appearance but so too do lesser-known sites and terrains in various parts of the world. Something of the sheer diversity of archaeological practice, its landscapes and social environments, is encountered.

The term "ethnography" as used in this book refers to the ethnographic method itself—the study of a way of life based on fieldwork (whether in the form of participant-observation, the conducting of questionnaires, or other ethnographic techniques). While not all methodologies employed by contributors conform to a strict definition of ethnography, there is a general emphasis throughout the book on ethnography as a way of *doing* rather than just as a way of *thinking*. In other texts, by way of contrast, the term is sometimes used to denote a loosely defined anthropological awareness of the social and historical contexts of archaeological writing, or to indicate a subtle reflexivity on the part of theoretical writers who might never venture out into the field to take up an ethnographic stance themselves. Or ethnography might be confused with the closely related field of the sociological analysis of the history of archaeological knowledge, often written from library research rather than actual fieldwork. In the context of this book, however, the conducting of ethnographic fieldwork is regarded as important precisely because it grounds theory in perceptual experience and material engagement with the world, bringing archaeology and anthropology into practical conjunction. To put it another way, it is only through the *being there* facilitated by the ethnographic method that the cultural encounters with archaeology referred to in the title take place.

As a corollary of this, the book has a strong primary focus on archaeological practice. "Practice" here means something more than just the writing or theorizing about the past; the term encompasses all aspects of the production of archaeological knowledge. It includes the digging and discovery of material remains, the management and conservation of sites, the interactions that take place between archaeologists and local communities or other groups, and so on. When viewed through an ethnographic lens, these are inevitably seen as social or cultural practices and are accorded no special privilege just because they could be described as part of scientific or academic activity. In that sense, at least, the disparate approaches of all seventeen authors in this book are united. Despite their different visions as to what ethnographies of archaeological practice are or what they should set out to achieve, the authors share the belief that archaeology—as a distinctive set of cultural activities—should not be exempt from ethnographic or sociological study.

The very act of ethnographizing archaeological practices is a significant one, for it symbolically places archaeology on a more equal footing with the multitude of other human cultures and cultural activities that have been objectified in this way. It acknowledges that, as cultural beings ourselves, we have something fundamental in common with all those peoples who are, have been, or will be the subject of anthropological and archaeological explanations, or from whose lives we have drawn analogies to shed light on past societies. And it implies a kind of reflexive equality or symmetry when it comes to the application of methods or theories about human behavior. If ethnography or ethnoarchaeology are appropriate methods through which to study material practices of the Dinka or the Inuit or the Mehinacu, it is equally appropriate to use such methods to study archaeological practices. If a general theory of material culture is relevant to the analysis of the material culture of exotic societies on the other side of the world—if it is truly general—it should be relevant to the analysis of our material culture too (the trowel, the context sheet, the camera, the computer). If Pierre Bourdieu's theory of practice is to be applied to an understanding of human action and material culture in the distant past, it should also be applied to our own present actions in constituting knowledge of that past. Indeed, that is the whole point of theory of practice. For, as Bourdieu himself would argue, how can we understand the object if we do not try to understand the principles of our relation to the object, which are partly constitutive of it?

Both ethnographic and archaeological methods embody ways of seeing that look outward and rarely inward, and which set up objectified fields that are not usually taken to include the very subjects who are doing the looking and the objectifying. The "ethnographic present" is one such field. In theory it includes all present peoples, cultures, societies, social groups, classes, communities (which might be constituted as the object of ethnographic study), but in practice it rarely includes anthropologists and archaeologists themselves.

This book is different. Here, the "ethnographic present" includes observers as well as observed, subjects as well as objects. The activities of archaeologists are seen to be as worthy of ethnographic study as those of any other cultural group. And this is not just because archaeologists are starting to use ethnography as a reflexive method; it is also because a few ethnographers, quite independently, are shifting the focus of their gaze onto archaeology. In the past, ethnographers practically never focused upon the presence of visiting archaeologists in ethnographic contexts, and certainly archaeologists never considered themselves as part of the social group or culture that an ethnographer might want to study. But a new generation of ethnographers—some of whom are represented in this book—is challenging these old practices and perceptions. They recognize that archaeology is interwoven with other social and cultural systems—that it is increasingly a constitutive part of the politics, economics, and identities of peoples in even the most exotic and far-flung places of the world, especially in areas where archaeological sites and remains are prominent parts of local landscapes. In such places, these ethnographers are turning their attention to the cultural exchanges that take place between local communities and archaeologists. They see these exchanges not only as key intersections in the social transformation of local communities but also as critical conjunctions in the production of archaeological knowledge. There is a dialectic taking place—a clashing and a merging of cultures. No wonder ethnographers are beginning to find such intersections of great interest.

How is it, we might ask, that archaeology was excluded (or excluded itself) from ethnographic observation for so long? Why did the range and scope of ethnography not extend so far as to encompass the work of archaeologists, even when they were working in the midst of indigenous peoples who were the object of the ethnographic gaze? The answer must be, in part, that archaeologists and anthropologists—experts in the analysis of forms of cultural production—have not always fully acknowledged or appreciated the fact that their own knowledge is itself culturally produced. There has always been an implicit assumption that our own mode of production and worldview is somehow of a different order and therefore not subject to the same forms of sociocultural explanations as other modes of production and worldviews. To put it in a nutshell: we could explain other cultures but not our own culture of explanation. The privileged viewpoint of the observer over the observed is maintained precisely through looking outward at some cultural Other—whether back through time into the past or across distances in space—rarely or never turning that outward-looking gaze back onto itself.

Ethnographies of archaeology presented here go some way toward changing that. In this sense, the chapters that follow are deeply subversive. The very fact that they focus on archaeological practice at all subverts ideas of the relationship between the explainers and the explained, and challenges the implicit assumption of the privileged standpoint of the observer over the observed. It blurs the boundary between subject and object. As you will discover, the observer can become the observed (and vice versa), the explainer can become the explained (and vice versa), the subject can become the object (and vice versa), and so on.

Bringing ethnographic perspectives back to bear on archaeological practice is a maneuver that has the power to surprise and discomfort. It turns our usual way of looking at the world on its head. The focus might still be on material culture but on our own as well as on that of some distant Other. The effect of twisting the conventional outward-looking gaze back toward familiar practices, and onto mundane objects that are rarely focused upon as things in themselves, is the very opposite of culture shock. For it leads to encounters with the familiar *as if* it were strange and exotic, rather than straightforward encounters with the strange. Such an approach might seem banal, even anti–common sense, if one does not appreciate the levels of irony involved. From the point of view of an archaeologist, it can be difficult to believe that there are cultural realms to be investigated right here in front of our eyes, in our very actions or words, or in the movements of the trowel. Or that the everyday archaeological routines and procedures that seem so ordinary to us might seem truly extraordinary if viewed from another standpoint. Yet the cultural processes of the production of archaeological knowledge by archaeologists are potentially of as much interest to ethnographers as witchcraft practices among the Azande or gift exchange systems that operated on Pacific islands over half a century ago. The seemingly impenetrable boundary of our own unquestioned assumptions and taken-for-granted expertise—even the commonsense attitude that protests against being constituted as the object of the ethnographic gaze—could perhaps be described as the new frontier of ethnographic and archaeological knowledge.

This book is all about crossing boundaries, pushing back frontiers, and extending the scope of the archaeological/anthropological imagination into hitherto unexplored or unreflected-upon domains of human experience. Papers collected here are initial forays into areas that are still hedged about by taboos, still resistant to incursions. As such, they do not in any sense represent a complete understanding of the potential field of study. Far from mapping out a territory the extent and shape of which is already known, they reveal the existence of vast continents that await further exploration and the potential for a multitude of hitherto unimagined re-encounters with archaeology. Although they do not go quite so far as to present an ethnography of archaeological practice carried out by an indigenous people themselves—with all the implications this would have for transformation of the ethnographic method—the possibility is nevertheless hinted at. There are many such possibilities, not all of which are foreseen here. For this is very much a field still forming, as yet unaware of its own boundaries. Indeed, insofar as it can be defined as a "field" at all, it is in the process of assembling and defining itself. And in this incipient state it is still experimenting with stances, perspectives, and forms of expression.

There will be those who argue that archaeologists should fix their attention on the past, not on the practices of studying the past in the present (as if it is possible to separate these two terms), and that anthropologists should focus their attention on cultures other than their own. They will insist that archaeological evidence should be viewed as a material reflection of past cultural activities, not at the same time a material reflection of the cultural activities of archaeological practice itself. They will say that ethnography should consist of an encounter with the Other, not at the same time a re-encounter with ourselves. There will be resistance to the inclusion of the activities of archaeologists and ethnographers within the objectified field we call the "ethnographic present." But this book stands by the belief that a more holistic archaeology and a more balanced anthropology must seek to gain knowledge not just of the cultural practices of others, but also of the cultural practices by means of which our knowledge of these cultural others is produced and reproduced. Strange though it may seem, the archaeological practices described here are all aspects of the objective pasts that, as archaeologists, we seek to discover and explain. Through opening up archaeological practices to ethnographic observation, the aim is to transform the way that archaeologists—and ethnographers—view their world and their role within it.

Matt Edgeworth

Acknowledgments

The book is based on an all-day session held at the Fifth World Archaeology Congress in Washington, D.C., in 2003, entitled "Ethnography of Archaeology." The session was coconvened by Denise Maria Cavalcante Gomes and me from an original suggestion by Joan Gero, who organized the congress as a whole. Various parts of the session were chaired by Robert Layton, Cornelius Holtorf, Denise, and me, and there was much lively debate between members of the panel and the audience, some of whom had already conducted ethnographies of archaeological practice themselves or have since gone on to carry out such work. It was the first time that ethnographers of archaeological practice working in different parts of the world had come together to discuss common themes and methodological issues.

Thanks to all those who took part in the session, as well as the many who have contributed to the project since. All papers have been radically revised and several additional authors invited to write further chapters for the book, which has evolved far beyond the parameters of the originating session. The support and advice of the series editors Heather Burke and Alejandro Haber have been invaluable. Adding further to the strong South American influence in shaping this volume, the detailed comments from Dánae Fiore led to many improvements in content and encouraged greater consideration of methodological issues. Another (anonymous) reviewer gave very helpful comments on the structure of the book as a whole. Claire Smith, Mitch Allen, Marian Haggard, Erik Hanson, and Sarah Walker are just some of those who have helped the book on its way to publication. Special thanks are also due to Joan Gero, Denise Gomes, Robert Layton, and Cornelius Holtorf for their encouragement at critical points in the early development of the book, and to Simon Edgeworth of Proper Websites for finding solutions to every problem encountered on the computer. In the long-standing tradition of the World Archaeological Congress publications, authors have donated all royalties from the sale of this volume to enable scholars from economically disadvantaged countries to travel to future WAC conferences.

The cover depicts an enigmatic stone carving of Celtic origin that stands on the Isle of Boa in Lough Erne, Co Fermanagh, Northern Ireland. This is the 'January God' of Seamus Heaney's poem of that name. Like the Roman door-god, Janus, the figure has two faces. One looks forward, the other looks back. At once subject and object, the sculpture is taken here to symbolize the need for our outward-looking focus on other cultures to be counter-balanced by a more reflexive inward-looking glance at our own culture of knowledge production. The photograph was taken by Jon Sullivan of PDPhoto.org.

1

Multiple Origins, Development, and Potential of Ethnographies of Archaeology

Matt Edgeworth

In order to set the scene for the chapters that follow, this chapter explores the multiple origins and development of ethnographies of archaeology up to now. Where do ethnographic perspectives on archaeological practice originate? Do the roots of these ways of seeing lie in anthropology as well as archaeology? How far back can the idea for this kind of study be traced? Can ethnographies of archaeology be described as just one of a range of reflexive methods used by postprocessual archaeologists? Or, do they amount to something more than that, a set of methods and perspectives that can serve other schools of thought and be applied to areas of archaeological practice outside of postprocessualism? How wide a range of approaches is currently in use? What problems are encountered and what common themes emerge? Only when we have considered these questions will it be possible to get some idea of the potential and future directions of this innovative mode of inquiry.

MULTIPLE ORIGINS OF ETHNOGRAPHIES OF ARCHAEOLOGY

The field of research was prefigured exactly fifty years ago in a small paper by American anthropologist Louis Dupree. He noted that by hiring workmen the archaeologist sets up an "artificial small group." Such a group includes both archaeologists and locally hired labor. Though artificially created, it becomes in time a "natural group" in the sense that—through its members' working together—it builds up "its own set of rules, its own internal equilibrium, and its own structure" (Dupree 1955, 271). It is also temporary insofar as it breaks up

once the archaeological project is over. Dupree clearly saw such groups as being worthy of ethnographic study. He envisaged that archaeologists should on
occasion take on a "dual role as technician and human scientist." And he was
not just talking about large excavation sites in Afghanistan or the Middle East—
an extension of a colonial anthropology. As he put it, "Why not make an inter-
actional study in the Jura Mountains of France or the Bann River Valley of Ireland? Or among Indians or other Americans in the United States?" (271).
Although Dupree never put these ideas into practice, artificial small groups or
communities of archaeologists would later be the explicit focus of ethnographic
study at Leskernick and other sites.

Dupree's suggestion, on the one hand, that archaeologists could take on the
role of anthropological observers and, on the other hand, that teams of archaeologists could be constituted as the object of ethnographic observation, immediately brings to the fore an important methodological problem. If (as I understand it) the site director is intended to be the anthropological observer of the
archaeological team, who observes the actions of the director? No study of the
social and political dynamics of the group would be complete without taking
the role of its leader into account. Is the director meant to include himself or
herself in the study, reflexively as it were, or to retain the role of a detached observer? We might call this, then, a problem of reflexivity. It is a problem that
reappears in one form or another, whoever the ethnographer is, in any ethnography of archaeology.

Perhaps the first time a sociological or ethnographic perspective was actually
taken up on archaeological practice was in 1967, when Ove Wall, Anita Christiansson, and Helena Wall carried out a sociometric study of cooperation in an
archaeological field team on an excavation in Sweden (Wall 1968, summarized
in Christiansson and Knutson 1989).[1] The project was initiated by site director
Hans Christiansson. In this case, then, the problem of reflexivity was put to one
side by delegating the observational work to others, thereby allowing the director to be included in the scope of the study. Issues addressed during fieldwork included the influence of different educational backgrounds of team
members on cooperation within the group, the relationship between the excavation team and its leader, and the interaction between groups working on different parts of the site.

In the 1970s and early 1980s the predominance of New Archaeology and emphasis on scientific objectivity may have discouraged further attempts. The only
paper to raise the possibility of an ethnoscience of archaeology was a light-
hearted and tongue-in-cheek portrayal of the archaeological community—as it
might appear from an ethnographic perspective—in "The Secret Notebook" by
Mary Sellars (1973). Kent Flannery's (1982) "Golden Marshalltown" paper was
similarly tongue in cheek. More parable than ethnography, it nevertheless con-
tained within it the notion that a kind of stepping back to look at the social activities of archaeologists might yield useful insights on the discipline of archaeology.

The late 1980s was a time when processualist and postprocessualist schools were coming into conflict in archaeological theory. Important work was being carried out in the new field of social study of scientific knowledge (Latour and Woolgar 1979; Knorr-Cetina 1981; Lynch 1985; Woolgar 1988). In social anthropology, experimental forms of ethnography were encouraged (Marcus and Fischer 1986), and Bourdieu's "theory of practice" was beginning to exert its influence (Bourdieu 1977, 1988).

It was in this theoretical context that, in the winter of 1989–1990, I carried out an ethnography of the excavation of a Bronze Age ring-ditch cemetery in the east of England (Edgeworth 1991, 2003). Although already a competent and experienced archaeologist, I spent ten weeks on the dig in the alternative guise of an ethnographer or participant-observer.

My fieldwork focused on the practical transactions between archaeologists and unfolding material remains, in which I observed two interlinked processes taking place. First, material patterns were emerging from the ground to be worked, shaped, interpreted, and transformed into data by archaeologists. Second, in the same everyday events of excavation, archaeologists were honing their digging skills against the resistance offered by that unfolding evidence. Crucially, it was not just physical skills that were being honed, but cognitive skills as well, both being part of the embodied expertise of excavators and bound up in the practical processes in which they were engaged (see Edgeworth 1990 for a discussion of the role of practical analogies in archaeological interpretation out in the field). Of especial interest to me was the emergence of surprising, unexpected, contradictory, or difficult evidence, which rarely appeared in fully fledged form all at once but rather unfolded over time as it was being worked. Existing archaeological knowledge was being applied to shape and make sense of the material evidence at the same time as the material evidence was reshaping the knowledge that was being applied. Such two-way transactions, mediated socially and through the use of tools, were rarely discussed in conventional accounts of excavation and were mostly written out of excavation reports. I called these transactions, where theory was effectively grounded in practice, "acts of discovery" (Edgeworth 1991, 2003).

The idea of ethnography of archaeology was emerging independently in other parts of the world at more or less the same time. In 1992–1993, Blythe Roveland employed a very different approach when she embarked upon work as leader of the excavation of a Late Paleolithic site at Pennworthmoor 1 in Germany (Roveland 2000). Unlike many other ethnographers of archaeology who later came in as relative outsiders, Roveland conducted her work as a situated inside observer, fully involved in running the site. She therefore had to address some of the difficulties entailed in being an ethnographer of one's own practices. She also pioneered the keeping of diaries by excavators as a reflexive excavation technique, which was later used at sites like Çatalhöyük and Leskernick. Her re-encounter with archaeology consisted in part of an increasing awareness of the material traces of previous (and present) archaeological activity as forms of material evidence in their own right. Her view of the archaeological record encompasses "not only the material remains of past societies but also successive interventions by archaeologists," including her own. In chapter 5 of this volume, Roveland summarizes the results of that important research project.

Also in 1992, the feminist archaeologist Joan Gero and the linguistic anthropologist Charles Goodwin carried out ethnographies of excavation at the site of Arroyo Seco 2, Argentina. While Gero's work has subsequently become well known and is cited in almost every discussion of postprocessual or gender archaeology, Goodwin's research (Goodwin 1994, 2000, 2002, 2003) is hardly cited at all in archaeological texts—though it is well known in other fields. A good example of his work is his seminal paper, "Professional Vision" (1994), which compares the work of archaeologists outlining a feature with lawyers highlighting evidence in a U.S. court of law. Based partly on ethnographies of excavation at various field schools in North and South America, his work addresses issues of social perception and action that—though wider than the traditional concerns of archaeology—draw insights from his experience of the materiality of excavation to shed light on other areas of professional work. As Goodwin puts it in chapter 4 of this volume, "My encounter with archaeology . . . led me to see that in my own research I had drawn an invisible analytic boundary at the skin of the speaking, embodied actors I was investigating, so that material structure in the environment was effectively ignored." As a result, he accords a significant role to material artifacts (alongside language, gesture, etc.) in his theories of human action. Chapter 4 in this volume provides a much-needed introduction to Goodwin's work for an archaeological audience.

A focus on the transmission and acquisition of craft skills or embodied expertise is central not only to Goodwin's work but also to that of other ethnographers of archaeology. Fieldwork carried out by the archaeologist David Van Reybrouck and the sociologist Dirk Jacobs at an archaeological field school near the Dutch town of Oss-Ussen in 1996 provides a good example. Their dual approach, juxtaposing the perspectives of a novice on the one hand and an experienced practitioner on the other, is both novel and effective. It yields important insights into the nature of practical competence and skill. As the authors explain in chapter 3, "Competence is not something which is given, but which accrues during research—very much like facts and reality." They go on to develop a sophisticated argument in which social and natural identities, far from being distinct, are mutually constitutive of each other.

If readers are looking for an easy and nonambiguous definition of "natural," they will not find one in this book. Archaeologists out in the field might use the term to denote all those things that are not the product of human action in the past, such as river-borne layers or glacial deposits. In the context of this book, however, the term means something quite different. It might refer, for example, to all those things that are not the product or instrument of the cultural activities of archaeologists in the present day. On these criteria, Paleolithic hand axes still undiscovered in the ground can be called natural, whereas a section cut by archaeologists through solid clay can not. However, a paradox of archaeological practice is that its natural object (the material remains "out there" that, at least up to the moment of discovery, exist quite independently of archaeological practice) consists in part of the products and outcomes and traces of past cultural activities. It is a further paradox that, as Roveland shows, some of these cultural traces are the result of previous archaeological interventions, including those of the very recent past (such as the trowel scrape performed only a moment ago). And, of course, it is a paradox of all science that in the very act of apprehending its natural object, that object is transformed into a cultural entity—an artifact of science itself. Thus we cannot uncover an ancient feature such as a pit or posthole without working and shaping it with our own tools, thereby making it a product of our own cultural activity as well as a product of cultural activity in the past. Material culture of past societies, through being appropriated in the very act of discovery, inevitably becomes a part of our material culture too.

The fact that artifacts and features discovered in excavation are double artifacts in this sense, at least partially fashioned by archaeologists in the present day, comes across very clearly in Joan Gero's ethnographic study of the excavation at Arroyo Seco in Argentina. She observed that male archaeologists tended to draw feature outlines much more confidently and clearly than women. In a famous example, she noted that one male made larger pedestals of soil for artifacts to stand on than female coworkers, drawing the attention of the site director more easily. She concluded that gender inequalities are to be found not only in social relationships and cultural interactions but also in the actual production of archaeological knowledge—even finding material expression in the form of data produced (Gero 1996).

An interesting feature of Gero's ethnography is that it prompted feedback from the excavation team who were the object of study. Gustavo Politis, the site director at Arroyo Seco, was generally positive about being constituted as Other by Gero and Goodwin, recommending the experience to all archaeologists. However, he suggested that Gero's interpretations of gender inequalities in excavation procedures were themselves inevitably conditioned by the assumptions and expectations of the ethnographer, who after all was coming to the work from a background in feminist archaeology. He went on to argue that the high profile of Gero's article was itself a reflection of power structures within the global structure of archaeology, specifically the dominance of European and North American discourse over voices from South America and other parts of the world (Politis 2001).

This exchange illustrates a major difference between ethnographies of archaeology and other more conventional kinds of ethnography. The latter might be described as one-way characterizations of a group of people by another group of people. In this case, however, some of the archaeologists who were the objects or subjects of the ethnographic investigation live and work in the same academic structures, broadly speaking, as the ethnographers themselves. Published results become a part of the very processes of the production of knowledge that they are about, open to be read by those who have been ethno-graphized. Within the various constraints identified by Politis, there is the very real possibility that interpretations made by the ethnographer will be challenged by the interpreted.

This not only brings about certain problems for the ethnographer in how to represent archaeologists in fieldwork reports (a major methodological consideration for most of the authors in this book), but it also raises the possibility of something approaching true, as opposed to contrived, reflexivity. There is the potential for a dialectical interaction to develop between observer and observed, in which the outward-looking ethnographic gaze is counterposed and reflected back onto the ethnographic study itself. Through such encounters and re-encounters a more holistic view of archaeological practice and its wider context emerges.

There is, of course, no sense in which ethnography provides a privileged vantage point from which the production of knowledge by archaeologists can be put into question without questioning how ethnographic knowledge of those processes is produced. Findings of ethnographies of archaeological practice, much like those of archaeology itself, are contingent (shaped to some degree by the social and historical conditions of their production). Thus this book is itself inevitably an expression of the global power structures and imbalances that Politis calls attention to. The greater number of English and American voices in the book relative to those from other parts of the world perhaps gives an erroneous impression of the formation of key ideas in dominant English-speaking countries at the "center" of theoretical discourse, only added to later by those from "peripheral" non-English-speaking countries. The reality, however, is almost certainly that early ethnographies of archaeological practice have been conducted in many of these nations, probably about the same time as the other pioneer works identified in this chapter (see, for example, Haber and Scribano 1993; Pizarro et al. 1995, based on project work carried out in 1991–1992 and only recently drawn to my attention). There must be further ethnographies of archaeological practice written in languages other than English; these are not included in the present narrative because they are inaccessible to me or not widely published (though I have done my best to track them down). It follows that there are other possible narratives that could be written on the origins and early development of the subject than the one put forward here.

ETHNOGRAPHIES OF ARCHAEOLOGY AND POSTPROCESSUAL METHOD

The use of ethnographies of archaeology as reflexive method, or set of methods, was taken up by postprocessualists as part of their general movement away from text and toward practice. Of the three most prominent proponents of postprocessualism, it is significant that Ian Hodder (at Çatalhöyük), Chris

Tilley (at Leskernick), and Michael Shanks (at Monte Polizzo) all integrated ethnographies into their excavation programs.

Many ethnographies of archaeological practice therefore have a strong post-processualist flavor. Anthropologist Carolyn Hamilton was invited by Hodder to carry out an ethnographic study of the construction of knowledge at Çatal-höyük in 1996, with a view to developing more reflexive excavation methodologies. Her "Faultlines" paper examines the structural breaks and tensions that can arise in the practices of excavation and recording—for example, between diggers and specialists. She deliberately engaged the archaeologists in discussions about their work and her reflections on it, thereby feeding the results of her research back into the developing excavation strategy, so that her work helped to shape the very practices she was documenting (Hamilton 2000).

Also at Çatalhöyük, Nessa Leibhammer studied visual conventions and representations that archaeologists use on-site in recording material evidence. In noting the great importance of images, which come to stand for and replace original objects and contexts encountered in excavation, she experimented with producing artistic visual representations alongside more conventional plans and sections (Leibhammer 2000). Two important papers by David Shankland examine the impact of the archaeological project on local communities at the nearby village of Küçükköy (Shankland 1997, 2000). Developing this theme, Turkish anthropologist Ayfer Bartu worked with the many different groups involved in the Çatalhöyük project, from tourists to New Age goddess worshippers to government officials, as well as local people and archaeologists themselves. Bartu's approach is interlinked with the work of postmodernist writers on multisited ethnography (Marcus 1995). A major insight here is that the excavation site itself can be seen as only one of multiple sites (overlapping and occupying the same space) at Çatalhöyük, all of which are involved in the construction of knowledge, but each of which has different cultural meanings for different social groups. There is also the emergence of multiple sites of knowledge production outside of the excavation site. All these sites are understood to be linked together at the intersection of local and global processes (Bartu 2000). Another Turkish anthropologist, Oğuz Erdur, has tried to "ethnographically ground" philosophical questions in archaeological practice, exploring from the perspective of the ethnographic stranger how archaeologists find meaning in the practice of finding meaning in the past (Erdur 2003a, 2003b).

In assembling this book, authors were encouraged to be daring and to take risks in developing their own versions of ethnography of archaeology, even if this meant breaking with traditional forms of academic writing. Indeed, one of the stated aims of the new Worlds of Archaeology series, of which this book is a part, is to encourage the development of new and unconventional literary styles that move beyond the straitjacket of hegemonic discourse. In chapter 9 of this volume, Erdur presents an innovative and experimental ethnographic narrative that does exactly that. It describes, in the stifling heat inside an excavation tent, the experience of ontological doubt that besets most ethnographers but is rarely reported upon.

By fictionalizing his narrative, and by giving "Indian" names to real archaeologists, Erdur attempts to strip the archaeologists of the power of their scientific presence and to problematize the uneven power relations between the observer and the observed. Archaeologists are portrayed as exotic members of a tribe of knowledge seekers, whose strange activities are observed by a native anthropologist. The paradox is that Erdur, as a kind of stranger-at-home, is himself part of the academic establishment, and his relation to both the diggers and locals he observes is full of ambiguities. This story of a day in the life of Everybody-Knows-Land is an ironic critique of a multinational excavation project, as well as a critical reflection on the nature of ethnographies of archaeological practice as a mode of study.

Erdur's experimental narrative style and its extreme irony will either enthrall or antagonize the reader. Any attempt to write something so radically different from the norm runs the risk that it will be dismissed out of hand because it is so unconventional. Yet at the same time it challenges us to break out of the conventions of traditional ethnographic reporting and its constructions of objective reality.

Other recent work at Çatalhöyük, brief accounts of which are available on the Internet, includes an ethnographic account of reflexivity in practice by Kathryn Rountree (2003) and an ethnographic study by Jackie Zak of collaboration between archaeologists and conservators (2004).

Another well-known archaeological site where the directors were keen to experiment with ethnographic perspectives as part of reflexive excavation methodologies was Leskernick on Bodmin Moor, UK (Bender et al. 1997). The principal focus of ethnographies here was the so-called artificial community of academics and professional archaeologists (echoing Dupree's concept of the artificial small group already discussed). Project sociologists Tony Williams and Mike Wilmore studied the artificial community in the context of the landscape within which the excavation took place, looking in particular at the many-layered perceptions of that landscape (Williams 1999, Wilmore 2001).

In chapter 10 Wilmore widens out the notion of landscape to include broader structures of class and power within which archaeologists work. As he puts it, "Archaeology is a social field structured through the exchange of various species of capital, at once economic, cultural and educational . . . and this means that differences between participants cannot be assigned only to 'beliefs, interests, or lifestyles.' The objective circumstances within which archaeologists live and work must be taken into account. Class may not be relevant to our understanding of Bronze Age society, but it is a vital component in our understanding of what occurs during archaeological research in the present day."

Ethnographic perspectives have also been developed in the context of postprocessual methodologies at the site of Monte Polizzo in western Sicily. Ashish Avikunthak demonstrated the great potential of video for this kind of research in a film that juxtaposes scenes from the excavation with old film footage (discovered in a roadside junkyard) of ceremonies and rituals of the middle-class India of the 1970s (Avikunthak 2001). His postmodernist style contrasts markedly with the more pragmatic use of video footage as an ethnographic recording technique by Goodwin, as outlined in chapter 4.

Cornelius Holtorf wrote an innovative and humorous paper about the life history of a potsherd found at Monte Polizzo, taking the moment of discovery as the beginning of its life and tracking it through various postexcavation procedures (Holtorf 2002). The life-histories approach can be applied to archaeological sites as well as objects. In terms of this approach, the life of the site can be taken to start when the archaeologists first arrive on the scene or at the moment the first spade cuts into the turf. Alternatively the archaeological activity can be seen as simply the latest phase in the history or life of the site. Either way it makes sense for there to be an ethnographer there to record this activity, hence Rachel Giraudo's work on the life history of the site at Monte da Igreja in Portugal (Giraudo 2002).

In chapter 7 Holtorf asks "what kind of experience project members have on an archaeological excavation project . . . what it means to participate in an archaeological project from the participants' point of view, and what it is they are actually learning during an excavation." As Holtorf points out, such questions are especially important when one considers that most multinational excavations are designed to facilitate student training. The author goes on to argue that training excavations like Monte Polizzo "are not only about acquiring professional skills and experience but also about learning a professional culture" and that transmission of this culture "occurs on excursions and beach visits as much as during working hours." In exploring the professional culture of archaeology in this wider sense, he examines both the stereotypes and the realities of "archaeology as adventure."

In these ways Holtorf effectively experiments with alternative strategies for conducting multisited ethnographies of archaeological practice (cf. Marcus 1995). In his paper on the life of the potsherd he "follows the thing" through multiple contexts and transformations, while in the latter part of chapter 7 he "follows the people," even when their various adventures and excursions take them away from what would normally be considered the archaeological "site."

A FOCUS ON THE MATERIAL CULTURE OF ARCHAEOLOGY

At both Çatalhöyük and Leskernick the project leaders chose to invite ethnographers in rather than to take on the role themselves. We might say that their reencounters with archaeological practice were negotiated by and mediated through these researchers. This is understandable, given the nature of the job of site director. All the same, it is interesting to speculate what kind of ethnography Chris Tilley, who wrote *An Ethnography of the Neolithic*, would have

written of the dig at Leskernick. Or to imagine what kind of ethnoarchaeological study might be conducted by Ian Hodder, who wrote *Symbols in Action*,
among all the material equipment and paraphernalia at Çatalhöyük. Would the
methods and techniques used to study patterns of decoration on pots in an
African village, or ancient artifacts from southern Scandinavia, be appropriate
to the study of the material culture of archaeologists?

Jonathan Bateman argues in his study of computer visualization in archaeology (Bateman 2000) that our theories of material culture should in principle be
reflexively applied to our own material culture too. This material culture is odd
in that it is rarely constituted as the object of the archaeological gaze. Trowels,
spades, planning grids, tapes, cameras, grids, theodolites, laptops, and so forth,
are all examples of artifacts involved in the production of archaeological knowledge. But as anyone familiar with excavation recording will know, these are not
meant to be viewed as objects in their own right. They are usually cleared out
of the way, for example, whenever a photo of objective evidence is about to be
taken. In my experience on sites in the United Kingdom, diggers first of all erase
the traces of their own actions in preparing the evidence for photography, such
as trowel marks. They then remove their spoil and tools and stand out of the
way so that their shadows do not fall within the frame of the picture.

In chapter 6 of this book Bateman repositions and refocuses the camera just
enough to capture, together with the archaeological evidence itself, the material
items and indeed the diggers normally removed from the scene—the instruments and agents of knowledge production. His photographs of the Gardom's
Edge excavation in Derbyshire, UK, portray a greater part of the archaeological
reality than we are accustomed to seeing represented in this media. The tools
that shape and record evidence, the shadows, footprints, and marks of archaeologists themselves, remind us of aspects of archaeological evidence—our own
role in constituting it—that we sometimes tend to deny. It is difficult to look at
these photos without getting a sense of the sheer tactility of excavation and its
materials. I find the images powerful because, even though I never worked on
this particular site, they reconnect me with my own experience of the realities of
archaeological fieldwork.

In a similar vein, Håkan Karlsson and Anders Gustafsson direct our attention
to the modern steps, paths, platforms, drainage gullies, and other aspects of site
layout that play such a major role in shaping the experience of visitors to archaeological monuments, yet like archaeological tools are rarely constituted as
objects of interest in themselves. In chapter 12 they look specifically at the signposts and information boards at the World Heritage listed site of rock-carvings at
Tanum in Sweden. By comparing these artifacts to totem poles, they use a similar metaphorical device to that employed by Erdur in his chapter, when he gives
real archaeologists "Indian" names. The irony of such a comparison is clear. By
making such familiar artifacts exotic and strange, Karlsson and Gustafsson
encourage us to re-encounter them, to rethink their uses, and perhaps to re-
design them or even replace them with something else. A focus on the material

culture of archaeology has major theoretical as well as practical implications. Hodder's conception of archaeology "at the trowel's edge" (Hodder 1997, 1999) is based upon a reconfiguration of our view of the humble trowel from mundane item of kit to an instrument of agency and power in the production of archaeological knowledge, as well as an instrument of human perception. It is amazing to think that most of our initial contacts with material evidence out on-site, our first encounters with that external reality until discovery exists independently of the cultural activities of archaeology—our very perceptions and active manipulations of emerging objects and features—are mediated through the use of the trowel (see Edgeworth 1991 and 2003 for detailed practical examples observed and analyzed from an ethnographic perspective). When the active agency of field archaeologists and their material culture is fully taken into account, fieldwork methodology itself may have to be rethought and redesigned (Chadwick 1998, 2003; Andrews et al. 2000; Hodder and Berggren 2003).

As Gavin Lucas (2001b, 42) acknowledges, recent consideration of archaeology as a *materializing* practice stems in part from perspectives afforded by ethnographies of archaeology. These perspectives have enabled archaeological practice to be understood as more than just a one-sided encounter, or "a subject encounter with an object" (Lucas 2001a, 15). To be sure, archaeologists shape and sculpt material evidence. But the object being worked acts back on the subject and shapes the very skills and techniques that are shaping it. There is a practical dialectic at work. Material "resistance" encountered in practice challenges and transforms archaeological knowledge (again, for many practical examples, see Edgeworth 1991 and 2003).[2]

Recently Thomas Yarrow introduced the important concept of "artifactual persons," emphasizing the interrelatedness of persons and things in excavation (Yarrow 2000, 2003), a point reiterated by several authors in this book. There are clear connections here, for example, with the argument developed by Van Reybrouck and Jacobs about the mutual constitution of natural and social identities. As this work shows, ethnographies of archaeology offer a potential means of moving beyond the opposition of subject and object, which has tended to characterize archaeological debate over the last few decades. In chapter 2, Yarrow describes his fieldwork at a Mesolithic site close to the famous site of Star Carr in Yorkshire. He points out that sites are made, in part, from the reputations as well as the actions of the people who excavated them (in addition to the actions of past human agents). But these people are also revealed in turn by the material properties of the archaeological site. In this closely argued chapter Yarrow looks at "how people create the site, and how they are in turn created by it."

Other aspects of the materiality of excavation are highlighted by John Carman in chapter 8, such as the hoardings that surround certain excavations, the baulks and wheelbarrows and other tools out on-site, and the beer that is drunk in the evenings. What emerges from a reading of Carman's chapter, where he sets out the perspectives of a social archaeology of archaeology, is a sense of just how strongly the social aspect of excavation is rooted in the material dimension, the two aspects being deeply intertwined with each other, perhaps far more so than in other areas of life. Social interactions and relationships in excavation practice can never be completely disembedded from this material matrix.

DEVELOPMENTS ON THE INTERFACE OF
ANTHROPOLOGY AND ARCHAEOLOGY

The impetus for the ethnographies of archaeology we have looked at so far has come largely from within archaeology. Ethnographic studies have for the most part either been carried out by archaeologists themselves or by ethnographers invited in by archaeological site directors. Either way, it is archaeological agendas that have mainly underpinned this type of research (with the notable exception of Goodwin's work).

However, a completely separate origin for ethnography of archaeology can be traced from within anthropology (at the points where it interfaces with or encounters archaeology). The Yucatán region of Mexico is a particularly fertile area in this respect. An important ethnography of the Mayan site of Chichén Itzá by Quetzil Castañeda (1996) challenged conventional views of archaeological sites. He regarded the material form of the site—with its temples, pyramids, ball courts, and so forth—as just as much an artifact of Western scientific practice as it is an artifact of ancient Mayan civilization. More to the point, the site is regarded as a key locale for cultural production in the present as well as the past, involving a complex web of activities and texts by archaeologists, local communities, landowners, tourists, tour guides, government officials, and other groups, through which the cultural identities of the Maya (and, we might add, those of archaeologists too) are produced and reproduced (Castañeda 1996).

It is perhaps not surprising, then, that anthropologists are beginning to situate their ethnographies in such places. The site of the production of archaeological knowledge is now becoming more and more the site of the production of ethnographic knowledge as well, with ethnographers and archaeologists both operating in the same space—their worlds overlapping, their views intersecting (or conflicting). Both Lisa Breglia (2002) and Timoteo Rodriguez (2001) have separately carried out recent ethnographies at the site of Chunchucmil, close to Chichén Itzá. Other projects that focus on the interaction between archaeologists and local communities, such as Angela McClanahan's ethnography of heritage management practices in the Orkney Islands, are being conducted independently elsewhere (McClanahan 2002). So here we have several scholars entering the field from new directions, with fresh approaches and new sets of research objectives. They widen out the perspectives of this book to encompass not just the archaeological site, and the practices that take place within and upon it, but also the wider landscape and its inhabitants (as well as outside influences such as heritage authorities and tourists) and the interactions between all these elements.

McClanahan focuses her attention in chapter 11 upon a region of Orkney that has been designated a World Heritage Site. Her ethnography reveals that the designation has caused some disagreement between local people and heritage managers. The numinous landscape of Orkney, dotted with extraordinary archaeological sites, is at once the setting, the instrument, and the object of dispute. As McClanahan states, "Through everyday, mundane action, the landscape of Stenness and Brodgar is lived and politicized, with many interest groups . . . negotiating different aspects of their identities and needs, with the landscape being used as both an explicit and implicit tool." Her sensitive ethnography uncovers some of the nuances of the relationship between local people and the rich archaeological landscape they inhabit.

In chapter 14, Rodriguez also discusses a contested landscape, in the equally exceptional setting of the Yucatán peninsula in Mexico. He shows how archaeological sites can be perceived quite differently by archaeologists and local Maya farmers, giving rise to cultural conflict between these two groups. As he explains, "a difference of understandings arose between local farmers and foreign scholars, constituting different perceptions of the same space through their different practices." Thus (reframing Marcus and Bartu) there are "different sites of cultural production in a local space." In documenting how the shared landscape is materially and symbolically contested, the author considers the question of the potential role of ethnographies of archaeology. He argues, following Laura Nader (1972), that such work can help us to study "up" as well as down, to produce an anthropology of the colonizer as well as the colonized.

Related themes are touched upon in chapter 13 by the Brazilian archaeologist Denise Gomes, who describes her ongoing project of excavation and survey in a remote area of Amazonia. This is an important chapter in the book precisely because it is written from the perspective of an archaeologist rather than from that of an ethnographer. Conducting research in difficult terrain, lone workers and small teams of archaeologists often do not have the rather luxurious option—enjoyed by large multinational research excavations—of taking along ethnographers of archaeological practice. This does not mean that the method is inappropriate. As Roveland and others have shown, it *is* possible to incorporate some form of reflexive ethnographic method into everyday archaeological activities; archaeologists *can* be ethnographers of their own practices.

Gomes develops an ethnographic awareness of her own work by taking on board the perspectives of local people (some of whom see archaeologists as foreigners or stealers of land). She highlights the important and usually neglected role of local people as hired workers in the production of archaeological knowledge, and the ways in which certain local groups may selectively appropriate archaeological findings into their cultural identities. Her achievement is that, while retaining the traditional archaeological focus on material culture of past societies, she places herself and the wider context of her work (including her unfolding relatiónships with local people) in the picture, and thereby attempts an essentially reflexive account of an archaeological project that takes place in a complex cultural and political environment.

Interesting correspondences emerge from chapters by Rodriguez, Breglia, and Gomes. All describe traditional communities who for different reasons do not regard themselves as descendants of the ancient peoples that occupied their land, and who therefore do not make a direct connection between themselves and the archaeological heritage that might be supposed to be theirs. This raises some ethical dilemmas about how archaeology and heritage work should be conducted in such places.

For Lisa Breglia in chapter 15, such dilemmas provide the rationale for developing and carrying out ethnographies of archaeology in the first place. She argues that "ethnography of archaeology begins by acknowledging this deep and often frustrating problem of how to carry out archaeology that meets both the standards of the discipline as well as the cultural context of the local community." Such research, involving new forms of collaboration between archaeologists and ethnographers, can help to build "a locally meaningful, ethical context" for archaeological and heritage work to take place.

Breglia's chapter, in configuring ethnography of archaeology as an ethical field of practice, situated on the interface between archaeologists and local communities, is an appropriate one with which to conclude the book. She rightly urges practitioners to move beyond the "closed hermeneutics of disciplinary self-reflexivity"—not that we should leave behind the reflexive project but rather that we try to open it up to encompass wider issues and realities. In envisaging that ethnographies of archaeology should explore hitherto uncharted areas of research on the boundaries of archaeology and ethnography, she sets a direction and trajectory for future research.

SUMMARY OF POTENTIAL

The potential of the "field" of ethnographies of archaeology lies in its capacity to facilitate alternative ways of looking at things, no matter what the prevailing orthodoxy might be. It is not a unified school of thought; nor is it a part of one. Individual proponents develop their version after their own fashion, to their own ends. Its great strength lies in its freedom from an encompassing ideology. As Rodriguez argues, it is better to conceive of it as an attitude or ethos rather than a doctrine.

That ethos is a reflexive and subversive one. Ethnographies of archaeology can help us to develop the kind of "critical ontology of ourselves" that Rodriguez, following Foucault, recommends. A general aim is to try and see ourselves (our activities and our material culture) as cultural Others see us, or as we see them. There is an imperative there to break down the established privileges of observer over the observed and to twist the outward-looking gaze back in on itself, so that an encounter with the cultural Other is also a re-encounter with archaeology or anthropology itself.

Fresh perspectives afforded by re-encountering our familiar world can quickly fade into established and orthodox ways of seeing, and things that stir our sense of wonder can soon become mundane and taken for granted. The use of the word "re-encounter" therefore refers to an ongoing process rather a finite event, and to what Breglia describes as "a continuously deterritorializing object of study." She envisages ethnographies of archaeology looking always to "the unexplored disciplinary interstices."

Participation of ethnographers like Breglia, Wilmore, and Yarrow as well as archaeologists like Gomes, Bateman, and Roveland means that the sites or fields where ethnographies of archaeology come into being are situated in the area of overlap right on the disciplinary boundary between anthropology and archaeology. These are liminal spaces of great creative potential, where ideas and techniques from both sides of the boundary can be combined. Hopefully, such spaces might also provide openings for the voices of local communities who inhabit archaeological landscapes to emerge—and not simply in the passive form of the "ethnographized." What archaeology and anthropology both currently lack is a critique of the disciplines formulated by local people themselves, empowered to engage on equal terms in intellectual discourse about archaeological sites and monuments on their land.

Perhaps one day—who knows?—there might be a Maya or Parauá ethnography of archaeological practice or an ethnoarchaeological study of the material culture of archaeologists, possibly carried out by an indigenous group or traditional community itself. Such a study might look not just at that material culture in its own right, but also at how it is used to shape (and through shaping, appropriate) the pasts of whole peoples, thereby fashioning also their present and the future. Or, as Rodriguez imagines it, there might be "an ethnography of ethnographers," perhaps conducted by those who were formerly the ethnographized. Appropriated by other cultures in this way (normally such cultural appropriation takes place in the other direction), the very practice of ethnography itself would be transformed.

As this book shows, ethnographies can constitute archaeological practice as the object of study from both outside or inside points of view, or any point in between. They can encompass both the very large and the very small, operating on a number of different levels or scales of inquiry. The method can be used to explore, for example, the microprocesses of the production of archaeological knowledge. It can penetrate into the tacit domain of embodied expertise—going right down, as Goodwin does, into the structure of a single sentence, gesture, or movement of the trowel. But at the other end of the spectrum ethnographies of archaeology can shift the level of focus and turn attention to the cultural and political interactions between archaeologists and local communities and other groups on a much broader landscape.

This is what ethnographies of archaeology enable us to do best—to shift in and out of focus, to change stances, to take up new perspectives, to reflect critically on established viewpoints, and to look at things in new and surprising ways. This work can add another dimension to the study of the past, enriching archaeological knowledge. By including the archaeological observer and the practical and social contexts of observation within the domain of study, ethnographies of archaeological practice can help us look more holistically at the past in the present and the present in the past.

NOTES

1. I am grateful to Cornelius Holtorf for pointing out the existence of this early work.
2. There are of course other "grounds" of archaeological knowledge apart from excavation practices. Ethnographers have been drawn to the study of excavation because of the extraordinary nature of the material engagements that it is possible to observe there, perhaps neglecting the study of survey and other modes of archaeological investigation (Bradley 2003).

REFERENCES

Andrews, G., J. Barrett, and J. Lewis. 2000. Interpretation not record: The practice of archaeology. *Antiquity* 74:525–30.
Avikunthak, A. 2001. Rummaging for pasts: Excavating Sicily, digging Bombay. Video film. *Stanford Journal of Archaeology,* archaeology.stanford.edu/journal/newdraft/ashish/index.html (accessed November 21, 2004).
Bartu, A. 2000. Where is Çatalhöyük? Multiple sites in the construction of an archaeological site. In *Towards reflexive method in archaeology: The example at Çatalhöyük,* ed. I. Hodder, 101–9. Cambridge, UK: McDonald Institute Monographs.
Bateman, J. 2000. Immediate realities: An anthropology of computer visualisation in archaeology. *Internet Archaeology* 8, intarch.ac.uk/journal/issue8/index.html (accessed November 21, 2004).
Bender, B., S. Hamilton, and C. Tilley. 1997. Leskernick: Stone worlds, alternative narratives, nested landscapes. *Proceedings of the Prehistoric Society* 63:147–78.
———. Forthcoming. *Stone worlds: Prehistoric and contemporary landscapes of Leskernick on Bodmin Moor.* London: UCL Press.
Bourdieu, P. 1977. *Outline of a theory of practice.* Trans. R. Nice. Cambridge: Cambridge University Press.
———. 1988. *Homo academicus.* Trans. P. Collier. Stanford: Stanford University Press.
———. 1990. *The logic of practice.* Trans. R. Nice. Cambridge, UK: Polity Press.
Bradley, R. 2003. Seeing things: Perception, experience and the constraints of excavation. *Journal of Social Archaeology* 3 (2):151–68.
Breglia, L. 2002. In situ collaboration: Ethnographers and archaeologists in the field. Unpublished paper presented at Symposium on Ethics and the Practice of Archaeology, University of Pennsylvania Museum, Philadelphia.

——. Forthcoming. *Monumental ambivalence: The politics of cultural patrimony.* Austin: University of Texas Press.

Castañeda, Q. 1996. *In the museum of Maya culture: Touring Chichén Itzá.* Minneapolis: University of Minnesota Press.

Chadwick, A. 1998. Archaeology at the edge of chaos: Further towards reflexive excavation methodologies. *Assemblage* 3, www.shef.ac.uk/assem/3/3chad.htm (accessed January 3, 2005).

——. 2003. Post-processualism, professionalization and archaeological methodologies: Towards reflective and radical practice. *Archaeological Dialogues* 10 (1):97–117.

Christiansson, H., and K. Knutson. 1989. The Bjurselet settlement III, vol 1, finds and features: Excavation report for 1962 to 1968. In *Societas Archaeologica Upsaliensis.* Uppsala, Sweden: Uppsala University.

Dupree, L. 1955. The artificial small group and archaeological excavation. *American Antiquity* 20 (3):271.

Edgeworth, M. 1990. Analogy as practical reason: The perception of objects in archaeological practice. *Archaeological Review from Cambridge* 9 (2):243–51.

——. 1991. The act of discovery: An ethnography of the subject-object relation in archaeological practice. PhD diss., University of Durham, UK.

——. 2003. *Acts of discovery: An ethnography of archaeological practice.* BAR International Series 1131. Oxford: Archaeopress.

Erdur, O. 2003a. On the "value of knowledge": The conditions and the possibilities of archaeological knowledge production in Turkey. In *Arkeoloji: Niye? Nasil? Ne icin? (Archaeology: Why? How? What for?),* ed. O. Erdur and G. Duru. Istanbul: Ege Yayinlari.

——. 2003b. Nietsche and the body of knowledge. *Stanford Journal of Archaeology* 2, archaeology.stanford.edu/journal/newdraft/2003_Journal/erdur/paper.pdf (accessed January 3, 2005).

Flannery, K. 1982. The golden Marshalltown: A parable for the archaeology of the 1980s. *American Anthropologist* 84 (2):265–78.

Gero, J. 1996. Archaeological practice and gendered encounters with field data. In *Engendering archaeology: Women and prehistory,* ed. J. Gero and M. Conkey, 251–80. Philadelphia: University of Pennsylvania Press.

Giraudo, R. 2002. The past less travelled: The dynamics of archaeological excavation. MPhil thesis, University of Cambridge.

Goodwin, C. 1994. Professional vision. *American Anthropologist* 96 (3):606–33.

——. 2000. Action and embodiment within situated human interaction. *Journal of Pragmatics* 32:1489–1522.

——. 2002. The semiotic body in its environment. In *Discourse, the body and identity,* ed. J. Coupland and R. Gwyn. London: Palgrave-Macmillan.

——. 2003. Pointing as situated practice. In *Pointing: Where language, culture and cognition meet,* ed. S. Kita, 217–41. Hillsdale, N.J.: Lawrence Erlbaum Associates.

Haber, A. F., and A. O. Scribano. 1993. Hacia una comprensión de la construcción científica del pasado: Ciencia y arqueología en el noroeste argentino [Towards an understanding of the scientific construction of the past: Science and archaeology in the Argentine northwest]. *Alteridades* 3 (6):39–46. Mexico.

Hamilton, C. 2000. Faultlines: The construction of archaeological knowledge at Çatalhöyük. In *Towards reflexive method in archaeology: The example at Çatalhöyük,* ed. I. Hodder, 119–27. Cambridge, UK: McDonald Institute Monographs.

18 *Matt Edgeworth*

Hodder, I. 1997. Always momentary, fluid and flexible: Towards a self-reflexive excavation methodology. *Antiquity* 71:691–700.

———. 1999. *The archaeological process: An introduction.* Oxford: Blackwell.

———, ed. 2000. *Towards reflexive method in archaeology: The example at Çatalhöyük.* Cambridge, UK: McDonald Institute Monographs.

Hodder, I., and A. Berggren. 2003. Social practice, method, and some problems of field archaeology. *American Antiquity* 68 (3):421–34.

Holtorf, C. 2002. Notes on the life history of a pot sherd. *Journal of Material Culture* 7:1.

Knorr-Cetina, K. 1981. *The manufacture of knowledge: An essay on the constructivist and contextual nature of science.* Oxford: Pergamon.

Latour, B., and S. Woolgar. 1979. *Laboratory life: The social construction of scientific facts.* Beverly Hills, Calif.: Sage.

Leibhammer, N. 2000. Rendering realities. In *Towards reflexive method in archaeology: The example at Çatalhöyük,* ed. I. Hodder, 129–42. Cambridge, UK: McDonald Institute Monographs.

Leskernick website. n.d. www.ucl.ac.uk/leskernick/forum/forum01.html (accessed November 19, 2004).

Lucas, G. 2001a. *Critical approaches to fieldwork: Contemporary and historical archaeological practice.* London: Routledge.

———. 2001b. Destruction and the rhetoric of excavation. *Norwegian Archaeological Review* 34 (1):35–46.

Lynch, M. 1985. *Art and artefact in laboratory science: A study of shop work and shop talk in a research laboratory.* London: Routledge and Kegan Paul.

Marcus, G. 1995. Ethnography in/of the world system: The emergence of multi-sited ethnography. *Annual Review of Anthropology* 24:95–117.

Marcus, G., and M. Fischer. 1986. Anthropology as cultural critique: An experimental moment in the human sciences. Chicago: University of Chicago Press.

McClanahan, A. 2002. Access and atmosphere: Practicing the construction of place in the Heart of Neolithic Orkney. Paper presented at the Theoretical Archaeology Conference, Manchester, UK, December 2002.

Nader, L. 1972. Up the anthropologists. In *Reinventing Anthropology,* ed. D. Hymes, 284–311. New York: Pantheon Books.

Pizarro, C. A., A. F. Haber, and R. D. Cruz. 1995. Diálogos en El Bañado. Relaciones socioculturales en la construcción científica y popular del pasado [Dialogues in El Bañado. Sociocultural relationships in the scientific and popular construction of the past]. *Revista de Ciencia y Técnica* 2. Catamarca, Argentina.

Politis, G. 2001. On archaeological praxis, gender bias and indigenous peoples of South America. *Journal of Social Archaeology* 1 (1):90–107.

Rodriguez, T. 2001. Maya perception of ancestral remains: Multiple places in a local space. *Berkeley Mcnair Research Journal* 9, www-mcnair.berkeley.edu/2001journal/Trodriguez.html (accessed January 3, 2005).

Rountree, K. 2003. Reflexivity in practice. Çatalhöyük 2003 Archive Report, catal.arch.cam.ac.uk/catal/Archive_rep03/a20.html (accessed May 8, 2005).

Roveland, B. 2000. Contextualizing the history and practice of Paleolithic archaeology: Hamburgian research in northern Germany. PhD diss., University of Massachusetts.

Sellars, M. 1973. The secret notebook for the practising archaeologist: With preliminary notes towards an ethno-science of archaeology. *Plains Anthropologist,* 140–48.

Shankland, D. 1997. The anthropology of an archaeological presence. In *On the Surface: The re-opening of Çatalhöyük*, ed. I. Hodder, 186–202. Cambridge, UK: McDonald Institute Monographs.

———. 2000. "Villagers and the distant past: Three seasons" work at Küçükköy, Çatalhöyük. In *Towards reflexive method in archaeology: The example at Çatalhöyük*, ed. I. Hodder, 167–76. Cambridge, UK: McDonald Institute Monographs.

Shanks, M., and R. McGuire. 1996. The craft of archaeology. *American Antiquity* 61:75–88.

Wall, O. 1968. Försök att studera samband mellan sociometriska val och interaktioner inom en arkeologisk grupp [The connection between sociometric choice and interaction in an archaeological excavation team]. PhD diss., Socialhögskolan, Umeå.

Williams, T., 1999. Imaging the self: Photography at Leskernick, www.ucl.ac.uk/leskernick/gallery/imaging/im-text.html (accessed January 3, 2005).

Wilmore, M. 2001. Far away, so close: Some notes on participant observation during fieldwork in Nepal and England. *Anthropology Matters* 3, www.anthropologymatters.com/journal/2001/wilmore_2001_faraway.htm (accessed January 3, 2005).

Woolgar, S. 1988. *Science: The very idea*. London: Tavistock Publications.

Yarrow, T. 2000. Excavating knowledge: The relational capacities of persons and things on an archaeological dig. PhD diss., University of Cambridge.

———. 2003. Artefactual persons: The relational capacities of persons and things in the practice of excavation. *Norwegian Archaeological Review* 36 (1):65–73.

Zak, J. 2004. Shared endeavors across disciplinary boundaries: Exploring collaboration between archaeologists and conservators. Çatalhöyük 2004 Archive Report, catal.arch.cam.ac.uk/catal/Archive_rep04/ar04_41.html (accessed May 8, 2005).

2

Sites of Knowledge: Different Ways of Knowing an Archaeological Excavation

Thomas Yarrow

SITES OF KNOWLEDGE

The first time I took part in excavation, in Troina, Sicily, I was struck by the almost imperceptibly subtle way in which ideas and relationships seemed to move from one form to another. For example, particular personal relationships between people on-site often became the basis for interpretations in the context of conversations that strung together talk about the weather or gossip with observations about the objects or features being excavated. Similarly, I was intrigued by the way thoughts and words gradually turned into understandings that were then objectified as drawings, diagrams, or text. Conversely the features that we were excavating often set up social relationships, as, for example, when the physical proximity they created between people led to conversations that would not otherwise have happened. What intrigued me about the site, more even than the beautiful glassy black obsidian blades we excavated, were the mobile ways in which aspects of people, ideas, and things became incorporated in or detached from one another in different moments.

While the finds from this site were taken to the local museum and interpretations of these later found their way into journals, it seemed that a lot was left unsaid in terms of the complex negotiation of relationships central to the endeavor. Some of the recent work in archaeology (e.g., Tilley 1989; Gero 1996; Bender et al. 1997; Hodder 1997) has attempted to recover something of these relationships by highlighting the social and subjective aspects of excavation. This approach clearly represents an important challenge to the excesses of an earlier empiricism, where a belief in objectivity obscured much of the work and creativity of people in the field. However, by simply offering "the other side" (cf. Lucas 2001, 15), the danger is that many of the same grounding assumptions are reproduced. The tendency has been to see social context as something that can be discovered, much as archaeologists themselves discover finds—as if the "social" empirically exists and the job is simply to reveal it.

Coming from an anthropological background, Shankland (1996) nonetheless shares many of these assumptions in an ethnography that examines how Çatalhöyük archaeologists and locals perceive each other and interact. As an anthropologist, who is "good at social contexts" (349), he is critical of archaeologists for their inability to integrate social context into their reports; on the other hand, the villagers are seen to be bound by their local context. The vision here is of "context" as a thing in a discrete sense that can be added to produce a more complete object. The social aspect is assumed from the outset to be distinct from the objective knowledge that the archaeologists produce.

In this formulation it is more or less explicitly assumed that people have a stable identity that marks them as separate from one another, as well as from the objects that they encounter. By implication, then, the site is also taken to be a relatively stable place with a fixed location. In looking at an archaeological excavation, my concern in contrast is with the nature of archaeological knowledge itself (cf. Edgeworth 1990; Lucas 2001; Holtorf 2002)—with the ways in which it is created and produced *through* particular relationships, people, things, and practices. As such, no distinction is presumed between the knowledge that is produced and the people that produce it or between the objective artifacts and the subjective people who excavate them. Rather I look at some of the ways in which these people and things are related, as well as at some of the relationships through which they are separated. The interest is in how people create the site and in how they are in turn created by it.

To this end, I take a conceptual lead from a relational model of sociality developed by a number of anthropologists working in Melanesia (e.g., Wagner 1986; Strathern 1988; Weiner 1988). Rather than seeing individuals as counterposed to society, and hence corporeally bounded bodies as counterposed to relationships (cf. Strathern 1995), the suggestion by these anthropologists is that in a Melanesian ontology people's bodies are themselves composed of the various other people and things with whom they transact. As Strathern (1991) puts it, "The physical body is composed of [things] as it is composed of relationships. The relationships appear intrinsic to the body" (76). People and things are therefore seen as being composed of different elements, literally of other parts of people or things, which may in various moments be hidden or discarded to produce particular effects. Such a model might seem misplaced when applied to an archaeological site in Europe: the archaeologists after all do not imagine themselves in these terms and this is therefore not an ontology that they share. However, by employing this analogy here, the idea is not to reveal points of similarity between these places.[1] Rather, it is to create the position from which the practices and conventions that archaeologists employ can be apprehended in terms other than the familiar (cf. Edgeworth 1990, 244–45).

FIELD WORK

On arriving at Scarborough station, it did not take me long to pick out the site director from the small crowd of hurrying commuters and dawdling tourists. Wearing a pair of dirty jeans and a shabby sweater and with a graying beard, he appeared to me at the time the very embodiment of an archaeologist. As we drove along winding Yorkshire lanes in the late-afternoon August sun he began to ask me about myself and, realizing that I was studying anthropology, we started talking about the differences between our disciplines. His jovial tone put me quickly at ease, but his point was serious: Where archaeology was a "good subject for understanding the world," anthropology was a subject of rhetoric and semantics; and where archaeology had a relevance beyond itself, being inclusive in its practice and widely comprehensible, anthropology was isolationist and exclusive—"very clever but not very useful," as he bluntly concluded.

In this instance, the journey came to enact a divisional form—evident in other aspects of the dig process—in which respective aspects of our identities were made visible relationally and oppositionally. Here our words were grounded by the disciplinary forms we imagined ourselves to embody: the encounter made me into an anthropologist just as it made him into an archaeologist. Yet the division held only for the duration of the journey, later to be erased as we pulled up to the farm campsite where I was to spend the month (and in subsequent years, others) camping with the volunteers. In this way, then, it was as though the field came to me (in the form of the site director) before I even arrived at the site.

In borrowing a conventional anthropological form of "arrival," I do not want to use this device to create the conventional distinction between fieldwork and theory that Gupta and Ferguson (1997) suggest it often has. Indeed the distinctiveness of my own field site—of the archaeological site as the locus for an anthropological enquiry—was evident to me only retrospectively. Although I was studying anthropology at the time, I did not participate in the excavation as an anthropologist: no formal interviews were undertaken, and moreover, I did not initially set out to formally observe the practices that I subsequently felt compelled to write about. The arrival then does not mark the beginning of my investigation as imagined at the time: it was not the moment at which I started to do fieldwork. And while the field season on which the bulk of my observations are based (and which I take to be the subject of this chapter) lasted one month, the end of it does not mark the end of my research either. Subsequent seasons participating on the same excavation, as well as time spent working as a contract archaeologist, also inform the remarks I make and the positions I arrive at. I did not, then, confront a field in which difference was self-evident, and to the extent that my account delimits a distinctive object of inquiry, I see this as an achievement of subsequent analysis, reflections, and thought. Just as the people participating on the site (myself included) were made into archaeologists through the processes of excavation we embodied and enacted, so my ethnographic perspective is one that comes from my choice to render this experience in terms of a particular set of theoretical commitments. I use these to abstract myself from the account, to distance and "other" it, and to define a subject, just as archaeologists themselves create their objects through the methodologies examined below. For me, the ethnography of archaeological practice is not simply a methodology to be applied or a way of doing fieldwork; however, it is not a perspective or theory either, if this presupposes the distinctiveness of ideas and interpretations from the people and things that they purport to describe. Rather, it deliberately calls into question the boundaries and distinctions through which the field, in both archaeology and anthropology, is constituted.

PERFORMING THE SITE

The following account focuses on the various people connected to a Mesolithic site in the Vale of Pickering, Yorkshire,[2] many of whom were present at the end-of-dig dinner. This was held in the barn in which volunteers ate and socialized in the evenings. However, by contrast to such informal occasions the dig dinner was an event through which people's roles and responsibilities were celebrated and their differences demonstrated: an event through which the people and relationships associated with the site were enacted simultaneously and as a whole.

These relationships were made visible in part through the arrangement of people at the tables, with more important people tending to sit nearer the head and less important people sitting closer to the ends. But their respective importance and differences were also more explicitly revealed through the speeches that followed the dinner. Thus the site director acknowledged the cooperation and generosity of the landowners along with the "crucial role of trustees and benefactors on which the excavation is entirely dependent." The importance of the academic findings and the good progress that had been made was testified to in a speech given by one of the site archaeologists. The volunteers' contribution was recognized through a series of awards.

People were therefore discursively placed in terms of their formal relationship to the site: trustees and beneficiaries who financially sustained the project; farmers who allowed or prevented access to land; the wider academic community who interpreted and made the site meaningful; and volunteers, who excavated and recorded the site. The dinner celebrated and made explicit the importance of various relationships, which remained invisible in much of the day-to-day practice of the site and in doing so revealed how these variously contributed to and shaped the form of the site. Indeed, as the site director himself acknowledged, without the various people present, "there would be no site."

Yet these roles and differences were not always made manifest but were created, sustained, and challenged in different moments, of which the dinner was but one example. Central to the negotiation and renegotiation of these relationships was an ability for people to act in different ways at different moments, making visible different aspects of the relationships in which they were composed (Wagner 1986) and hence having their words and actions grounded to different effects in different moments. The following account examines in more detail some of the people who were involved with the excavation, looking at various discourses and practices through which the site is differently imagined and constructed.

VOLUNTEERS

A common way in which archaeological sites are imagined is as a place that is an object of knowledge. Underpinning this understanding is the assumption that the site, composed of artifacts, is itself also an object or artifact. As Edgeworth (1990) interestingly points out, it is a characteristic of artifacts that "once they have been shaped, they can be released, so to speak, to stand for themselves" (250). But if the site is indeed distinct from the various archaeologists who are involved in its production, how is such a distinction brought into being?

As I have discussed elsewhere in more detail (Yarrow 2003), part of the answer is that people on-site adhered to archaeological conventions. For example, volunteers all employed the same kinds of techniques to excavate spits and adhered to a particular set of procedures to record and identify finds. In this way, although there were a variety of different people with a range of skills and perspectives, their actions were made to be in certain respects the same. By erasing certain differences between people, these site conventions made it possible to elicit objectivity in the various finds that were encountered. The site was thus created as an object distinct from the relationships and people through which it was excavated only because all that was recovered was turned into an instance of archaeological method.

Yet if these conventions generated equivalence between the various people on-site, they also acted in certain moments to foreground distinctions between them. For example, the trench was sometimes seen as an extension of the actions of the person excavating it, as when comments were made about the flatness or neatness of particular people's spits or conversely about people who excavated shoddily or found very little.[3] When this happened, the physical form of the trench was taken not as an object but rather as a measure of the ability of the person who excavated it (Yarrow 2003). Similarly, volunteers' knowledge was made visible through their ability to distinguish various kinds of artifacts, as seen when finds were excavated that could be recognized only by particular people.

In these instances people had different capacities for foregrounding aspects of the relations of which they were composed (Wagner 1986). The internal capacities of different people—knowledge, skill, and ability—were therefore made visible by the various objects that they encountered. As with the artifacts themselves, these differences and comparisons between volunteers were made possible by the shared archaeological conventions and understandings that existed on-site.

However, in more overtly social contexts, such as in the pub or on the campsite, similarities and differences between people were made manifest through a different set of conventions. The construction of a community and the extent to which the dig was seen to bring together a broad cross-section of people was often positively remarked upon and given as an explicit reason for participation. As one volunteer commented, "The best thing about archaeology is the people you meet." In a similar way people often fondly recounted memories of past years of excavation in terms of particular characters or social occasions and many of the volunteers told me that the social life was a big part of the reason for their participation. Part of the good social life was put down to the equality that existed among different volunteers and the way in which it was therefore possible to meet "people that in ordinary life you might not." In social contexts, such as in the pub where people often went in the evenings or the campsite where the volunteers stayed, this equality was created through a number of social conventions. For example, tasks such as washing up were strictly shared through a rota; all volunteers received the same subsistence pay and all camped in the same place. In this way, aspects of liminality (Van Gennep 1908) or *communitas* (Turner 1967) were created, with normal kinds of roles—and the distinctions and hierarchies implicit in these—being suspended through social conventions that acted to erase them. This is not to suggest that such social conventions made everybody the same. Rather, they created the context in which social differences were made visible against a background of equality.

Interestingly, in these social contexts, a further consequence of the creation of a community of equals was that the authority of archaeology was subverted as one perspective among many. Archaeological matters would often be talked about in the evenings as people would chat about such things as the day's events or particular unusual or interesting finds. Yet here discussions were not grounded by the same conventions and shared archaeological understandings that pervaded on-site. Consequently a student's assertion that archaeology was irrelevant or pointless could be placed on an equal footing to the site director's or specialist's riposte. The efficacy of the words spoken in these moments—the force of particular arguments—was constituted not through reference to a set of shared assumptions about archaeology but rather through the ways in which archaeology itself was talked into being. Here, then, as the conventions on-site created the context in which differences emerged between artifacts or people, so, too, social conventions enabled differences of opinion or perspective to be articulated in ways that would not have been possible in other contexts.

ACADEMICS

By contrast to these overtly social interactions, in academic contexts the importance of archaeology was not itself in doubt;[4] however, the significance of particular artifacts or features often was. For example, a controversy surrounded a
wooden structure found on the nearby site of Star Carr, and this has been given
a number of very different interpretations. While Clark (1954) suggested that it
could have been used as a platform for living on, Pitts (1979) by contrast argued
that it might have been a tool for tanning hides. At one level, such different theories assume the existence of an object—or more generally, a site—whose material properties are taken to be independent of the interpretations that are made
of it (see Lucas 2001, 212–14). But there are ways in which properties of the site
and "properties" of the academics associated with it mutually elicit one another.

One side to this is that academics and specialists were central to maintaining
the perception of the site as academically important. Although not necessarily
involved in the excavation at a practical level many different people were associated with the site in a variety of ways. For example, a renowned professor
was on the board of trustees; many of the flints and other finds were interpreted
elsewhere by various specialists; and the site has been interpreted and used in
a large number of academic accounts. These people might normally be considered external to the workings of the site itself, and in a related way it might be
assumed that the number of important people interested in the site was simply
a function of the site's own importance. But perhaps it was only because of the
various positions such people occupied and the different kinds of knowledge
or skill that they were seen to possess that they were able to authenticate or
make visible particular aspects of the things that were recovered. The site's academic importance is not due to the material properties of the artifacts alone
but also to the properties—their academic roles or positions, publications, reputations, and so on—of the various specialists and academics who have produced and interpreted these.

As one of the site specialists noted, the importance of the nearby site of Star
Carr is not due primarily to the site's "dazzling material inventory" but to the
work and reputation of Grahame Clark who originally excavated it (Conneller
2003). Indeed, this interpretation has been pivotal for subsequent approaches,
shaping the scope of excavations at the site and the methodologies employed.
In this way, then, it could be argued that the site drew its importance from the
importance of Grahame Clark himself. The fact that Clark was the most eminent
Mesolithic archaeologist of the time is in part why Star Carr has been established
as the most important Mesolithic site.

He did not therefore simply interpret the site, but was instrumental in its creation
in a very literal sense. It should be noted that his theoretical preoccupations—for
example, with economic theory and seasonality—have influenced the kinds of
methodology employed and hence the material properties of the site itself (Conneller, pers. comm.). But in pointing to the interdependence of the site and the the-

ories of it, I do not simply want to make the familiar point that this is a kind of bias. Rather, I want to suggest that the very objectivity of the site itself comes from the people who interpret it and the capacities that they are regarded as having.

On the other hand, the properties of the site were also capable of revealing aspects of the people who interpreted it. Indeed, this relationship between archaeologists and the things that they excavate was interestingly brought to light by the reexcavation of a site originally dug in 1950. Although I was not present when this happened, the site director described how the trench sides were "as clean as a whistle," with "nothing at all in the backfill." Through what was effectively an "archaeology of archaeology" (cf. Lucas 2001, 201–2) the trenches made explicit the objectivity of those who initially excavated them, causing the site director to remark that "he must have been a brilliant excavator." By revealing the material properties of the site, the contemporary archaeologists also revealed properties of the original people who excavated it.

LANDOWNERS AND TRUSTEES

In contrast to these academic contexts, where the importance of archaeology as an endeavor was for the most part assumed, the same could not be said for landowners and farmers, for whom the activities of the site were largely incidental or even considered a nuisance. Yet the cooperation and help of these people was of fundamental importance to the physical construction of the site. In this context, then, the value of the site had to be established. The dig dinner was one important expression of the site's value and significance and, to this extent, much care was taken to present site activities in a positive light. Yet the importance of the site was not the same for all farmers and landowners concerned.

One of the trustees was a keen deer hunter and he explicitly drew parallels between the activities of Mesolithic hunters and his own. Thus the evidence of deer hunting in the Mesolithic came to legitimate his own activities in the present and "man's natural urge to hunt," as he put it. For him, then, the site provided evidence of timeless and unchanging aspects of humanity. In contrast, one of the farmers I spoke to was a keen amateur archaeologist, who collected flints from his farm. He possessed a detailed knowledge of archaeological theories pertaining to the site, and for him, the interest lay more in the way in which he saw things in the past as being different from those in the present. For him the flints and the meanings he attached to them seemed a way of asserting and creating a connection with the past and spoke to him of where he had come from. Yet for one of the trustees the importance of the site lay largely in the fact that it could be used as a means of campaigning against modern farming techniques, which she told me were leading to the destruction of the wetland habitat. For her the site's interest did not lie so much in a particular set of meanings or understandings as in the very fact that it was important.

For some of the landowners and farmers, then, the form or aesthetic of the excavation seemed to be of greater interest than the results or objects it produced. That the dig was archaeological, scientific, or, as I was told, "contributing to knowledge" was seen by some as more significant than any specific instances of meaning that were produced archaeologically or scientifically.

Interestingly, however, these kinds of imagining were not simply of trustees' or landowners' own making but were often facilitated and played with by the site director and volunteers. For example, with the arrival on-site of trustees, landowners, or other archaeological specialists, people would often adopt a rigor and meticulousness that, as some acknowledged, far exceeded any function in terms of the accuracy of the results. Trench sides would be hurriedly straightened, loose earth would be cleared away, and conversation would be reduced to minimal comments about finds. By embodying science, academic rigor, and objectivity I would suggest that the actions of those excavating enabled them to connect a source of authority and legitimacy beyond the specificity of particular objects or people on the site.

Through the different actions and words of people associated with the excavation, "the site" came to literalize different things for different people. In these ways, the site would come at various moments to stand for different ideas and concepts: science and progress, heritage, local identity, academic endeavor, and so on. But if the site was changed by the different ways in which people saw it, then it in turn created the context in which aspects of people's identities, ideas, or relationships were also transformed. In this sense, different people were able to make claims, perform particular identities, or assert ideas through their association with the site—identities that would not otherwise have been possible.

MULTIPLE SITES?

Through examining the activities of different people associated with a particular archaeological site, this account has demonstrated some of the ways in which the site was imagined and some of the different instances in which it was constructed and enacted. In this way, the intent was in part to challenge more bounded or monolithic visions of what an archaeological site is.

Superficially, this might appear a similar approach to that of an increasing number of anthropologists advocating multisited ethnography (Marcus 1998; Gupta and Ferguson 1997).[5] With its roots explicitly in postmodern thinking, this critique has called into question the vision of discrete cultures or places and the corresponding formulation of anthropological fieldwork as the study of one of these. In place of this site-specific approach, anthropologists such as Marcus have argued for the need to adopt strategies that come to terms with the purportedly global world,[6] in which different groups are more and more connected through various "logics of association" (Marcus 1998).

Ayfer Bartu (2000) explicitly adopts just such an approach in her ethnography of Çatalhöyük. Starting from the premise that "the excavation of the site is only one of the sites in which a particular kind of knowledge is being produced," she goes on to explore some of the "multiple groups and sites through which knowledge about Çatalhöyük is produced and consumed" (101). These include the World Bank office in Washington, a local wedding ceremony, and the local annual agricultural ceremony, leading to the conclusion that "rather than one single monolithic site, we see the dispersion of the site" (103). In place of the vision of the site as a single place, then, the image is of multiple people and contexts. Where previous formulations privileged archaeological knowledge of this site over others, here the argument is rather that there are simply different competing claims and different kinds of knowledge. Although the focus is different, a similar logic underpins the approach of Hamilton (2000), who discusses the fault lines or tensions that existed between different groups at Çatalhöyük. Tringham and Stevenovic (2000) in the same volume similarly develop the idea that different "windows" are created on Çatalhöyük by the contrasting methodological approaches that American and European teams adopted.

Importantly, these accounts focus on the question of what an archaeological site is and on the nature of knowledge produced and consumed in relation to it. In doing so, they call into question the relatively static and bounded way in which sites have often been conceived. As Bartu importantly notes, the idea of the site needs to be reformulated to account for nonarchaeologists' and nonspecialists' implication in it. Similarly, Hamilton and Tringham and Stevenovic make the important point that the site itself is not a place that is known and constructed in one way but is rather a place of contestation and difference.

Yet, in privileging multiplicity over singularity, fundamental problems remain. Starting from the premise of multiple and diverse groups of people, Bartu outlines some of the ways these groups of people imagine what the site of Çatalhöyük is. Central to this argument is the idea of "context" and the implication that explanation lies ultimately in the contextualization of different ways of knowing. What is left unanswered from this perspective, however, is the question of how one is to ever mediate or adjudicate between these. The local understandings of villagers, it is argued, are no less valid as a perspective on the site than the archaeological understandings that we would normally privilege. And yet there is no concerted attempt to interrogate the logics or conventions under which competing claims are actually made. In place of the vision of one objective site we are left with one that sees the site multiply apprehended from different subjective viewpoints.

Against this, I have suggested the need to interrogate different social and archaeological conventions that work not simply *in* different contexts but as the very things that create them. This is to argue for a more nuanced appreciation of how people associated with archaeological sites themselves construct the conditions under which different kinds of knowledge are brought into being and, sometimes, contested. For example, while *archaeological* conventions on-site created the context through which volunteers' different capacities and knowledge could be compared, various *social* conventions created the context in which archaeological authority was erased. In this sense rather than taking context as an explanatory concept, the point was rather to demonstrate the mobile ways in which different kinds of contexts were themselves brought into being by the actions of various people associated with the site. To put this in a slightly different way, since the distinction between the social aspects and the objective aspects of the excavation was not fixed but was itself a product of the work of the various people associated with the site, such a distinction should not be taken as the tacit basis of analysis. This distinction can only be *understood* through a focus on the practices, people, and conventions through which it is made.

Yet if the site was created by the actions of people associated with it, then aspects of these people were in turn revealed by the material properties of the archaeological site. This was apparent in the moments when the volunteers' own abilities were evinced by the material form the trench took; when particular artifacts were used to demonstrate the efficacy of a particular academic theory; or when trustees and landowners co-opted the site into their own self-understandings. In this sense, then, people and things need to be comprehended not as self-evidently distinct but as oppositions that are contingently made and fluidly negotiated through the practice of archaeology.

NOTES

1. It is important to distinguish this use of ethnography from some of the ways in which it has commonly been used within the discipline of archaeology. For example, ethnoarchaeology proceeds from known ethnographic examples and uses these to comprehend relatively unknown archaeological sites. Such analogies rest on there being a similarity between the two, and so, the veracity of arguments will always rest in part on the ability to demonstrate the basis of similarity on which the analogy turns. In this chapter, by contrast, I reveal how the apparently familiar practice of excavation can be apprehended differently to the way in which it is conventionally imagined.

2. The research was undertaken over three successive seasons, each a month in total, in the Vale of Pickering, North Yorkshire. The excavation, funded by the Vale of Pickering Research Trust, is undertaking extensive survey work around the prehistoric Lake Flixton in order to identify patterns of Mesolithic activity in their environmental setting.

3. Gero (1996) discusses similar instances from a different perspective. She points out the different gendered ways in which people excavate and hence how the archaeological record reflects different subjective ways of acting.

4. It is important to emphasize that this distinction is not a sociological one in any straightforward way and that the change I want to signal is rather concerned with differences in convention. People's identities were in this sense mobile and contextually negotiated. For example, some of the specialists were also academics; some of the aca-

demics, specialists, and trustees were also volunteers; and some of the academics were also trustees.

5. Hodder (1999) and Lucas (2001, 143–44) advocate that such an approach can also be usefully applied within archaeology.

6. For critiques of the conceptualization of the "global" in such formulations, see, for example, Weiner (1999), who notes that the effect of multisited ethnography is to shift familiar concepts such as culture to a different scale. In doing so, he argues that it retains many of the grounding assumptions of earlier paradigms.

ACKNOWLEDGMENTS

This chapter came out of work in the Vale of Pickering, North Yorkshire, not in the first instance conceived as research. I therefore wish to apologize to those with whom I lived and worked for any apparent sleight of hand and thank those who have generously accepted my retrospective renegotiation of relations. Unfortunately, I cannot thank all of my fellow diggers by name, whose insights and creativity, I hope, are apparent in the text. However, I would like to particularly mention Tim Schadla-Hall, who has engaged my ideas even when he has not always shared them. A number of people have read and commented on earlier drafts of the text, and the insights of Chantal Conneller, Duncan Garrow, Tony Crook, Paola Filippucci, and Marilyn Strathern were particularly instructive. Lastly, I would like to acknowledge my grandfather, Gresham Dodd, who would not have recognized himself in my words but who is there nonetheless.

REFERENCES

Bartu, A. 2000. Where is Çatalhöyük? Multiple sites in the construction of an archaeological site. In *Towards reflexive method in archaeology: The example at Çatalhöyük*, ed. I. Hodder, 101–9. Cambridge, UK: McDonald Institute Monographs.
Bender, B., S. Hamilton, and C. Tilley. 1997. Leskernick: Stone worlds, alternative narratives, nested landscapes. *Proceedings of the Prehistoric Society* 63:147–78.
Clark, J. G. D. 1954. *Excavations at Star Carr*. Cambridge: Cambridge University Press.
Conneller, C. 2003. Star Carr re-contextualised. In *Peopling the mesolithic in a northern environment*, ed. L. Bevan and J. Moore, BAR S1157. Oxford: Archaeopress.
Edgeworth, M. 1990. Analogy as practical reason: The perception of objects in excavation practice. *Archaeological Review from Cambridge* 9 (2):243–52.
Gero, J. 1996. Archaeological practice and gendered encounters with field data. In *Gender and archaeology*, ed. R. Wright, 126–39. Philadelphia: University of Pennsylvania Press.
Gupta, A., and J. Ferguson. 1997. Discipline and Practice: "The field" as site, method and location. In *Anthropological locations: Boundaries and grounds for a field science*, ed. A. Gupta and J. Ferguson. Berkeley: University of California Press.

Hamilton, C. 2000. Faultlines: The construction of archaeological knowledge at Çatalhöyük. In *Towards reflexive method in archaeology: The example at Çatalhöyük*, ed. I. Hodder, 119–27. Cambridge, UK: McDonald Institute Monographs.

Hodder, I. 1997. Always momentary, fluid and flexible: Towards a self-reflexive excavation methodology. *Antiquity* 71:691–700.

———. 1999. *The archaeological process*. Oxford: Blackwell.

Holtorf, C. 2002. Notes on the life history of a pot sherd. *Journal of Material Culture* 7 (1):49–71.

Jones, A. 2002. *Archaeological theory and scientific practice*. Cambridge: Cambridge University Press.

Lucas, G. 2001. *Critical approaches to field archaeology: Contemporary and historical archaeological practice*. London: Routledge.

Marcus, G. 1998. *Ethnography through thick and thin*. Chichester: Princeton University Press.

Pitts, M. 1979. Hide and antlers: A new look at the gatherer-hunter site at Star Carr, N. Yorks, England. *World Archaeology* 11 (1):32–42.

Shankland, D. 1996. Çatalhöyük: The anthropology of an archaeological presence. In *On the surface: Çatalhöyük 1993–1995*, ed. I. Hodder, 349–58. Cambridge, UK: McDonald Institute Monographs.

Strathern, M. 1988. *The gender of the gift: Problems with women and problems with society in Melanesia*. London: University of California Press.

———. 1991. *Partial connections*. Lanham, Md.: Rowman & Littlefield.

———. 1995. *The relation*. Cambridge, UK: Prickly Pear Press.

Tilley, C. 1989. Excavation as theatre. *Antiquity* 63:275–80.

Tringham, R., and M. Stevenovic. 2000. Different excavation styles create different windows into Çatalhöyük. In *Towards reflexive method in archaeology: The example at Çatalhöyük*, ed. I. Hodder, 111–18. Cambridge, UK: McDonald Institute Monographs.

Turner, V. 1967. *Forest of symbols: Aspects of Ndembu religion*. Ithaca, N.Y.: Cornell University Press.

Van Gennep, A. 1908. *Rites of passage*. London: Routledge.

Wagner, R. 1986. *Symbols that stand for themselves*. Chicago: University of Chicago Press.

Weiner, J. F. 1988. *The heart of the pearlshell: The mythological dimension of Foi society*. Berkeley: University of California Press.

———. 1999. Afterword: The project of wholeness in anthropology. *Canberra Anthropology* 22 (2):70–78.

Yarrow, T. 2003. Artefactual persons: The relational capacities of persons and things in the practice of excavation. *Norwegian Archaeological Review* 36 (1):65–73.

3

The Mutual Constitution of Natural and Social Identities During Archaeological Fieldwork

David Van Reybrouck and Dirk Jacobs

Excavations are not only places where observations are turned into facts but also where individuals are turned into archaeologists. Ethnographers of archaeology, however, have so far given much more attention to the social construction of facts than to the factual construction of social agents. This is probably because they are generally accomplished archaeologists who have turned the ethnographic look inward. In order to overcome this methodological problem, we did ethnographic fieldwork at the excavation of a prehistoric site in the Netherlands from an insider/outsider perspective. Participant observation by both an archaeological novice and an experienced practitioner allowed a much better documentation of how scholars make facts and how facts make scholars. Following Latourian actor-network theory, this chapter argues that the socialization of individuals into scholars cannot be detached from the objectification of observations into data.

SAVING HOUSE 10

To surf the website of the Maaskant project, go to maaskant.leidenuniv.nl/alms1 .htm. Click on Sites, Almstein 1995, and Late Iron Age, phase A to download a map of House 10 (the caption says "c 250 BC").

We were there. We worked at the house. It happened ten years ago, in the southern part of the Netherlands. Almstein was the name given to a real estate building project near the town of Oss. It was also the name given to the rescue excavation of 1995, which formed part of the ongoing excavations at Oss, which in turn formed part of the Maaskant project—a long-standing regional research project in Dutch archaeology (Fokkens 1996; Jansen and Fokkens 1999). The campaign yielded a fair amount of archaeological features, dating from the early Iron Age to the Roman period. Most features were estimated to have been built between 250 and 100 B.C. "In total 8 house plans were recovered," says the website. "They belong to a settlement with probably two contemporary houses that were rebuilt every 25 years or so on almost the same spot." That this valuable prehistoric evidence was going to make it into the present was far from evident. Imminent building plans aside, the place had been used for garbage dumping. According to the website, "Since this had been done in the recent past, excavation here was a very smelly business, and messy as well. To complete this description of *couleur locale*, imagine temperatures of over 30 degrees Celsius, and you get the picture."

But now, the house is there, on the website, readily visible for the worldwide Internet community. It has been saved.

BEYOND THE RESCUE METAPHOR

One of the many metaphors underlying archaeological fieldwork is the idea of "rescuing." This applies to "salvage archaeology" and other forms of emergency digging, but also to fieldwork as a whole. According to this very common metaphor, excavations are conceived as operations for *salvaging* fragments from the past. Researchers in the present, much like members of a rescue boat, are portrayed as extricating evidence from a sea of oblivion. They try to salvage the past before it drowns.

This might very well be the case; it is presumably the metaphor with which most field archaeologists would describe what they do. Yet more could be at stake. The rescue metaphor assumes that the prehistoric evidence is already out there, drifting on the waves, waiting to be hauled up. In recent years, sociologists of science in general, and ethnographers of archaeology in particular, have convincingly demonstrated how facts are not simply *given* but are actively *construed* in scientific practice. Facts are, quite literally, that which is being made. In a landmark paper, Cornelius Holtorf (2002) persuasively described the processes through which a particular thing found at an excavation in western Sicily was gradually transformed into an ancient potsherd. Excavation seems not so much a process of *salvaging* but of *solidifying*. In the case of Almstein, we did not really find an early Late Iron Age house; we found discolorations in the sand that became House 10. Archaeological facts are not floating on the tide of time but only become factual once they are picked up. If the past is a sea, it must be a sea of melted wax where things solidify only once they are lifted out.

We must even go further, for excavations are not only places where observations are turned into facts but also where individuals are turned into archaeologists (Yarrow 2003; see also chapter 2, this volume). "Archaeology," Shanks

(1992) has rightly argued, "is immediately biography" (130). This is certainly the case for the majority of digs where unearthing the past goes hand in hand with training students. In Almstein, for instance, prehistory was being created simultaneously with a new generation of prehistorians. This dual process also takes place at strictly professional excavations, since the professional identity of scholars is never fully established. Professional identities (e.g., someone's status as a competent specialist) might be challenged and transformed during a fieldwork season. If facts are more fluid than we commonly think, so are the social actors whom we commonly indicate as archaeologists. The received idea of stable, unshakable social actors is readily contradicted by dramatic cases of entire academic careers built on a single find. Not only do scholars make facts, but facts also make scholars.

No, an archaeological excavation is not necessarily an emergency operation performed by a rescue team. Facts and archaeologists all seem to be floating, drifting in an ocean of contemporary situated practice. Prehistoric houses are still only observations of discolorations; archaeologists are simply flexible social actors. In this sea of observations and actors, some alliances will be crafted. Some observations will be turned into a prehistoric house, some individuals will be transformed into competent scholars. But others will disappear from sight. Next to a social construction of facts, there is also a factual construction of society. It would be erroneous to privilege social actors above factual constructs, since both are the result of situated practice (Van Reybrouck 2002).

BEYOND SOCIAL CONSTRUCTIVISM

Let us return to the Iron Age house in Almstein. We could very easily investigate the processes through which this house was made—not in prehistory but in the present. We would, as Bruno Latour suggested in his earlier works, go upstream from the neat established fact toward the messy context of discovery (Latour 1987; Latour and Woolgar 1979). We would retrace history, from the highly formalized digital map on the worldwide web accessed in November 2004, to the vague discolorations observed between June 5 and 9, 1995, in a field near a small town in the Netherlands (Bateman 2000).

And yes, we would refer to a recent major synthesis on the prehistory of that region, which says that the "excavations at Oss-Almstein exposed a small cluster of farmsteads of the Late Iron Age" (Gerritsen 2001, 59). Checking bibliographic references, we would see how Gerritsen's canonizing statement relied on an earlier doctoral thesis on the Oss settlement system (Schinkel 1998) and on two unpublished undergraduate theses, written by students who were very actively involved as fieldworkers in the Almstein excavations (Beek 1996; Jansen 1997).

We would go even further back in time. We would look at how these theses helped to "construct" House 10. We would see how their drawings and descriptions were solidified versions of field drawings and notes. And we would go to the latter to see how the idea of a house gradually emerged during the campaign. We would compare them with original photographs taken during excavation, if only to see how messy reality can be and how selective our drawings are (thereby forgetting, for the sake of convenience, that photographs are equally constructions of reality). Doing so, we would understand how faint colors in the sand are transformed into postholes, postholes into houses, and houses into settlement history.

Yes, we could do that, were it not that this sort of work has already been done (Holtorf 2002) and were it not that such an approach encounters important theoretical challenges. By focusing on how one object (a potsherd, a house plan) travels through time, this approach runs the risk of reducing the social dimension to a mere explanatory level. Facts might be mutable, but social actors are depicted as the steadfast members of the rescue boat. The flexible nature of social dispositions tends to be disregarded. (Recent research has discussed the intrinsically social aspects of archaeological excavation—see Holtorf, chapter 7, and Carman, chapter 8. But the emphasis on archaeological cultures of drinking, quarrelling, and social bargaining is so detached from actual data construction that it is difficult to grasp the interrelationship between processes of socialization of scholars and the objectification of facts.)

Holtorf (2002) is quite successful in analyzing how a thing becomes a find, yet the protagonists in his narrative seem immutable. The finder of the sherd, Erica Grijalva, is described as "an undergraduate student in Mechanical Engineering from Stanford University, California," while the analyst, Emma Blake, is said to have "a lot of experience, and a lot of intuition" in determining ceramics (Holtorf 2002, 59, 61). As competences and credits seem to be taken for granted, these social identities are never really problematized. In this analysis, the potsherd *becomes*, but the archaeologists simply *are*. In fact, it is because they *are* that the find *becomes* an ancient potsherd. The social realm is thus suggested to determine the natural realm. Against an objectivist view of reality we are presented with a social constructivist view. Both have their limitations.

THE DUAL CONSTITUTION OF THE SOCIAL AND THE NATURAL

Though Bruno Latour has been a key thinker within the social constructivism of the 1980s, he has also been the first one to abandon it. Social constructivism, he argued, is a weakness that characterized much early sociology of science and science studies (Latour 1993, 1999). As there were no good reasons why social factors would be more real (that is, more stable, less fluid) than natural causes, the a priori distinction between nature and society created an unnecessary asymmetry. He suggested a principle of symmetry: "Our general symmetry principle is thus not to alternate between natural realism and social realism but to obtain nature and society as twin results of another activity, one that is more interesting for us. We call it network building" (Callon and Latour 1992, 348).

The resulting actor-network theory offered an alternative for unilateral social constructivism (Latour 1999, 2005). The key idea is that of the dual and simultaneous constitution of the natural and the social order. Social actors do not precede natural constructs but are as much the outcome of scientific practice as are facts (Van Reybrouck 2002). What takes place at an archaeological excavation is not the objective discovery of natural facts, nor the social construction of an empirical reality, but the mutual constitution of actors and facts. These entities, regardless of whether they are postholes or prehistorians, are interrelated in a network. Only by allying themselves to each other can they become powerful nodes in the network. Powerful nodes are those that gain reality, that is, those that are recognized as being real. A discoloration in the sand becomes a true posthole through association with a reliable undergraduate student. An undergraduate student becomes a reliable observer at a dig through association with a clearly delineated posthole. They mutually articulate each other; they emerge simultaneously from actual practice.

The same holds true for an established scholar. Take Emma, the ceramic expert looking at Cornelius's sherd in western Sicily. Of course, the social and professional identity of Emma did not entirely depend on the way she classified this single sherd—in fact, a misclassification would have been unlikely to jeopardize her career. Yet the continuous feed of potsherds reproduced her status as a competent ceramic expert. The sherds needed her, for sure, but she needed the sherds as well. Take the sherds away and her professional status would rapidly dwindle.

Since more attention has been given to the social construction of facts than to the factual construction of social actors (cf. Yarrow 2003; Yarrow, chapter 2; Bateman, chapter 6), we decided to do ethnographic fieldwork at the Almstein excavation from an insider/outsider perspective. Whereas one of us (David Van Reybrouck, a graduate student in archaeology at the time) was implicated as a field school lecturer, the other one (Dirk Jacobs, then a graduate student in sociology) was a complete novice to archaeological fieldwork. This has an advantage: the latter's participant observation might help us to see how attempts to articulate oneself as an archaeological fieldworker go hand in hand with the articulation of certain facts.

THE SOLITARY SOCIOLOGIST

How does one become a field archaeologist? When Dirk Jacobs arrives in Oss on the evening of June, 6, 1995, he joins the group of archaeologists, field school students, and lecturers in their lodging quarters at an old farm a few kilometers away from the site. The excavation in which he is going to participate is considered a routine dig. Project leader Harry Fokkens of Leiden University has no objections to the presence and participation of a sociologist. All participants are informed of the goal and nature of Dirk's presence: a participant observation of archaeology in action. Throughout the ethnographic experiment, he takes field notes that form the basis of our present analysis.

Like all novices to the field, Dirk has never worked on an archaeological site before and does not quite know what to expect. On the train to Oss he has reread the instruction manual (Fokkens 1995) that had been prepared for participants of the field school. In this manual a wide range of practical information is offered, ranging from the financing of excavations and dangers of potential cables and pipelines on the site to digging and data registration procedures. The text is clearly written, but practical knowledge and manual skill disclose themselves badly in the format of a verbal discourse. It is like learning to drive a car from a textbook.

In order to give him a better idea of the work, the implicated lecturers (David being one of them) show him drawings of the excavation that have been made today. When first looking at them, Dirk sees only randomly scattered dots. The archaeologists explain to him how he should read the map. The dots represent postholes, they say, and an arrangement of postholes refers to a settlement feature, like a house or a granary. In the absence of an unmediated contact with the material, Dirk can only write down what he is being told: "David points to a number of typical discolorations that have been baptized as 'sock structures'; they indicate the entrance [to the house]" (field notes, June 6, 1995). As long as the novice has not allied himself with a number of emerging facts, his professional status as a field archaeologist is nil. At this point, Dirk is still a solitary sociologist, lost in a farm full of archaeologists. Yet what the archaeologists tell him is a first step in formatting his vision. He has not yet seen the facts but representations of them—and these representations will determine how he construes facts in the future. He is learning to see before he has to look.

LOOKING FOR ALLIES: SELECTION AND REIFICATION

The lessons of the previous night have taken effect. When Dirk arrives at the site in the morning, he has a first look at the different pits. He sees a multitude of color patterns and is able to spot the house: "In one of the pits, I can recognize the traces of a settlement feature. That is, if I had not seen the map yesterday, I would never have noticed it" (field notes, June 7, 1995).

A major step in the development of a professional vision entails the ability to discern relevance. Though still a newcomer, Dirk has already moved one step up from complete outsiders. The previous night, local youngsters have tried to vandalize the site by scratching a large skull and the word "Metallica" in the sand of pit 70. Almost proudly, Dirk notes that these graffiti have been drawn "in a recent disturbance of a pit which is not very interesting" (field notes, June 7, 1995). The vandals would have been much more successful had they actually disrupted the network created between archaeologists and data, for instance, by destroying discolorations deemed relevant by the archaeologists. Dirk already sees that this has not been the case.

Attributing relevance to certain observations (and consciously neglecting others) is a crucial prerequisite for the creation of socioempirical alliances. On his first day, Dirk discovers that excavation is not just about retrieving but also neglecting information. Every physical feature could be turned into a fact (Holtorf and Schadla-Hall 1999), but he notices how archaeologists systematically select and favor certain categories over others. Digging is selection. On their maps, the archaeologists make a sharp distinction between prehistoric and recent traces. Dirk is surprised to learn that everything post-Roman is unhesitatingly considered "recent noise." He understands that making alliances with such "noise" will not grant him many credits.

After certain patterns have been favored, they are increasingly reified through various procedures, of which *highlighting* is the most typical (Goodwin 2002). In essence, archaeologists draw a line in the sand with their trowel around a presumed feature, thus reifying the object that they assess to be visible in the color patterning in the soil. When Dirk asks the senior archaeologists why they do this, they explain that the color patterns are best visible shortly after the layer has been opened. Contact with the air tends to fade the colors away, it is said; so, the contours must be marked in the soil for future relocation. Highlighting seems an essential step in turning observations into data—Hodder (1999) calls it "interpretation at the trowel's edge" (92). Yet to recognize a feature is far from an easy task for novices to perform. In their daily field reports, first-year undergraduates complain that it is a painstaking practice at first and that it takes a lot of practice before it becomes an automatic procedure. Being able to efficiently highlight discolorations in the sand yields better data—as well as better archaeologists.

REINFORCING ALLIANCES, LOSING ALLIANCES

It becomes clear to Dirk that establishing evidence (the single most important activity for establishing oneself as a field archaeologist) entails more than a passive registration of given data. It involves a highly active commitment to crafting data, and this crafting, as Edgeworth (2003) convincingly argues, is mediated by the use of instruments. Archaeologists rarely discover data with their bare hands; they construe them through the use of material culture. Trowels, cameras, pencils, sheets, plastic bags, and so forth, are all instruments for articulating facts. Learning how to deal with instruments is therefore an integral part of student training. On his second day, Dirk learns to handle some of these instruments.

As a matter of exercise the undergraduates have to do measurements with an instrument called the *theodolite*. The new students all seem to have difficulties with it. They do not fully understand instructions and pick up the correct procedure only by trial and error. The lecturers are clearly impatient and dissatisfied. They complain. "'Hey, I am talking Dutch, you know,' one of the instructors shouts at the students. It is striking that the junior students are supposed to practice with the old instruments, while the senior students are all working with sophisticated digital stuff" (field notes, June 7, 1995). The association between find and finder becomes stronger if it is mediated by instruments, but the quality of the alliance also depends on the quality of the instruments.

Dirk's vision is showing signs of incipient professionalism, especially when it comes to appreciating discolorations as postholes and using simple instruments. However, becoming an archaeologist entails the acquisition of a whole range of competences. When he observes that black sand from the postholes is being collected in bags, he is surprised to learn it is charcoal that might be used for dating. He is also told that pieces of ceramics have been found but he notes: "I don't see it. For me these are strange pieces of stone which are being collected" (field notes, June 7, 1995). Later that day, Dirk is given the opportunity to increase his familiarity with potsherds: "In the evening I first looked and then helped with washing the finds." It is also an opportunity for further establishing his credentials by extending his socioempirical network, though some alliances are not easily crafted: "Apparently I broke a considerable piece of ceramic. 'A recent crack,' one of the older students says. Out of courtesy it is not said directly, but the indirect hints are clear enough: 'It is a pity.'" Whether this diminishes the value of the data, Dirk cannot assess (he is still a novice, after all), but that it may diminish his value as an archaeologist is clearly felt: "I cannot really judge by myself if it is a big deal or not and I do not feel like asking explicitly. I am wondering whether I will be confronted with it again at a later stage" (field notes, June 7, 1995).

QUESTIONING ALLIANCES

How could there not be a dual constitution of natural facts and social actors? If Dirk breaks a sherd, he also breaks some of his credentials. If he highlights a posthole, he equally articulates his competences. On the third day of the field school, he starts to recognize patterns and potsherds by himself, thus creating new socioempirical alliances of his own. Yet he also begins to question alternative alliances. Network building does not only involve manufacturing new links but also challenging existing ones. As he gets more involved, his field notes become more critical (field notes, June 8, 1995). He notices pictures are not being taken every time and wonders why this is the case. He starts to disagree about interpretative decisions on color patterns. He witnesses substantial disagreements in interpretation between the senior professional archaeologists and a local amateur archaeologist who is visiting the site. Most of all, he is struck by the fact that medieval traces are simply disregarded and are considered to be uninteresting. A lecturer tells him the same happened in the past with

Roman traces, until someone started taking an interest in them. Dirk knows it is risky to associate oneself with "noise," yet he realizes that the definition of noise is a relative one. It suffices to build a powerful, alternative network with so-called noise for it to become respectful—and for *him* to become respectful. This will be even more so when it is coupled with an attack on previous alliances.

Socioempirical alliances become stronger if they succeed in incorporating multiple nodes without falling apart. Yet the price one pays for strength is the danger of dissidence (Van Reybrouck et al. 2006). Networks can be challenged by individual nodes that have escaped the alliance. At the end of the day, an incident illustrates how labor intensive the creation and maintenance of alliances is: "Just before 5 p.m., David finds an unregistered posthole. In another trace (a doorpost) a weaving weight is being discovered. The person in charge seems to be panicking due to the lack of registration. It is decided to do some extra work" (field notes, June 8, 1995). Excavations turn out to be battlegrounds where allies are sought, found, disputed, and lost. Luckily, an overlooked posthole is an easy dissident to deal with: some extra work will do to get it in line.

THE RECOGNITION OF COMPETENCE

Of course, one does not become a field archaeologist in one week. Yet after less than a week, Dirk notices how his participant observation has clearly passed the stage of mere observation and analysis. In the course of the morning he switches to another trench where a Roman ditch has been found. He is working hard to clear one of the three sections across the ditch. Some ceramics are found and, equipped with his fresh professional vision, he confidently notices how different they are from "those of the Iron Age postholes" (field notes, June 9, 1995). The sections are being cleared until ground water is struck. Then the usual drawing and photographing begin. Recording is central to the recognition of the alliance between finder and find. But Dirk becomes quite frustrated when it turns out that a section of the pit in which he has been working is being given much less attention: "Some sections are given priority. Two are extensively photographed and drawn. For a third one, photos are taken but no drawing is made (this is shitty: it was my section)" (field notes, June 9, 1995).

Interestingly, Dirk shifts to the past tense when expressing his frustration: "it was my section." The moment the section is not properly documented, it ceases to be *his* section. He might as well not have excavated it. In the absence of full recording, the section does not make it into a proper fact—and his efforts do not yield a public recognition of competence. The alliance, which could have helped to articulate the particular nature of the ditch as well as the particular value of Dirk, was broken. It was a useless networking effort.

What is the benefit of being considered competent? Trustworthiness, that is, the right to speak and the chance of being heard. Yet there is more. It is Friday afternoon; Dirk notices the work everywhere is getting sloppy. When confronting the senior archaeologists about this, they first jokingly dismiss the remark. Finally, they claim that this is more or less allowed in this phase of the work. What could they mean by that? During the past couple of days, Dirk has tried to convert his ignorance into the beginning of competence and now that he has obtained some, it does not seem to matter anymore. Competence is not something which is given but which accrues during research—very much like facts and reality. The next step is perhaps nonchalance. Nonchalance can never be the attitude of the novice, unless he or she wants to be considered incompetent. Nonchalance is what settles in once sufficient credentials have been acquired, once the network nodes are strong enough to allow a degree of indulgence. Nonchalance, Dirk realizes, is the luxury of the competent. It is not yet within his reach.

CONCLUSION

Has the House of Almstein been rescued? No. The place where discolorations were observed ten years ago has now been converted into a new suburban neighborhood of Oss. The house has not been rescued, but it has been "realized"; that is, it has acquired a virtual existence (on maps, in publications, on the Internet), which is in many ways more real than ever before (Van Reybrouck 1998). The network that operated in Almstein has proved solid enough to guarantee the undisputed reality of the house ten years after its discovery. It is almost certain that if the house had been unearthed by Dirk *alone*, its life would have been much less stable.

Has Dirk become a full-blown archaeologist? No. He has recently been appointed a professor of sociology at the Université Libre de Bruxelles in Belgium. His presence at an archaeological excavation was too brief, his alliances with finds too flimsy, and his incipient socioempirical networking too weak to establish him as a competent field archaeologist. Yet this fluidity of competence was really quite fortunate for our ethnography of archaeology. Just as one has to travel upstream to discover the transformation of flexible observations into solid data, one also has to go back to the stage where professional competence is still open and undecided. This is not always easy, especially when the ethnographic perspective is that of a professional archaeologist, but collaboration with a nonarchaeologist offers new opportunities. Our participant observation from an insider/outsider perspective (using both a novice to archaeology and a competent practitioner) has proved a valuable procedure for understanding the dual and simultaneous constitution of natural and social entities. Seen from this angle, it becomes clear that archaeologists, like facts, need to be established and that the socialization of scholars goes hand in hand with the objectification of facts.

ACKNOWLEDGMENTS

We wish to thank project leader Harry Fokkens for allowing us to do this research at the Oss excavations. In the field, Zita van der Beek, Richard Jansen, and Piet van de Velde welcomed our presence and generously helped us around. Fokke Gerritsen and Dieke Wesselingh kindly supplied us with additional material.

REFERENCES

Bateman, J. 2000. Immediate realities: An anthropology of computer visualization in archaeology. *Internet Archaeology* 8, intarch.ac.uk/ journal/issue8/index.html (accessed November 12, 2004).

Beek, Z. van der. 1996. *Een nederzetting uit de Late IJzertijd: Het verslag van de opgraving Oss 1995* (A late Iron Age settlement: The report of the excavation Oss 1995). MA thesis, Universiteit Leiden, the Netherlands.

Callon, M. 1986. Some elements of a sociology of translation: Domestication of the scallops and the fishermen of St. Brieuc Bay. In *Power, action, and belief: A new sociology of knowledge?* ed. J. Law, 196–233. London: Routledge and Kegan Paul.

Callon, M., and B. Latour. 1992. Don't throw the baby out with the Bath School! A reply to Collins and Yearley. In *Science as practice and culture*, ed. A. Pickering, 343–68. Chicago: University of Chicago Press.

Edgeworth, M. 2003. *Acts of discovery: An ethnography of archaeological practice.* Oxford: Archaeopress.

Fokkens, H. 1995. *Opgraven in zand: Grootschalig nederzettingsonderzoek. Een handleiding voor de opgravingspraktijk* (Excavating in sand: Large-scale settlement research. A practical manual for the excavation). Leiden, the Netherlands: Universiteit Leiden.

———. 1996. The Maaskant project: Continuity and change of a regional research project. *Archaeological Dialogues* 3 (2):196–215.

Gerritsen, F. 2001. *Local identities: Landscape and community in the late prehistoric Meuse-Demer-Scheldt region.* PhD diss., Vrije Universiteit, Amsterdam.

Goodwin, C. 2002. Professional vision. In *Qualitative research methods*, ed. D. Weinberg, 281–312. Malden, UK: Blackwell.

Hodder, I. 1999. *The archaeological process: An introduction.* Oxford: Blackwell.

———. 2002. The interpretation of documents and material culture. In *Qualitative research methods*, ed. D. Weinberg, 268–80. Malden, UK: Blackwell.

Holtorf, C. 2002. Notes on the life history of a pot sherd. *Journal of Material Culture* 7 (1):49–71.

Holtorf, C., and T. Schadla-Hall. 1999. Age as artefact: On archaeological authenticity. *European Journal of Archaeology* 2 (2):229–47.

Jansen, R. 1997. *Van grondspoor naar nederzetting: Een reconstructie van IJzertijdnederzettingen in Oss-Mettegeupel* (From trace to settlement: A reconstruction of Iron Age settlements in Oss-Mettegeupel). MA thesis, Universiteit Leiden, the Netherlands.

Jansen, R., and H. Fokkens. 1999. *Bouwen aan het verleden: 25 jaar archeologisch onderzoek in de gemeente Oss* [Building the past: 25 years of archaeological research in the municipality of Oss]. Leiden, the Netherlands: Universiteit Leiden, Faculteit der Archeologie.

Latour, B. 1987. *Science in action: How to follow scientists and engineers through society*. Cambridge, Mass.: Harvard University Press.

———. 1993. *We have never been modern*. Cambridge, Mass.: Harvard University Press.

———. 1999. *Pandora's hope: Essays on the reality of science studies*. Cambridge, Mass.: Harvard University Press.

———. 2005. *Reassembling the social: An introduction to actor-network-theory*. Oxford: Oxford University Press.

Latour, B., and S. Woolgar. 1979. *Laboratory life: The social construction of scientific facts*. London: Sage.

Schinkel, K. 1998. Unsettled settlement: Occupation remains from the Bronze Age and the Iron Age at Oss-Ussen. The 1976–1986 excavations. In *The Ussen project: The first decade of excavations at Oss* (Analecta Praehistorica Leidensia 30), ed. H. Fokkens, 5–305. Leiden, the Netherlands: Leiden University, Faculty of Archaeology.

Shanks, M. 1992. *Experiencing the past: On the character of archaeology*. London: Routledge.

Van Reybrouck, D. 1998. Imaging and imagining the Neanderthal: The role of technical drawings in archaeology. *Antiquity* 72:56–64.

———. 2002. Boule's error: On the social context of scientific knowledge. *Antiquity* 76:158–64.

Van Reybrouck, D., R. De Bont, and J. Rock. 2006. Spreading stones and showing bones: The material rhetoric of prehistoric archaeology. In *The fabric of the past: Historical perspectives on the material culture of archaeology*, ed. N. Schlanger. Oxford: Berghahn.

Wesselingh, D.A. 2000. *Native neighbours: Local settlement system and social structure in the Roman period at Oss (the Netherlands)* (Analecta Praehistorica Leidensia 32). The Netherlands: Leiden University, Faculty of Archaeology.

Yarrow, T. 2003. Artefactual persons: The relational capacities of persons and things in the practice of excavation. *Norwegian Archaeological Review* 36 (1):65–73.

4

A Linguistic Anthropologist's Interest in Archaeological Practice

Charles Goodwin

In this chapter I will briefly describe what led me, a linguistic anthropologist, to become interested in archaeological practice (in essence because I don't think one can build an adequate picture of human beings unless you take into account both human language and the social practices through which we transform the environments we inhabit on an extended time scale). I will then briefly describe some of my ethnographic research at archaeological field schools in the United States and Argentina. Finally I will present an example of how archaeologists construct the discursive objects that sit at the heart of their profession (such as features in the earth, maps of those features, categorizations of relevant phenomena, etc.) through socially organized practice that encompasses embodied action, language, and structure in the environment.

In 1976 my wife, Marjorie Harness Goodwin, and I arrived at the anthropology department of the University of South Carolina as their new linguistic anthropologists. The same year the department also hired two new archaeologists. This was when the work of Lewis Binford and the theories of Marvin Harris seemed about to usher in a new era of rigorous, empirical science in archaeology. On the other hand, linguistics, under the influence of Chomsky, was increasingly focusing on mental phenomena and competence rather than the messy, degenerate language found in actual talk. My own approach to human language, strongly informed by both linguistic anthropology and the analysis of conversation initiated by the sociologist Harvey Sacks and his colleagues (Sacks 1995; Sacks et al. 1974), was more concerned with the social and cultural organization of talk in human interaction. My data consisted of videos of people talking in natural settings, and I was interested in human language as a form of public social practice rather than as a symbolic structure located in the psychological organization of the human mind. Nonetheless, one of my most influential teachers, a man I still revere, was Ward Goodenough. He was Marvin Harris's perennial opponent in an ongoing debate (sometimes leading to confrontational sessions at the annual meetings of the American Anthropological Association) about what work should consist of in anthropology. Could serious study of what is important about human beings focus on invisible mental life, emic phenomena, as Goodenough's did, or should it, like archaeology, devote its attention to what could be held, weighed, and measured empirically, and to the larger social processes that had given human societies their distinctive shapes over extended time periods? (By way of contrast I wrote papers about what occurred during the unfolding of a single sentence.)

In retrospect, I believe that the anthropology department at the University of South Carolina was an ideal place to grow intellectually. We included all four fields that make up American anthropology: sociocultural anthropology, biological anthropology, archaeology, and linguistic anthropology. This diversity led to friendly but intense debates between the new hires when we arrived ("you're just mental and emic," etc.). Initially I could ignore such claims about the importance of structure in the material world as irrelevant to my own intellectual interests. However, because we were a small department the entire faculty went to the colloquia of all guest speakers, not just those in their own specialty. Years of such talks provided an ideal way of becoming acquainted with the issues being debated within contemporary archaeological thinking and, more crucially, with what animated the lives of archaeologists intellectually and how they worked and made arguments. The central importance of not only what they were doing, but also how they viewed the world, at last began to sink in.

In essence, archaeologists and linguistic anthropologists took two radically different views of what it means to be human. For those interested in language, it is human language that defines us as a species, differentiates us from all other animals on the planet, and provides the crucial infrastructure for the cultural and cognitive worlds that we inhabit. However, for archaeologists, what defines us as human beings and separates us from all other animals is our ability to structure our material environment in ways that dynamically organize social life on very large time scales. Consistent with such a view, a few cognitive scientists have recently come to recognize the crucial importance of material artifacts, such as maps and tools, in the organization of human cognition in the wild. Hutchins's (1995) analysis of how navigation is accomplished on a naval ship provides an excellent example.

I eventually came to see that while each of these perspectives—one focused on language structure, the other on material structure—offers a crucial insight into what we are as human beings, each perspective is at best a partial truth. Any attempt to adequately describe what it is to be human, and what makes us distinctive as a species, must encompass both. Moreover, such a framework must also take into account how both language and the use of structure in the environment are organized as collaborative social practice, that is, as something that separate individuals do and use together within a public arena of meaningful action.

To try to work out how the ways in which I had studied language in human interaction could be expanded to include material structure in the environment, I began to do fieldwork and videotaping in a number of tool-saturated work settings, one of which was archaeology. The settings I have investigated include the following: (1) I spent two years (1989–1991) at Xerox's Palo Alto Research Center (PARC) as part of the Workplace Project organized by Lucy Suchman (Goodwin 1996; Goodwin and Goodwin 1996). We focused on work practices in various settings at a medium-sized airport (ground operations rooms, the ramp, the ticket counter, etc.). While there I became much more deeply acquainted with contemporary work in social studies of science, and these perspectives have deeply informed my ethnographic approach to the study of archaeological practice. (2) With the aid of Willard Moore, in 1989 I videotaped the geochemistry lab of an oceanographer in South Carolina (Goodwin 1997) and then in 1990 videotaped the work of a group of oceanographers on a research ship in the mouth of the Amazon (Goodwin 1995). (3) I am currently participating in a project organized by Timothy Koschman focusing on the education of surgeons. The data consists of recordings of operations being performed jointly by a senior and junior surgeon. The senior surgeon wears a small video camera on his or her forehead that provides a record of where he or she is looking and thus of the unfolding surgery. (4) I am part of a project organized by Elinor Ochs at the anthropology department of UCLA that is recording the daily lives of families with two working parents in Los Angeles. In addition to the project's videotaping and interviews (psychological, health, family network, and education), our project team includes several archaeologists who draw maps of each family home, record who is present in each space and what activities they are engaged in at ten-minute intervals throughout the filming, and make an extensive photographic inventory of all objects in the home.

Finally, I have recorded work and interaction at a number of archaeological field excavations and labs (Goodwin 1994, 1999, 2000, 2003a, 2003b). First, with the generous aid of Gail Wagner at the University of South Carolina, Marjorie Harness Goodwin and I recorded students working in Wagner's lab in the fall of 1991 (approximately thirty-four hours of tape); then, we recorded at a series of field schools in South Carolina that she directed in the summers of 1992, 1994, and 1996 (approximately thirty-nine hours of tape); we also recorded briefly at an excavation directed by Stanley South in 1994 (approximately eight hours of tape). Second, in the spring of 1993 I recorded a short field school in southern California directed by Jeanne Arnold at UCLA and some of the lab work that followed the field school (approximately twelve hours of tape). Third, in the spring of 1992, Joan Gero, who was then at the University of South Carolina, and I recorded a week of fieldwork at Arroyo Seco, a site being excavated on the pampas of Argentina by Gustavo Politis of the Universidad Nacional De La Plata (approximately twenty-four hours of tape). Joan also introduced me to the then unpublished work of Matthew Edgeworth (2003). At the moment I am preparing for fieldwork at two archaeological excavations with Evangelos Kyriakidis. I am deeply indebted to all of the archaeologists and their students who made this research possible by allowing my colleagues and me to record and investigate the details of the work they were doing.

My encounter with archaeology has thus informed my own research in two different, though interrelated ways. On the one hand, sustained exposure to the work and presentations of archaeologists, and to workplace settings, led me to see that in my own research I had drawn an invisible analytic boundary at the skin of the speaking, embodied actors I was investigating, so that material structure in the environment was effectively ignored. I gradually recognized that an adequate perspective on human action had to encompass both multiparty, multimodal embodied language use and the way in which historically sedimented structure in the environment organized human action and social life in local interactions and on large multigenerational time scales. On the other hand, the work practices of archaeologists themselves, during field excavations and in the laboratory[1] has provided a perspicuous site to investigate the consequential organization of embodied action that encompasses both language and structure in the environment. Figure 4.1, in which two young archaeologists are using a Munsell color chart to classify the color of the dirt they are excavating, provides an example.

Color classification has been a major topic in linguistic and cognitive anthropology. The analysis of Berlin and Kay (1969) remains one of the classic works in the field. They demonstrated that underneath the great variety of ways in which different societies segmented and categorized the color spectrum there was a universal pattern. This was visible in the way in which languages added color terms. If a language had only two they would be white and black (or light and dark); the next to be added would be red, followed by green and yellow, and so on. Despite its power, this analysis was based upon a particular geography of cognition, one that located all relevant phenomena within the mental life of the language user, or in the semantic systems of different languages. Berlin and Kay never looked at how people use color categories to pursue a relevant course of action in the consequential scenes that make up their lifeworld. By way of contrast, the archaeologists in figure 4.1 are classifying color because it is a task posed by the work of excavation they are engaged in. Their cognitive activities are embedded within a larger ensemble of work practices that includes not only categories for classifying color but also tools such as trowels, vernacular documents such as the coding form they are filling out, and a Munsell color chart (a physical artifact that transforms the task of color categorization from an entirely mental activity into a process of comparing what is to be classified to a visible standard sample).

I have analyzed how the Munsell chart structures cognition and social action in archaeological excavation in more detail elsewhere (Goodwin 1999, 2000).

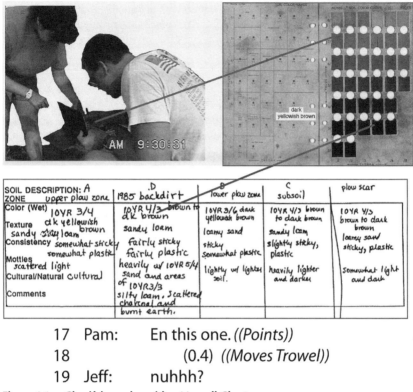

SOIL DESCRIPTION: A ZONE upper plow zone	.D 1985 backdirt	B lower plow zone	C subsoil	plow scar

Color (Wet) 10YR 3/4
Texture   dk yellowish
   sandy clay loam brown
Consistency somewhat sticky
     somewhat plastic
Mottles
   scattered light
Cultural/Natural cultural
Comments
	10YR 4/3 brown to
	dk brown
	sandy loam
	fairly sticky
	fairly plastic
	heavily w/ 10YR 5/4
	sand and areas
	of 10YR3/3
	silty loam, scattered
	charcoal and
	burnt earth.
		10YR 3/6 dark
		yellowish brown
		loamy sand
		sticky
		somewhat plastic
		lightly w/ lighter
		soil.
			10YR 4/3 brown
			to dark brown
			sandy loam
			slightly sticky,
			plastic
			heavily lighter
			and darker
				10YR 4/3
				brown to dark
				brown
				loamy sand
				sticky, plastic
				somewhat light
				and dark

17   Pam: En this one. ((Points))

18   (0.4) ((Moves Trowel))

19   Jeff: nuhhh?

Figure 4.1.   Classifying color with a Munsell Chart

Here a few points will be briefly noted. First, the two archaeologists in figure 4.1 are engaged in very active cognitive work. However, the origins of that cognitive activity are not to be found inside the skulls of the actors but rather within the organization of the larger activity in which their work is embedded. They are intently scrutinizing a tiny bit of dirt because they are faced with the task of filling in a box on a form asking for the color of the dirt. The actions of the senior archaeologist who constructed the form, long before the current actors got to the field site, are organizing in fine detail the perceptual and cognitive activities of those doing the excavation. The way in which the structure visible on the form is constructed through the collaborative work of two different kinds of actors (the senior researcher who constructed the form and the current fieldworkers) occupying quite different social and temporal positions is visible in the contrast between the printed text of the category names and the handwritten entries of the current excavators. The orientation of the current participants to the coding form thus links their local work to distant sites, including both the construction of the form in the past and future use of the form in the lab in the analysis of data and the writing of papers, long after the excavation itself has been shut down.

Second, the Munsell chart itself constitutes a historically structured architecture for perception. With its precise color samples it incorporates into a portable physical object the results of a long history of scientific investigation of the properties of color. It exists not only as a symbolic structure but also as a concrete object constructed in a physical medium, and this is crucial to its organization. Thus a small hole is cut into the paper next to each color patch. The fieldworker using the chart moves a trowel with a small sample of the dirt to be categorized on its tip from hole to hole until the best match with the color of an adjacent patch is found. By doing so she creates what Foucault (1986) calls a *heterotopia*, a juxtaposition of two radically different kinds of space. Actual dirt, a bit of the primordial world that is the focus of the archaeologist's scrutiny, is framed by a theoretical space for the rigorous, replicable classification of color. The mundane moment when this juxtaposition occurs might at first glance seem trivial and quite distant from larger archaeological theory and argument. However, it is precisely here that nature is transformed into culture, or more properly where dirt, the raw material of the world that is the distinctive focus of archaeological investigation, is transformed into the analytic categories and documentary materials (e.g., an entry on the coding form that will be brought back to the lab) that will provide the infrastructure for subsequent analysis, publication, and theory building.

A Munsell page provides not one, but three complementary systems for identifying a reference color: (1) the actual color patch; (2) a page name that specifies hue followed by numeric coordinates specifying a particular patch on the page for that color, for example, "10 YR 3/4"; and (3) color names. These systems are not precisely equivalent to each other. For example, a single color name might include several different color patches and grid descriptions. Thus, on the page reproduced in figure 4.1, the color name "dark yellowish brown" includes four color patches.

Why does the Munsell page contain multiple, overlapping representations of what is apparently the same entity (e.g., a particular choice within a larger set of color categories)? The answer seems to lie in the way that each representation makes possible alternative operations and actions and fits into different kinds of activities. Both the names and numbered grid coordinates can be written and thus easily transported from the actual excavation to the other work sites, such as laboratories and journals, that constitute archaeology as a profession. The outcome of the activity of color classification initiated by the empty square on the coding forms is a set of portable linguistic objects that can easily be incorporated in the unfolding chains of inscription that lead step by step from the dirt at the site to reports in the archaeological literature (see also Hutchins 1995, 123). However, as arbitrary linguistic signs produced in a medium that does not actually make visible color, neither the color names nor the numbers allow direct visual comparison between a sample of dirt and a reference color. This is precisely what the color patches and viewing holes make possible. Moreover, as discrete, bounded places on the surface of the page, they can be identified not only through language but also by pointing. In brief, rather than simply specifying unique points in a larger color space, the Munsell chart is used in multiple overlapping activities (comparing a reference color and a patch of dirt as part of the work of classification, transporting those results back to the lab, comparing samples, publishing reports, etc.) and thus represents the same entity, a particular color, in multiple ways, each of which makes possible different kinds of operations because of the unique properties or each representational system.

Unlike most other animals, human beings have the ability to secrete cognitive organization into the world they inhabit in ways that create new forms of both knowledge and action, while transforming the environment within which relevant activities are accomplished. The Munsell page is simultaneously a material object and conceptual tool. It relies upon the specific properties of material media to build cognitive structure that could not exist within the confines of the skull, for example, the arrangement of possibilities for color classification into an ordered grid that can be repeatedly scanned, the production of actual reference samples that can be visually compared both with each other and with the material being classified, and so forth. All of these operations depend upon the properties of specific physical objects. However, such objects do not exist, and could not exist, in a pure, natural world, for instance, a domain not structured by human practices. By juxtaposing unlike spaces, but ones relevant to the accomplishment of a specific cognitive task, the chart creates a new, distinctively human, kind of space. Moreover, with its view holes for scrutinizing samples, the page is not simply a perspicuous representation of current scientific knowledge about the organization of color but is also a space designed for the ongoing production of particular kinds of action.

Third, when multiple archaeologists work together, as in figure 4.1, the full resources provided by the organization of talk-in-interaction for shaping intersubjectivity within processes of coordinated action are mobilized. Language structure, the sequential organization of action within temporally unfolding human interaction, the body, and material structure in the environment are seamlessly integrated into the relevant courses of action that constitute the lifeworld of a particular community. In line 17 Pam proposes a particular color patch as the solution to their classification task. Rather than naming the patch she identifies it with a deictic expression: "this one." Deictic terms, which point toward something else (they are also called indexical expressions), require that features of the surrounding context be taken into account for their proper understanding. Pam's action in line 17 includes two different aspects of the physical context. First, her talk is accompanied by an embodied action, a pointing gesture; second, that gesture indexes a particular square on the Munsell chart in front of them. Such environmentally coupled gestures (Goodwin 2003a) build multimodal, multisemiotic, meaning-making packages in which sign systems in diverse media are brought together to create a whole that goes beyond any of its constituent parts.

Pam's proposal makes relevant a response from Jeff, and indeed in line 19 he rejects it. However, there is a significant gap in the talk before he answers (line 18). Rather than being empty silence, that time is occupied by embodied work necessary for the competent production of the requested answer: moving the dirt sample to the hole next to the indicated color patch so that a comparison can be made. This brief sequence offers an opportunity to investigate human culture (the distinctive ways in which a particular social group views and categorizes the phenomena that are the focus of its work and attention), cognition, and social organization from an integrated perspective that includes embodied action, the details of language use, and historically structured physical artifacts. Rather than locating the cognitive properties of color categorization in the brains of individual actors, or the semantic systems of different languages, such a perspective opens up to investigation the historical processes through which social groups both provide solutions to repetitive tasks by secreting built, enduring structures into the environment (such as the Munsell chart) where they provide frameworks for the organization of action by their predecessors (Hutchins 1995), and articulate those structures to build relevant action through situated talk-in-interaction.

This provides one example of how I have found it useful to use ethnographic analysis of archaeological practice to investigate how human beings build the actions that constitute the social and cognitive worlds they inhabit together. I am particularly interested in developing frameworks for analysis that include both the details of language use and structure in the environment, as well as embodied action. I will briefly note several aspects of this process.

First, unlike many ethnographers I do not depend primarily upon interviews or my own field descriptions and notes (though I do find such resources invaluable as secondary aids to analysis). I am less interested in what people say they do than in what they do, or rather in where their saying is part of the activities being done and not a gloss or description to an outsider. I view language as a form of social action in its own right. My ethnographic methodology therefore consists of extensive videotaping of whatever people happen to be doing in a setting. Videotaping is always selective, partial, and imperfect, but it does provide records that permit detailed analysis of situated, temporally unfolding actions in which the details of language use, embodied action, and structure in the environment mutually inform each other. My point of departure is an analysis of talk-in-interaction. Thus at Arroyo Seco there was a division of labor in which Joan Gero made extensive observations, field notes, and interviews, while I spent just about all of my time videotaping teams doing excavation. In this process audio is crucial and frequently difficult to record clearly. I have thus constantly changed how I tape based on accumulating experience. In subsequent fieldwork, for a range of reasons I eventually came to favor, though not exclusively, a situation in which a wireless microphone was placed on the senior archaeologist as she went from team to team to inspect their work. My use of video has also forced me to develop ways of representing the data that include not only the talk spoken but also relevant aspects of the participants' bodies and phenomena they are attending to in the environment.

Second, though I consider archaeology a most important site for my research, it is not the only one. Indeed, in order to demonstrate that the practices used to build the specific events that are the focus of a community's attention are in fact quite general, I have frequently compared the work of archaeologists with that in other settings that might initially seem quite different. In "Professional Vision" (Goodwin 1994) I described how a range of practices (highlighting, coding schemes, and the articulation of graphic representations) used by archaeologists to transform the very complex visual field provided by the dirt they were excavating into the discursive objects of their profession were also used by lawyers defending the policemen who beat Rodney King to structure what the jury saw on another complex visual field, the videotape of the beating. In "Action and Embodiment" (Goodwin 2000) I compared archaeologists' embodied work with the Munsell chart with the use of a hopscotch grid to organize action and embodied movement by preadolescent Latina girls. I was attuned to the social importance of coding forms, such as that found in figure 4.1, because of my encounters with similar forms at the airport studied by the Workplace project. The importance of architectures for perception was first impressed upon me on the oceanographic ship, a site in which maps also played a central role in the construction of action and knowledge. Most centrally the organization of embodied action within talk-in-interaction, my original area of research, deeply informs both the methods and the theoretical perspectives of all of my analysis. While archaeology is a central site for my research, I am less interested in what is unique about archaeology than in the way in which the work done by archaeologists sheds light on quite general practices used by human beings to construct social organization, culture, and cognition, and expands our understanding of language structure and use by taking into account a consequential material environment.

Third, topics that I have focused on in my analysis include the social organization of categorization and professional vision. Such phenomena are clearly central to the work of many others (see, for example, Edgeworth 2003). For me they emerge in part from my interest in the organization of collaborative action. In order to build multiparty action together, separate individuals must in some relevant sense construe a world in common. While some of the resources for this are provided by public artifacts, such as the Munsell chart, much of it consists of particular ways of seeing and categorizing the world for which members of a community hold one another accountable. Any competent archaeologist is expected to be able to see features such as post moulds in diffuse color patterns found in the dirt being excavated and to map such features, and so forth. Insofar as such seeing is social, an important part of what it means to be a particular kind of social actor, an archaeologist, its organization is not to be found in the psychology of the individual. To investigate how such vision is organized as public practic, I have found it useful to record the very early days of a field school, where ways of seeing and acting that will later be taken for granted emerge as not only problematic but also as the topic of instruction and repair in interactions between senior archaeologists and newcomers.

I had planned to include a second example demonstrating how vision and embodied tool use were organized as public social practice through specific interactive arrangements. However, I do not have space to do this. I will therefore briefly sketch the argument without providing a specific example (for a more detailed demonstration of these points see Goodwin 1994; 2003a; 2003b). First, I am especially interested in situations where a senior archaeologist is observing and commenting on the work of a newcomer during actual excavation. Typically in such situations the senior archaeologist can observe both the environment that is the focus of archaeological work (for example, the dirt being excavated) and the operations of the newcomer on that environment. These operations can take many different forms, from drawing lines in outlining features, to map making, and to categorization. In all cases the newcomer must put into practice her ability to both see the world as an archaeologist and use that seeing to build the artifacts, such as a map, which are constitutive of archaeology as a profession. Such professional vision is expected of any competent archaeologist; it is an essential part of what it means to be an archaeologist. The senior archaeologist can approve, challenge, modify, and so forth, the work done by the newcomer and indicate other phenomena that must be taken into account in order to accomplish the tasks in progress. A rich array of different kinds of sign systems and meaning-making resources, including language structure, gesture, embodied participation frameworks, and the ability to create new structure in an environment that can be scrutinized together, are used in conjunction to accomplish action in such settings. For instance, after a young graduate student outlines a feature in the dirt, the senior archaeologist not only says that she would have drawn the line in a different place but also demonstrates this by using her finger to draw another line next to the student's. Through such embodied joint work by a newcomer and someone who is already a competent practitioner, the ways of seeing and doing that constitute being an archaeologist are calibrated as public, social practice. The relevant unit for the analysis of the intersubjectivity that occurs in such encounters, the seeing of a world in common by multiple participants, is not specific to individuals as isolated entities but to archaeology as a profession, a community of competent practitioners, most of whom have never met each other but who nonetheless expect each other to be able to see and categorize the world in the ways that are relevant to the work, tools, and artifacts that constitute their profession.

In summary, linguistic anthropologists and archaeologists focus on very different kinds of phenomena and, indeed, inhabit quite separate cognitive worlds. For one community the uniqueness of human cognitive life, what defines us as a species, is language; for the other community what is distinctive about human beings is the ability to act within and upon the material environment and to re-shape it in ways that shape human life and social organization on very long time scales. My sustained encounters with archaeologists led me to see the importance of trying to develop analytic frameworks for the study of human action and cognition that would encompass both perspectives. Archaeology itself provided one very crucial site for investigating how human action is built through the simultaneous use of language, embodied action, and structure in the material environment.

NOTE

1. I have not so far examined the writing of academic articles, the political organization of the profession, the relationships between archaeologists and the inhabitants of the local communities where they do fieldwork, and so forth. I consider these and the other phenomena that make up the working life of archaeologists most important.

REFERENCES

Berlin, B., and P. Kay. 1969. *Basic color terms: Their universality and evolution.* Berkeley: University of California Press.

Edgeworth, M. 2003. *Acts of discovery: An ethnography of archaeological practice.* Oxford: Archaeopress.

Foucault, M. 1986. Of other spaces. *Diacritics* 16:22–27.

Goodwin, C. 1994. Professional vision. *American Anthropologist* 96 (3):606–33.

———. 1995. Seeing in depth. *Social Studies of Science* 25:237–74.

———. 1996. Transparent vision. In *Interaction and grammar*, ed. E. Ochs, E. A. Schegloff, and S. Thompson, 370–404. Cambridge: Cambridge University Press.

———. 1997. The blackness of black: Color categories as situated practice. In *Discourse, tools and reasoning: Essays on situated cognition*, ed. L. B. Resnick, R. Säljö, C. Pontecorvo, and B. Burge, 111–40. Berlin: Springer.

———. 1999. Practices of color classification. *Mind, Culture and Activity* 7 (1). Originally published 1996 in *Ninchi Kagaku* (Cognitive Studies: Bulletin of the Japanese Cognitive Science Society) 3 (2):62–82.

———. 2000. Action and embodiment within situated human interaction. *Journal of Pragmatics* 32:1489–1522.

———. 2003a. The body in action. In *Discourse, the body and identity*, ed. J. Coupland and R. Gwyn, 19–42. New York: Palgrave/Macmillan.

———. 2003b. Pointing as situated practice. In *Pointing: Where language, culture and cognition meet*, ed. S. Kita, 217–41. Hillsdale, N.J.: Lawrence Erlbaum Associates.

Goodwin, C., and M. H. Goodwin. 1996. Seeing as a situated activity: Formulating planes. In *Cognition and communication at work*, ed. Y. Engeström and D. Middleton, 61–95. Cambridge: Cambridge University Press.

Hutchins, E. 1995. *Cognition in the wild.* Cambridge, Mass.: MIT Press.

Sacks, H. 1995. *Lectures on conversation, Vols. I and II*, ed. G. Jefferson. Oxford: Basil Blackwell.

Sacks, H., E. A. Schegloff, and G. Jefferson. 1974. A simplest systematics for the organization of turn-taking for conversation. *Language* 50:696–735.

5

Reflecting upon Archaeological Practice: Multiple Visions of a Late Paleolithic Site in Germany

Blythe E. Roveland

In 1992 I embarked upon a project that considered the practice of Paleolithic archaeology from historical and reflexive points of view. The focus was on a Hamburgian site, Pennworthmoor 1 in northern Germany (Roveland 2000). By weaving documentary and collections research, and by bringing reflexive and ethnographic perspectives to an excavation on which I participated as field supervisor, I attempted to gain a deeper, more contextual understanding of archaeological practice. The research deliberately incorporated elements of present and past practice in order to convey a sense of the various contexts in which archaeology operates. Here, I share one dimension of that research by describing the use of ethnography and reflexivity as tools in understanding archaeological practice.

I began my inquiry with the working assumption that the archaeological record is the product not only of past human societies but also of recurring and changing priorities, strategies, expectations, techniques, and day-to-day activities of archaeologists. Thus, my view of the archaeological record encompasses not only the material remains of past societies but also successive interventions by archaeologists. All archaeologists face the challenges presented by the conglomerate archaeological record, which has been constructed within various historical, intellectual, ideological, economic, and sociopolitical contexts. As practitioners, we encounter and evaluate the archaeological record through a number of access points including archaeological reports and publications, field notes, collections, and our own fieldwork—each of which has been shaped to some extent by these contexts.

The determination of what is recognized as meaningful and collected as data is influenced by a number of factors, including archaeology's accepted practices and expectations at a particular time and place. Also of significance are the excavator's personal history, his or her previous experiences (both at the site and elsewhere), the sequence of events and discoveries, and the daily occurrences that continually affect interpretation at the "trowel's edge" (Hodder 1997, 694).

At the time that I carried out my fieldwork at Pennworthmoor 1, there were few published ethnographic studies of archaeology on which I could model my own (see Edgeworth, chapter 1, for a discussion of the development of such work). The abstract for Matt Edgeworth's dissertation (1991) did not appear in *Dissertation Abstracts International* until 1993 and other studies from which I could have benefited, such as those by Joan Gero (1996) and Ian Hodder (1997), appeared later and thus did not influence my own fieldwork. Nonetheless, their analyses have affected my thinking on the topic of fieldwork after the fact.

These examples do not precisely parallel the context in which my own ethnography of fieldwork was carried out. Gero was the observer in her study but did not participate fully in the daily archaeological excavation. Like me, both Gero and Edgeworth faced the challenge of being an "ethnographer of the familiar" (Edgeworth 1991, 42). As such, one tries to stand outside of a world one normally inhabits. Hodder, on the other hand, directed the fieldwork but did not act as ethnographer. Neither Gero nor Hodder make extensive comment on their own part in the "drama" in the field.

Edgeworth's study was the closest to my own because he both participated on the dig and acted as ethnographer. However, he did not supervise the excavation as I did. In retrospect, the difficulties presented by the dual roles of participant and observer, combined with the added burden of being the site supervisor in my case, proved difficult to overcome.

A BRIEF BACKGROUND TO HAMBURGIAN ARCHAEOLOGY AND PREVIOUS WORK AT PENNWORTHMOOR 1

The Hamburgian was first defined as a Late Paleolithic cultural complex on the North European Plain in the early 1930s. Throughout its research history, avocational archaeologists have played a prominent role in the discovery and interpretation of the Hamburgian record. The most influential of these amateurs was Alfred Rust, whose fieldwork at the now classic sites of Meiendorf and Stellmoor in northern Germany was carried out at the very inception of Hamburgian research. His discoveries inspired a host of other explorations of Hamburgian sites in northern Europe and shaped subsequent expectations and interpretations about this prehistoric period. These findings were eagerly followed by an interested public and were the source of intense regional and national pride during the unique social, political, and economic climate between the World Wars in Germany.

Among the early investigations that followed upon the heels of Rust's work was the excavation of Pennworthmoor 1 in Cuxhaven-Sahlenburg by another self-trained archaeologist, Paul Büttner. Büttner spent his free time riding his bicycle around the countryside to look for prehistoric sites. In 1935, on one such trip, he noticed a newly dug, meter-deep drainage ditch between a dirt farm track (*Feldweg*) and a potato field. Upon closer examination of the walls of the ditch, Büttner found what he had been looking for—Paleolithic stone tools in their primary context (Büttner 1936, 1940a, 1940b). He proceeded to excavate approximately twenty square meters on and around the *Feldweg* on evenings and weekends during 1935 and 1937. His efforts at Pennworthmoor 1 yielded about two thousand artifacts, two hundred of which were diagnostic tools. He had dreams of launching a large-scale excavation of the site and into the adjoining moor (to find another situation like Meiendorf), but this did not come to pass.

I studied documentary evidence and extant artifactual collections to reconstruct Büttner's activities at the site and the broader contextual issues surrounding them—how he excavated, what he recovered, what was recorded, what was saved, and how he interpreted the site. Aside from his own articles (Büttner 1936, 1940a, 1940b, 1942) and letters, several regional newspapers chronicled his finds. I gained an even greater insight into his work when, fortuitously, I had the opportunity to participate as field supervisor in archaeological testing around the Pennworthmoor in 1992 and 1993, nearly sixty years after Büttner's discoveries.

EXCAVATIONS AT PENNWORTHMOOR 1 IN 1993

During the four-week 1993 season, a small team and I concentrated exclusively on Büttner's Pennworthmoor 1 site—seeking evidence of both the Hamburgians and Paul Büttner. In addition to those goals, I wanted to study our own fieldwork in a similarly critical way, to illustrate the complexities and effects of daily practice involved in data recovery and interpretations that cannot easily be gleaned from publications and other historical records.

The landowners granted permission to excavate both on the *Feldweg* and in the fields to the east and west. However, an oat field that could be reached only via the *Feldweg* had to be harvested sometime during the course of our excavations. The timing of the harvest depended on the weather and the farmer's other obligations. Therefore, excavation of a large area on the *Feldweg* could not be undertaken.

We embarked, as all excavations do, with a set of idealized methods and strategies intended for our campaign. However, these methods and strategies varied to accommodate changing circumstances. The decision of where and how to dig was structured partly by me, partly by the visions of other archaeologists, partly by the farmer's needs, and even partly by the weather. It rained on twelve of the twenty-one workdays.

We were unsure of the exact location of the 1930s excavation because Büttner's maps were not to scale, and only an *X* marked the spot. Test units that measured one square meter and were largely noncontiguous were excavated during 1993. We proceeded digging in fifty square centimeter quadrants within a square meter unit at ten-centimeter arbitrary levels. For finer control, in the levels below the fill on the *Feldweg*, each quadrant was to be dug out in three buckets full. Each removal (*Abtrag*) or spit represented approximately 3.3 centimeters. The buckets of sediment were sieved through a one-half centimeter mesh screen. Ideally, any artifact larger than two centimeters was to be left in situ, mapped in three dimensions, and given a separate find number. Much of the documentation of daily activities was recorded on standardized forms. In addition to the more formal means of documentation, I kept my own personal notebook, as did the crew.

That year, there were five of us in the field, two Americans (one woman and one man) and three German students (one woman and two men), with varying amounts of field experience. In some ways it often felt as if a sixth crew member was present, since the traces of Paul Büttner's excavations, and even mere thoughts of him at the site, continually influenced our experiences. As time progressed and we detected more signs of his activities, encountering them nearly overshadowed the thrill of finding Hamburgian artifacts. Coming upon traces of previous excavation added another dimension to the encounter with material remains of Paleolithic people. We had examined Büttner's publications, in which we could see him digging on the *Feldweg*. We had held artifacts that he recovered from the site, now housed on museum storeroom shelves. Both were part of the record of what we knew as Pennworthmoor 1. But the realities of his "doing" of archaeology were never as clear to us as when we witnessed the evidence of that activity emerging from the ground. We became more self-conscious that we, too, were adding to, rather than simply revealing, evidence at the site. Gavin Lucas (2001) describes a comparable experience of coming face-to-face with past and present archaeological practice in his discussion of the re-excavation of a Viking site in Iceland. He asks the question, "What if we see excavation as part of the archaeology of the site—and not just an earlier excavation, but the one happening now. . . . As we uncover the site we also add to it" (202).

We surmised about the record that we would leave for future archaeologists. Furthermore, when one of our test units cut slightly into one excavated the previous year, we confronted ourselves in a material way. These thoughts entered ever more into our consciousness as the weeks progressed. The profile of our excavation unit was an intersection of three points in time that left material traces at the site. The outline of two of Büttner's trenches visibly bracketed vestiges of Paleolithic find layers. Our excavation unit revealed both of these instances and at the same time left behind our own mark in the ground.

There was a great deal of disturbance evident in the excavation units and this, too, led to alterations in our plans. Some of the disturbance could be accounted for as traces of Büttner's excavations from the 1930s. Other areas had been untouched by his shovel, but centuries of accumulation of material on the *Feldweg* complicated the picture.

During the course of the fieldwork, I attempted to note adjustments to the idealized methods and intended plans, as well as my reactions to them. The crew members were, likewise, encouraged to reflect upon their experiences and record them in their diaries. In the following section, I present some excerpts from these diaries and my observations about these multiple reflections. These excerpts illustrate the nature of the work and the decision-making process. Similar types of scenarios described here may well have operated on other Hamburgian excavations, perhaps even on those carried out by Büttner. Although I identify my own passages, the other crew members are referred to by the letters *A* to *D*.

WEEK ONE

Monday

ME: I explained [to the farmer's wife] that I needed to know when the oats would be harvested. . . . She said definitely not this week and probably not next.

[It] started raining so we went inside [the] trailer. This happened repeatedly during the course of the morning. . . . The Feldweg has changed so much in just a year—looks like fill had been added—that's why we couldn't find last year's marker at first. . . . All three [German crew members] are from further south where the presence of flint indicates human intervention. We talked about the difficulties of recognizing artificially [versus naturally] worked pieces. I said better to save it and we can throw it out later.

B: First day of excavation. . . . Despite the constant rain showers we were able to at least set up the excavation grid. A rather small crew. Therefore, I think we'll work effectively.

Tuesday

ME: Mood was positive today even though we didn't find much. . . . C had questions about what was and wasn't an artifact so we screened together a lot. D also had questions about "artifact or not an artifact," B less so. A only asked a couple of times. . . . No one takes unnecessary breaks—I like this crew.

A: I'm not sure if the heavy mottled fill at thirty centimeters is Büttner's back fill or not.

B: Most of us did not sleep well last night. It rained on the tents almost the entire night and the thunder kept us awake. Despite this we are all quite fit, perhaps because it was the first real day of the excavation. In the western portion . . . is a band of yellow sand [that] looks like a[n] animal burrow but it is very straight. . . . I'm having trouble with all the roots in the eastern portion. . . . I have the feeling that I have hit upon the boundary of the old excavation with the yellow sand in the eastern part.

D: My first live contact with Paleolithic material. [I had] seen it, and not really extensively, behind display cases in France last year. That said, I stood before the screened material like a blind man and ran the risk of [attributing] every piece of flint with sharp edges to the . . . Reindeer Hunters. I had to ask almost constantly; most of it was natural junk. . . . I require a long time at the screen. . . . Roots are a nuisance. Larger rocks that I am ripping out with [the roots] are ruining the profiles a little. . . . We've become a very good team in this short time. . . . I hope, but don't believe, that we'll find good [things] tomorrow. My guess is that Büttner . . . turned a lot of ground upside down [in the entire area].

Wednesday

ME: Everyone found some artifacts today although most in disturbed levels . . . Büttner's backfill? . . . Everyone is working very well, but I'm discouraged about how slow it is going.

A: Still not sure of the origin of the mottled fill. However, it looked like stratigraphy one sees in backfilled excavations that have been screened.

D: I frittered away a lot of time at the screen again; still have to ask about almost everything.

Friday

ME: B's new unit is in the middle of the road. Hoping that the farmer can drive over it. . . . I'm getting anxious that at the end of the first week we haven't even completed four units.

A: I had a number of finds I had to map in so I took notes in the rain on a small find card and went back to the work trailer to fill out find cards and draw them on the plan map.

C: Work in level 8 is rather tiring and is not as fun as yesterday and the day before yesterday.

D: I am reluctant to bag any questionable pieces of flint because one could think that I am not looking carefully.

The week began with a good deal of optimism in spite of the rain, and the first Hamburgian artifacts caused great excitement. The excavation procedure changed daily and sometimes more frequently as a different picture emerged about the site. Some of the changes in strategy were prompted by the pressures of time and productivity. Even after this short amount of time, I expressed a self-consciousness and anxiety about the farmer's arrival and about expectations regarding the number of units that should be dug in a week. It was this uneasiness, and not only the data that we were uncovering, that prompted changes in strategy. The identification of ambiguous-looking flints caused difficulty and anxiety. The crew's notes implied that they were feeling inept in some ways. This was the reason behind D's reluctance to collect any questionable pieces of flint for fear of what others might think of him as an archaeologist. Such revelations prompt one to question what might have been lost in the process. Other sources of errors could have come from finishing excavation documents in the trailer out of the rain, but also out of view of the unit.

Each crew member's interpretations about what he or she was finding changed through the course of a unit's excavation, and from unit to unit. The sequence of discovery certainly influenced subsequent expectations about what would be found next and how the data were interpreted. Additionally, each person viewed what was unfolding through the lens of his or her constellation of knowledge and previous experience. For example, A's suggestion about the mottled fill was based upon prior observations on other excavations. My own brief encounter with the site the year before confused the picture for me initially because a Hamburgian artifact had been found much closer to the surface of the *Feldweg* that year. I expected a similar situation during the current season. Also, although I had worked on other Paleolithic sites, I had not encountered so many naturally occurring flints that hampered progress at a site. Other crew members had never excavated in northern Germany or at a Paleolithic site.

Everyone anticipated Büttner's disturbance, formulating and reformulating what it would look like. This may actually have served to deflect attention away from the primary aim at hand: recovering Hamburgian remains in situ.

WEEK TWO

Monday

A: Today was warm and pleasant. It seemed to almost lull the crew into a sleep; but of course it was a Monday. . . . I was excited to find the first complete shouldered point. . . . Overall the majority of the finds appear to be coming from the same level discussed by Büttner. I still think most of this level was intact except maybe in the eastern third.

D: [I'm] sharing a cell next to B.

Tuesday

ME: B preferred to work in the rain. . . . B and D built makeshift tent over their units. A and C finished their units . . . which was a relief. They can begin digging in the field. I'm worried about opening too much in the road.

B continued to have interesting/colorful disturbances in his level 7—B is convinced that [it is] Büttner's disturbance.

D: Here and there are quite small flakes. They are so small that it could very well be that they were overlooked in the earlier excavation.

Wednesday

ME: C was dragging today. . . . D kept finding artifacts 1.99 cm long so he didn't have to map them in!

A: I finally noticed a line in the north wall and . . . [a] floor where the unit from last year had been. So we seem to be on grid from last year.

B: At first it wasn't clear to me which one I should view as the disturbed area and which one was the undisturbed area. . . . Small quantities of blades and flakes came from [the area of Büttner's old excavation] as if there had been enough material there that he had overlooked some. . . . At first I didn't believe that Büttner had "forgotten" remainders of the original level between his excavation pits. But in my unit there is evidence that he dug in the north and the south [of the unit]. There was a fifty-centimeter-wide area that remained undisturbed.

Thursday

ME: D throws a lot of his artifacts into his work tray and labels them later on. I don't know how good his memory is to judge the possible source of error.

Friday

ME: The morning was rainy and it became impossible to work—dirt stuck in screens—units filled with water.

The constant questioning of what might have constituted Büttner's disturbance illustrates the rethinking that occurs during most excavations. Emerging interpretations about the way in which Büttner had dug the site illuminated not only his methods but ours as well. B at first did not anticipate that Büttner might have left gaps between his excavation units. In his publications, the avocational archaeologist stated that he would pick up exactly where he had left off the time before. We were also surprised to find relatively few (and small) artifacts in Büttner's backfill. Since he had used only a screen while excavating a few of his units, I expected him to have missed more finds.

D had the annoying habit of finding artifacts that did not quite measure two centimeters and, hence, did not have to be piece plotted. Perhaps he was following this "rule" too strictly (or perhaps he was conveniently mismeasuring them ever so slightly). Another excavator might have erred in the other direction and might have mapped these borderline artifacts. Comparisons between the plan maps of units would then give the impression of a greater density of significant artifacts in the latter case. However, one could also ponder the arbitrariness of this figure of two centimeters in the first place.

The impending threat of the harvest continued to determine the choice of the placement of units. There were several potential sources of error during the week like the problems screening the muddy sediment. At the end of the previous week and throughout the second week the burden of taking personal notes along with all our other duties was already becoming too great. Some of my diary entries were written days later.

WEEK THREE

It continued to rain almost daily into the third week of excavation and the farmer still had not come to harvest the oats, so we continued to be afraid to dig more units in the *Feldweg*. C summarized it nicely one day: "The morale was rather low this morning." And B commented, "I am sick and tired of walking back and forth to the trailer every time it rains. This afternoon I was so perturbed that I opened up my new unit in the pouring rain."

Digging and drawing under makeshift tents had become commonplace occurrences. These cannot be considered optimal conditions in which to work. The plastic tents diminished visibility, and this might have led to some things being overlooked. It was also quite uncomfortable to work under the tents for long, and so there was a tendency to rush the activity in order to be free of discomfort.

This week's personal notes emphasized the nature of fieldwork, not only as a practical and intellectual exercise but also as a social one (Edgeworth 1991, 118). The tensions mounted as the week progressed. One instance of this can be noted from the following diary passages.

Friday

ME: Today I told C that she would screen and D would dig in her unit on the road. . . . D missed a double borer that was later found in the screen.

C: I'll only say one thing: Borer . . . and it didn't go much better in B's unit. . . . Because my walls were really terrible according to D, I screened the entire day. I can't do more than try my best.

B: C screened for me today. Unfortunately that takes a while because she looks in the screen for a long time so that she doesn't miss any flakes.

C's slowness at the screen was annoying to B, who attributed it to her lack of experience and archaeological knowledge. However, there might have been more to it than that. It may have been a way for C to demonstrate her competence in finding every possible artifact in the screen (and likewise to demonstrate other crew members' shortcomings). The fact that the crew members were beginning to be at odds with each other might have stifled some potentially useful cooperation and idea sharing.

WEEK FOUR

By the last week, fatigue, pressure, and the weather had taken their toll. Tensions among the crew continued to mount and it was probably fortunate that this was the last week of the dig.

The pace had picked up to the point of noticeably affecting the quality of our work. A long blade ended up in the screen, profiles were not drawn, and the number of unscreened levels had increased. It is likely that certain careless errors would not have occurred had it been the first week of the excavation, when expectations were high, questions were many, and the crew erred on the side of caution. Three days before the end of the dig, the farmer arrived on his combine to harvest the oats. We kept a few units open in the middle of the *Feldweg* in the hope that the combine wheels would straddle them. Unfortunately, the weight of the combine collapsed the walls, requiring us to rush to backfill the units and then reexcavate them after the harvest.

Note-taking activity had dropped off even more dramatically, and I became one of the primary culprits. My personal diary entries ended on the day of the combine disaster. This seems to be one of the first things to be neglected when time and energy are scarce, although it is, of course, an important activity. Edgeworth (1991, 85) also found that it was difficult to keep up with his own ethnographic notes of an excavation as the tempo increased toward the end of the project. Even at Hodder's (1998) state-of-the-art field project at Catalhöyük, which offered the crew networked computers rather than old-fashioned pencil and paper, personal note taking became less systematic.

CONCLUSION

The difficulties involved in being a kind of ethnographer of one's own practice are clear. It is difficult from an intellectual standpoint to distance oneself from the familiar. It is also challenging from a practical standpoint—it is yet another task added to an already burdensome suite of daily duties.

I find it remarkable that this crew was so candid in their notes even though they knew of my purpose for them. I remain skeptical whether this approach would be effective in other contexts with other participants. The hierarchical nature of many excavations might serve to suppress true reflection on the part of the crew (Chadwick 1998). This particular exercise was carried out as part of my doctoral research, which presented certain limitations in terms of power relations and expectations. Critiquing one's own research is not a practice that is regularly rewarded in academia through gaining employment or being promoted. I ran the risk of suggesting that because I was a student and because Büttner was an amateur, our research warranted scrutiny, while that of other experts would not. Therefore, even in an attempt to reveal, certain issues and events remain shrouded, consciously and subconsciously.

Additionally, the admission of errors and personal disputes during fieldwork is not encouraged, although they occur all the time, however much denied. If mistakes are not revealed in personal field notes, site reports, and other publications, knowledge about potentially serious sources of error is suppressed. Like any archaeological team, we brought our own strengths, expertise, and shortcomings to a situation in which we did not always have complete control.

Büttner likely encountered some situations that affected his work at Pennworthmoor 1 that were similar to those we experienced. He, too, lacked adequate funding and resources. While we do not know about the other people who might have participated in his dig, they would have brought their own sets of skills and limitations. In his publications, it is clear that his work had been affected by the farmer's use of the *Feldweg* and by the weather. Because it was a tourist area at that time, too, various onlookers also would have influenced his day-to-day practice, as they did ours. On the other hand, Büttner had a different worldview, training, and working assumptions about the Hamburgian record. He had no previous experience on a Paleolithic site, and Hamburgian archaeology itself was in its infancy. Whatever the similarities and differences in our experiences on that particular site, each campaign left its permanent mark, simultaneously drawing from and adding to the archaeological record (Lucas 2001).

Through the process of critically evaluating past practice and assumptions, I began increasingly to question my own practice and those of my contemporaries. As in previous research, retouched artifacts held an importance that other artifacts did not. Uncovering a retouched tool in situ was reason for jubilation, while one found in the screen evoked consternation. Although we had been trained to think differently than Büttner about artifact distributions, concentrations of artifacts were still more interesting to us than dispersed patterns.

In other ways, however, our working assumptions probably diverged. Whereas Büttner might have erred on the side of discarding ambiguous, nonartifactual flints, I likely erred in the other direction by encouraging the crew to save pieces that may have been naturally "worked."

It would seem that by carrying out the excavation as we did, we had inherited the view that Paleolithic distributions (and, likewise, hunter-gatherer behavior) are and were meaningful at the centimeter scale. We think little about the true benefits of plotting artifacts and features to the nearest centimeter, but we take great pains to do so. Would it make much difference if a shouldered point had been mapped two centimeters away from its actual location? We obsess about such details but dismiss other details as insignificant.

We are trained to keep records in the field of day-to-day events. Yet much of this information is missing in the final report and can be retrieved only with much time and effort. The mistakes, daily strategy changes, decision making, difficulties, and reports on the weather will be lost as well. Yet these are important in understanding the "what's, why's, how's, and therefore's" of the excavation, as Tilley (1989, 279) has suggested.

Archaeological fieldwork, data, and interpretations are influenced by a complex web of factors operating on many different levels. If we were to take the time and effort to include such information in our reports at the outset, we would be making a significant contribution. We would be acknowledging that these issues are relevant to any understandings of the data and interpretations presented.

ACKNOWLEDGMENTS

I am indebted to Dr. Stephan Veil and Andreas Wendowski-Schüneman for allowing me to carry out fieldwork at Pennworthmoor. Martin Wobst has provided remarkable guidance over many years. I am grateful to Matt Edgeworth for persuading me to take part in the WAC session and the present volume. Barrett Brenton has been my rock and contributed immeasurably to the fieldwork in Germany and all the other fine messes I've gotten him into. My research was supported in part by a Deutsche Akademische Austauschdienst (DAAD) Grant, a Wenner-Gren Foundation Grant for Pre-Doctoral Research, and a University of Massachusetts Graduate Fellowship. Any omissions or errors are strictly of my own doing.

REFERENCES

Büttner, P. 1936. Ein eiszeitlicher wohnplatz am Pennenmoor bei Cuxhaven. *Mannus* 28 (4):501–10.

———. 1940a. Der eiszeitliche wohnplatz am Pennenmoor bei Cuxhaven (Schlussbericht). *Mannus* 32 (3):448–54.

———. 1940b. Ein eiszeitlicher wohnplatz an der elbmündung. *Jahrbuch der Männer vom Morgenstern* 30:7–13.

———. 1942. Wie ich zur vorgeschichte kam: Die geschichte der entdeckung der steinzeitlichen wohnplatz bei Cuxhaven. *Die Kunde* 10:54–59.

Chadwick, A. 1998. Archaeology at the edge of chaos: Further towards reflexive excavation methodologies. *Assemblage* 3, www.shef.ac.uk/~assem/3/3chad.htm (accessed June 15, 2003).

Edgeworth, M. 1991. The act of discovery: An ethnography of the subject-object relation in archaeological practice. PhD diss., University of Durham, UK.

Gero, J. 1996. Archaeological practice and gendered encounters with field data. In *Gender and archaeology*, ed. R. Wright, 251–79. Philadelphia: University of Pennsylvania Press.

Hodder, I. 1997. Always momentary, fluid and flexible: Towards a reflexive excavation methodology. *Antiquity* 71:691–700.

———. 1998. Introduction and summary. Çatalhöyük 1998 Archive Report, catal.arch.cam.ac.uk/catal/Archive_rep98/hodder98.html (accessed January 18, 2005).

Lucas, G. 2001. *Critical approaches to fieldwork: Contemporary and historical archaeological practice*. London: Routledge.

Roveland, B. 2000. Contextualizing the history and practice of Paleolithic archaeology: Hamburgian research in Northern Germany. PhD diss., University of Massachusetts, Amherst.

Tilley, C. 1989. Excavation as theatre. *Antiquity* 63:275–80.

6

Pictures, Ideas, and Things: The Production and Currency of Archaeological Images

Jonathan Bateman

The drawings that are produced by archaeologists occupy a pivotal point in the complex of relationships that develop around excavations. The act of putting pen or pencil to paper or film has come to underpin the visual language upon which archaeology relies for its everyday discourse. And beyond the role drawings have as structuring elements of the discipline's visual vocabulary, they are also of great interest in understanding the social and intellectual arena in which they are conceived—the excavation.

Excavation plans, section drawings, and maps are among the strongest common currency of archaeological illustration. The traditional, developed forms of these illustrations are allied in their reliance on visual codes derived from the hand-drawn, inked line—their shared roots lying in the development of archaeological draftsmanship as a craft. These traditional, quite commonplace, monochrome images form the basic building blocks of archaeology's visual vocabulary, but their role within the discipline can be seen to reach far beyond that of illustrative tools and simple visual prompts. The mechanisms that create these images are not subservient or subsidiary to the overall processes of archaeology that create narratives of the past but are in fact central to such production. And although the crafted drawn form is prevalent in many of archaeology's illustrative realms, it is its relationship with the excavation process that has established its position as the visual lingua franca of archaeology.

The illustrative practices that surround and accompany excavation can be seen as a crucial link between that mechanism of destruction (excavation) and the mechanisms of preservation (record) that form an uneasy relationship through

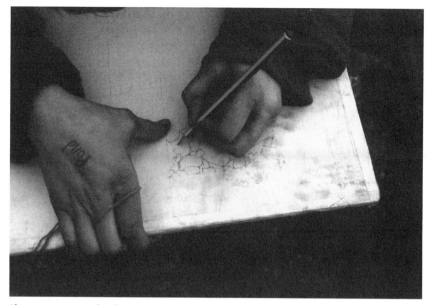

Figure 6.1. Drawing in progress. Archaeological drawing has an intimate and personal relationship with the materiality and the embodied processes of excavation. (Photo by Jonathan Bateman)

archaeological excavation. Excavation technique and process have developed with the notion that record is as important a rationale as that of discovery. Archaeological drawings can be conceived of as, at once, both reasons for the destruction entailed in excavation and saviors of that which is destroyed—through record and through preservation.

This intimate relationship between the destructive and creative processes that are excavation, and the archaeological drawings that both drive and witness them, puts the act of drawing at a conceptually crucial stage in the archaeological production process. The potency of this interpretive step is further reiterated by the social positioning of the drawing process within the discipline and the techniques and technologies through which these images are reproduced and manipulated. In this way, drawing, as an interpretative step, becomes inextricably intertwined with both previous and later interpretative and creative stages, such as the physical excavation itself and the writing of narratives of the past based on that excavation.

Unraveling how the drawing process, along with its products and its material culture, has reached and maintains its position within the intricate web of relationships and processes of excavation is a complex task. But we need to come to an understanding of the role of archaeological drawing in the discipline to fully illuminate how the interlacing of knowledge, people, practice, and things constructs archaeology—in physical, social, and intellectual forms.

Figure 6.2.   Supervisor watching diggers. Drawing is entwined with the social production of archaeology throughout the creative process. (Photo by
Jonathan Bateman)

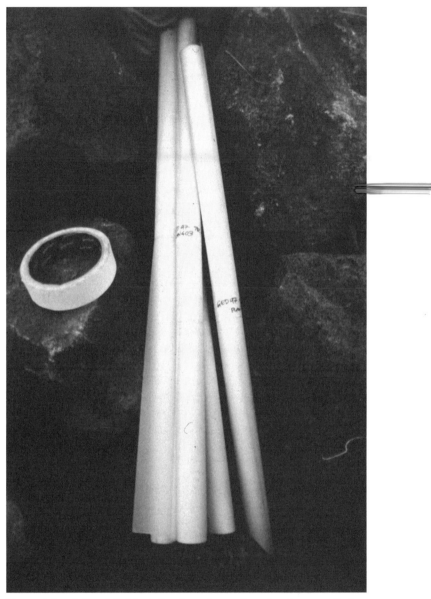

Figure 6.3. Rolls of finished drawings. Excavation drawings rapidly become recognizable artifacts of the archaeological process. (Photo by Jonathan Bateman)

Critical to understanding the relationship of drawing to the excavation process as a whole is the character of its production and materiality. Among the material products of excavation, drawings can be conceived of as being the most objectified if we exclude excavated material itself. Excavation plans are very physical things, unwieldy to unwrap and view and sensual to touch, sight, and even smell. They often bear the material essence of the excavation itself, stained with dirt and scarred from the very processes of their production. In their distinct and unwieldy nature they have also become the last bastion of analog recording—the hardest of archaeology's record products to mold into digital forms.

In their first incarnation, fresh from the board, they represent the excavation process's most artifactual product—the one output of digging that most meets the criteria of artifact. Most other products of the recording process are quickly subsumed into files, both paper and digital, but excavation drawings remain a dirty, cumbersome presence, characteristics both resented and fetishized by those who come into contact with them.

Along with many other aspects of the excavation process, recognizing that drawings have both intellectual and material resonance, as well as being embedded within and reflecting complex social relationships, is an important step in developing understandings of the production of archaeological knowledge. Accepting their complexity as objects—as artifacts of the archaeological process—and embracing it as we would the intricacies of recovered artifacts is a critical step.

A useful example of such a step is Alfred Gell's (1996) essay "Vogel's Net," in which he conceptualizes anthropologically sourced traps as artworks—in particular a bundled Zande hunting net. Gell conceptualizes the hunter's trap as a surrogate for the hunter himself, so that "the hunter's skill and knowledge are truly located in the trap, in objectified form, otherwise the trap would not work." He describes traps as devices that

> embody ideas, convey meanings, because a trap, by its very nature, is a transformed representation of its maker, the hunter, and the prey animal, its victim, and of their mutual relationship, which, among hunting people, is a complex, quintessentially social one. That is to say, these traps communicate the idea of a nexus of intentionalities between hunters and prey animals, via material forms and mechanisms. (29)

Gell establishes essentially functional items as potential carriers and embodiments of complex ideas, meanings, and intentionalities. He gives an inclusive definition of an artwork, discarding traditional definitions, to reach a point where artworks are fundamentally "objects that are scrutinized as vehicles of complicated ideas" (36)—objects that potentially reward such scrutiny because they embody "intentionalities that are complex, demanding of attention and perhaps difficult to reconstruct fully" (36). Such an approach to objects is not far from many archaeological paradigms that offer ways of encompassing the

Figure 6.4. Tapes, strings, and planning frame. The complexity of the material production of drawings reflects their intricate relationship with both the material and the social production of archaeology. (Photo by Jonathan Bateman)

complex aesthetic codes and explicit functionality of material culture into our understandings of its social context.

Gell's conceptualization seems both a development and an operationalization of Pierre Bourdieu's (1971) notion of the "cultural unconscious" (180). This is the term that Bourdieu applies to the inherent influence the social context of production has upon creative endeavor, upon the "artist."

Jonathan Bateman

It is the extent to which he forms part of an intellectual field by reference to which his creative project is defined and constituted, by the extent to which he is, as it were, the contemporary of those whom he wishes to communicate and whom he addresses through his work, referring implicitly to a whole code he shares with them—themes and problems of the moment, methods of argument, manners of perception, etc—that the intellectual is socially and historically situated. (180)

It is essential to Bourdieu's concept that the meanings (the intentionalities, potential meanings) that the social and historical situation embody in a cultural product cannot be considered as divisible from any other meaning intended by the artist. It is not something added on to an already existing intention (an artist's "intended" meaning) as any artistic intention is, in fact, conditional upon its position within this unconscious cultural landscape. In this instance, this goes a long way to helping us conceptualize the notion of cultural meaning embedded within functional products, where the codes of expression are considered as givens, so deeply embedded in practice that they are considered beneath (or perhaps beyond) complex consideration.

> This culture consists of credos which are so obvious that they are tacitly assumed rather than explicitly postulated. Examples are ways of thought, forms of logic, stylistic expressions and catchwords (yesterday's existence, situation, authenticity, today's structure, unconscious and praxis) which seem so natural and inevitable that they are not properly speaking the object of a conscious choice. (Bourdieu 1971, 180)

Archaeological drawings help to establish their creators as archaeologists and their subjects as archaeological facts and knowledge, and the association of one with the other aids both. Archaeologists are so because they create archaeology, and that archaeology is so because it is created by archaeologists. Thus the illustration of archaeological material has become part of a hermeneutic system that acts to both initiate and reinforce the knowledge-creation structures of the discipline.

This can be seen throughout the process by which survey and excavation are transformed to published book, report, or journal. At each stage the process is intertwined with other intentions, desires, and expressions of those intentions and desires. During excavation, illustrative practices and activities can be seen as a crucial arena in which archaeological identities are created and maintained. This is particularly visible in relation to the tools and materials used by archaeologists. Just as the choice of tools and materials is an important element of the illustrator's positioning within the production process (a point that is emphasized in many traditional manuals of drawing technique: Hope-Taylor 1966, 1967; Adkins and Adkins 1989), so those involved in the illustrative processes of excavation use drawing tools and materials to establish and maintain archaeological identities.

This is manifested in the personal toolkits developed by individuals on excavations. The selection or deselection of illustration tools within these kits is a

Figure 6.5.   Pencil, board, and eraser. Drawing tools are representations of personal and professional experience, knowledge, and belonging. (Photo by Jonathan Bateman)

mechanism through which individuals can position themselves in relation to the illustrative aspects of excavation practice. This is one way in which these practices are aligned with personal archaeological identity. You can see this with particular clarity on excavations where a wide range of people brings a variety of desires and expectations to the site (Bateman 2004).

Figure 6.6. Balancing while drawing. The act of drawing offers opportunities to demonstrate intimacy with the archaeological process. (Photo by Jonathan Bateman)

During observation over a number of years of an excavation project at Gardoms Edge in Derbyshire, England—which involved professional archaeologists, university-based archaeologists, experienced and inexperienced students, and amateur volunteers—it became clear that the illustrative practices were a key area in which archaeological identity and the roles that individuals aspire to were established and expressed. Those wishing to be perceived within the social group as professional archaeologists could be seen to express this through their choice, acquisition, and use of illustration tools and materials. I saw this as related to the responsibility that is placed upon those involved in the recording aspects of excavation, of which drawing is one. An alignment with these practices was a demonstration of willingness to accept this responsibility—this responsibility itself being one of the key elements of the professional identity to which these individuals aspired (see also Van Reybrouck and Jacobs, chapter 3).

Conversely, those who wished to establish and confirm other identities onsite were seen to exclude these materials from their practice, demonstrating that these responsibilities did not fit into their aspired role in the excavation. This was observed with respect to "amateur" volunteers, whose expected role involved excavation but not the responsibility involved in recording. Similarly the relationships that inexperienced students demonstrated with the material culture of the site were explicit demonstrations of their experience or inexperience in specific practices. The familiarity or otherwise with tools and materials could

Figure 6.7.   Preparing pencils. The authenticity of field illustrations is always tempered by the anticipation of the reproductive processes that await them. (Photo by Jonathan Bateman)

be seen as quite public reflections of the students' desires for tutoring or mentoring relationships, while the students were also beginning to establish their own nascent professional archaeological identities.

In the context of archaeological production we can see that those producing—and indeed reproducing—images are using them and the situation of their production in different ways. The production of archaeological drawings in the field is an intimate negotiation between the drawer, the materiality of excavation, and the social relations that surround them. Here, very personal desires and intentionalities become entwined with the images, closely tied to their authenticity. These images reflect the situatedness of those who create them—they reflect the distinct nature of the author's relationship with their material and social surroundings. Through archaeology's illustrative practices—the tracing, redrawing, and inking—these images are transformed into images for reproduction, images for public consumption. At this point the intimate relationship between the image, its creator, and those who see the image cannot be reconstituted as it was, and in fact, the transformed image could be understood as having no use for these relationships.

In this sense, it is the act of creation, the authorship of the image in the field, that has value to those concerned—this value is lost when the image enters the reproductive processes of archaeology. But here the image takes on new, wider, more public values and resonance.

Drawings made on-site are created with the knowledge and expectation that they will be reproduced in multiple forms. In archaeology this does not mean only that they will have copies made for distribution. The processes through which these drawings are incorporated into archaeological discourse and embedded in archaeological narrative are processes both of reproduction and of reiteration. The pencil drawings made in the field are drawn with an awareness that they will be traced and redrawn, probably by someone else, to become part of a more inclusive whole. Inked reference plans, composite plans and sections, archive drawings, drawings for reports, and drawings for final publication are inked up in the drawing office—lacing together the dispersed dialogues with the archaeology that the raw field drawings represent.

These reproductive processes of archaeological illustration can be related to Walter Benjamin's conception of art as taking on political value when it leaves the ritual context of its production and enters the uncontrollable, public realm of its dissemination (Benjamin 1970). Here the authenticity of the image is no longer of value, so it is no longer questioned by the reader. The continually reproductive process of archaeological illustration has produced a representation of archaeological truth. Now the social and political value of the image lies in its form and context, the references between it and other images, and the links between it and the text around it. The content—the archaeological information represented by the image—has limited social power, but the manner of its representation has the ability to enforce or undermine professional (and intrinsically therefore social) relationships and identities.

These meanings and intentionalities in the published archaeological product are not unrelated to, or divorced from, those intimate desires embedded through the initial drawing process, but the shift in the manner and scale of their expression determines that they function in fundamentally different ways. The reiterative process through which site drawings are transformed into illustrations for publication gradually separates the image from the subjective interpretive process that was at the root of its inception. The conscious and unconscious decisions that were part of the image's creation become embedded more deeply within the knowledge authority structures of the discipline. The fuzzily drawn lines are sharpened and the hesitantly drawn boundaries are strengthened and defined through the repeated tracing and redrawing of the original field drawing. But as this strengthening of the archaeological veracity of the image is underway, the counterpoint is the increasing entanglement of the authorship and authenticity of the image.

Communal authorships become masked by the veneer of the drawing office's consistency of style and then also by the declared authorship (through signature or acknowledgement) of the final publication illustrations. While the transition between the ritual and the political (in Benjamin's terms) has taken place, the ritual meanings—the desires and intentionalities of all those surrounding the production of the image—are not cast off but become part of a complex of

Figure 6.8.   Looking, thinking, and drawing. Drawings are the artifacts of some of the critical interpretive steps between excavation and narrative. (Photo by Jonathan Bateman)

meanings and references that is embedded within the archaeological narratives of which these images form a part.

In light of this, we can better understand how archaeological drawing, as practice and product, has become the building block of the discipline's visual language. In a reiterative cycle the reverence that the discipline has for the drawn form can be seen as a symptom of the importance of illustration to the discipline and the reason for that importance. Individuals use the practices that surround illustration to establish and maintain personal and professional identities because these practices have a valuable social currency in the discipline, and simultaneously such use of these practices enhances their value in this context.

But more importantly, understanding these practices allows us to approach understandings of how the production of archaeological pasts and knowledge is entwined with the personal and social situations of all those who make up the discipline.

Just as I forged both professional and personal identity in the creation of the photographs that form part of this discussion (Bateman 2004), so in creating drawings, archaeologists are negotiating relationships with both the archaeological material and those around them. Both the drawings and these photographs embody these negotiations, and evoke the complex intentions and desires of their creators. Without these intentions and desires the images would not complete their transformation from drawing to archaeological truth.

REFERENCES

Adkins, L., and R. A. Adkins. 1989. *Archaeological illustration*. Cambridge: Cambridge University Press.

Bateman, J. 2004. Wearing Juninho's shirt: Record and negotiation in excavation photographs. In *Envisioning the past: Archaeology and the image*, ed. S. Smiles and S. Moser. Oxford: Blackwell.

Benjamin, W. 1970. The work of art in the age of mechanical reproduction. In *Illuminations*, ed. H Arendt, 219–53. London: Jonathan Cape (originally published in 1936, *Zeitschrift für Sozialforschung* 5 [1]).

Bourdieu, P. 1971. Intellectual field and creative project. In *Knowledge and control: New directions for the sociology of education*, ed. M. F. D. Young. London: Collier-Macmillan.

Gell, A. 1996. Vogel's net: Traps as artwork and artwork as traps. *Journal of Material Culture* 1 (1):15–38.

Hope-Taylor, B. 1966. Archaeological draughtmanship: Principles and practice, part II: Ends and means. *Antiquity* 40:107–13.

———. 1967. Archaeological draughtsmanship: Principles and practice, part III: Lines of communication. *Antiquity* 41:181–9.

7

Studying Archaeological Fieldwork in the Field: Views from Monte Polizzo

Cornelius Holtorf

Ethnography of archaeology is a new but fast-growing field of interest and approach, investigating the practice and materiality of professional archaeology. Often the focus is on archaeological fieldwork, as the present volume illustrates. My own contribution addresses the question of what kind of experience project members have on an archaeological excavation project. Besides the way a project can be described in academic terms, for example in field reports, I will be asking precisely what it means to participate in an archaeological project from the participants' point of view and what it is they are actually learning during an excavation. This matters particularly when excavations are designed as student training excavations, making it pertinent to study the learning experiences and outcomes.

My case study consists of the ongoing excavations at Monte Polizzo in western Sicily (Morris et al. 2001; Prescott and Mühlenbock 2003; Mühlenbock and Prescott 2004). This large international coproject involving partners in Italy, Norway, Sweden, and the United States[1] is committed to a joint research strategy including common ways of digital recording, scientific sampling, and finds administering. My research extends and complements a number of other studies that have focused on the character of archaeological fieldwork at Monte Polizzo (Avikunthak 2001; Pearson and Shanks 2001, 28–32; Shanks 2001–2003; Holtorf 2002; Shanks 2004, 497–99).

During the summers of 1999 and 2000 I took part in the Monte Polizzo project for four and three weeks respectively. My methodology consisted mostly of participant observation, aided by my camera and a journal. In addition, near the end of both my stays I distributed two-page questionnaires (in English and Italian) to as many project participants as possible. In 1999, I received forty completed questionnaires, in 2000 only eighteen. The questions were a mix of queries about possible improvements for future seasons and questions specifically designed to explore the experience of participating in the project. All my own research was conducted openly and I answered many questions about it. I believe that it was widely understood that everybody could speak to me openly without their interests or reputations being harmed as a consequence, which is why I have anonymized most references to specific people in this paper.

At the time of my research, the community of archaeologists at Monte Polizzo consisted of about fifty-five (in 1999) and over eighty (in 2000) project participants from many countries. About three-quarters were students or recent graduates. Although it was not a homogenous group, but one that differed vastly in academic experience, ranging from undergraduates in other disciplines to various research students in archaeology, anthropology, orclassics, all will be called "students" in this chapter. The group of students was the largest and also the one easiest to observe by freely mingling among them, so that it became the main focus of my research. Another reason for not taking into account to the same extent the experiences of the project leaders and various independent experts was that I had no access to their meetings and discussions and a lot of the time I was guessing—with the students—about their true agendas and the precise character of the evidently existing disagreements between them. Since I began my research in 1999, two senior members have resigned from the project.

Overall, my experience in this project was very positive. I met many interesting people from diverse backgrounds, worked at some great locations, was surrounded by much challenging and exciting archaeology, undertook some fantastic excursions to various sites in the area, and benefited a great deal from the good organization of the project. The overall evaluation of the project by other participants was similarly positive. Nevertheless, for heuristic reasons only, I will be saying unproportionally more about those tensions and frictions that arose.

ON ARCHAEOLOGICAL CULTURES

Fieldwork has always been considered a crucial part of archaeology's identity, both inside and outside the discipline (Welinder 2000, chapter 4). Among archaeologists, those who do not do fieldwork are often mocked as armchair archaeologists. It is therefore not surprising that practical fieldwork is widely considered of central importance for the training of students. In the field, students become "real" archaeologists by learning the practical skills and methods of academic archaeology. The various universities cooperating at Monte Polizzo made this aspect of fieldwork the key content of their project descriptions. The 1999 field prospectus for Monte Polizzo by Stanford University is an ambitious document, making much of the academic potential of both the site and the project, and again emphasizing field methodology. Likewise, The Sicilian Archaeo-logical Field School run by Michael Kolb of the Northern Illinois University (NIU) invites students to "Learn how to excavate, survey and conduct lab analy-sis," gaining them six hours of anthropology credits.

When in international coprojects teams from various countries—with their own disciplinary traditions—apply different research methodologies to their own trenches, all sorts of faultlines can emerge that run right across the entire project, creating tensions and animosities on all levels (see, e.g., Hamilton 2000). At Monte Polizzo, as elsewhere, students learned very different kinds of archaeological practice depending on which team they happened to be work-ing with. I remember the disbelief with which a senior team leader looked down on the methodology applied in one particular working area by another team (Pearson and Shanks 2001, 29). I also remember the dismay that was caused when it emerged that the recording of the entire site, managed fully electronically by one team, was duplicated by another team that apparently thought that only their own, traditional recording system could be relied upon. Moreover, there was one area of excavation that some observers considered to be conducted with a very poor excavation methodology indeed.

Going into the field can be considered the principal initiation rite for an ap-prentice archaeologist, where the professional culture of the discipline is trans-mitted from one generation to the next (Moser forthcoming; Welinder 2000, 54–60; Carman 2004; see also chapters by Bateman, Carman, Van Reybrouck and Jacobs, and Wilmore in this book). There students learn the unspoken rules, attitudes, and lore of their discipline and they, too, can differ strongly be-tween different archaeological traditions. Stories about the hardship of archae-ological fieldwork and anecdotes about students or colleagues that derive from a shared experience of being in the field are popular subjects of conversations among archaeologists of all ages. Personal friendships (and animosities) with future colleagues are established in the field too. The professional culture of ar-chaeology also encompasses such elements as

- ritual feasts;
- digging songs (see also Eibner et al. 1996);
- site-specific vocabulary referring to food (combat bread, cf. Avikunthak 2001), people (Don Kolbo, Pop Karin, Lolita), places (the Swedish hill), things (Banks mobil), or larger issues (the Kristianisation of western Sicily);
- oral traditions, for example, about how the professor bought large num-bers of Kinder chocolate eggs in order to get to the toys inside, or how X and Y were secretly interested in each other;
- and behavioral norms including eating manners and dress codes, for vari-ous occasions.

Learning such rules of the game, or tacit knowledge, can be of crucial signifi-cance in determining whether or not students relish becoming archaeologists

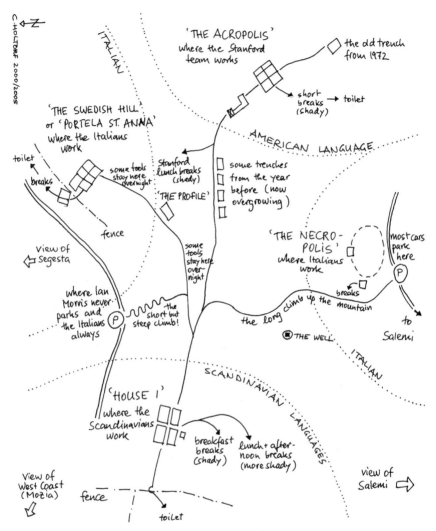

Figure 7.1. A sketch map of Monte Polizzo (Cornelius Holtorf 2000/2005)

and succeed in their subject or not. For "competence in the cultural life of the discipline . . . functions as an informal sorting device, often without the sorters and the sorted being aware of the fact" (Gerholm 1985, 2; see also Becher 1989). It is mainly this dimension that makes archaeological fieldwork so significant in educational terms: you learn how to "do" excavation (Carman 2004, 49).

At Monte Polizzo (in 2000), different archaeological cultures could be studied by focusing on distinct working areas on the site (figure 7.1). The American NIU team engaged in survey work and small excavations at some distance around the main site, so that its members were not normally in sight of the others during working hours. On Monte Polizzo itself, a Scandinavian team of Norwegians from Oslo and Swedes from Göteborg excavated at House 1 and in some trenches nearby. A local Italian team from Palermo dug at Portela St. Anna. A small group of other Sicilians investigated the Necropolis. Finally, another American team, from Stanford University, occupied the Acropolis area and ran the finds lab in the excavation base back in the town of Salemi. Since the various teams did not generally share all their tools and equipment, they might even be kept apart on the basis of their material culture alone and thus be identifiable as archaeological cultures in the conventional sense. The same cultural differences were also manifested in language boundaries that effectively ran both across the mountain and, back in our base in Salemi, across the long table where we ate our main meals together.

In 1999 students were encouraged (and in 2000 allowed) to move between the various working areas of the different teams, in order to be confronted with the variety of traditions and learn about different methodologies, but many never made use of this opportunity. Even those students who did rotate were never left uncertain about which archaeological culture they belonged to themselves. In their questionnaire answers, many mentioned that the student rotation scheme was not working as it should and wished that it be better coordinated by the senior team leaders. My own cultural affiliation was not simple. In 1999, I lived in Göteborg and felt close to the Swedish participants but was officially part of the Stanford team. In 2000, I came from England but was officially part of the Norwegian team.

FIELDWORK AS A SOCIAL EXPERIMENT

In the evenings and on weekends, the existing cultural distinctions were played out socially. Sometimes, what members in one team found appropriate was considered offensive, bizarre, or downright embarrassing by others. Toward the end of the 2000 season, for example, the Stanford students publicly awarded various fun awards to members of their team—what others felt would have been appropriate on a scout camp but hardly on a professional excavation project. On another occasion, they commemorated the U.S. Independence Day (July 4) by singing loudly the American national anthem on top of the Italian mountain (see also Holtorf 2002, 68)—to the complete astonishment and disbelief of various onlookers. Some Scandinavians and NIU students, in turn, were considered unwelcoming and cold, even aggressive, because they did not project sufficient friendliness and seemingly lacked requisite small-talk abilities ("Can she actually smile at all?" somebody wondered about a Swede). In another significant episode, one person decided to set fire to the maypole that the Swedes had erected for their midsummer celebrations, even though this was not the Swedish custom and explicitly resented by some of them.

As a result of such experiences, social mixing between members of the various teams only went so far. Sometimes even at the beach they were sitting in separate groups. The reasons for the existing social divisions among the various groups of students were manifold and partly also linked to

- varying durations of participation in the project (in 1999, many Stanford students stayed a considerably shorter time than most others);
- age differences (Scandinavian students were older on average than American students);
- varying personal motivations (for most Stanford students, the project was a holiday experience and a chance to visit Europe—whereas the Scandinavians and NIU students participated in order to advance their archaeological careers);
- the variation in students' social backgrounds and in status of their universities (especially ordinary NIU versus Ivy League-caliber Stanford);
- associations with different Western regions and cultures, and the prejudices associated with them (directed mostly against the Californians);
- varying linguistic abilities and ambitions (whereas some Italians struggled with English as the project's lingua franca, few others were trying to pick up conversational Italian, and the Scandinavians occasionally fell back on their own languages); and
- quite simply the specific mix of characters and personalities involved in each year.

The emerging social tensions were neither unusual nor unexpected. Indeed, one educational rationale for such international cooperation is the desire to confront students with complex social situations, since arguably the experiences gained will help them in their future lives and professional careers. I have no reason to challenge this assumption. But I am not sure if these are merely side issues—however desirable—of international coprojects in archaeology, the main task of which is to understand the past, or if they in fact become the main concern for the project members, against which the daily digging and surveying might seem fairly inconsequential and insignificant. In 1999, every other American who completed my questionnaire described the multinationality of the project in negative terms, and more than half of my sample had reservations about the overall atmosphere within the project.

Tensions can be particularly strong when it comes to perceived or real hierarchies of privileges. By that I do not mean that somebody who returned to the site in the following year could gain status from inside knowledge about the project and life in Salemi, and might thus be able to occupy a particularly prestigious seat at the dinner table (cf. Yarrow, chapter 2), or the supposedly best spot in the house to spend the hot Sicilian summer nights. Problematic, rather, was the fact that the students attended the project under very different financial conditions depending on where they came from. In the Scandinavian tradition, education is provided free of charge and in addition students are eligible for favorable loans to meet their living costs. Most of them participated on the basis that their costs were paid (for instance, by research grants from their university), but a few had paid their own costs in order to participate. Stanford students had everything paid for and additional resources to spend as they needed them, but they of course also paid tuition fees of close to thirty thousand dollars per academic year. NIU's Sicilian Archaeological Field School charged each student several thousand dollars (in 2003, $3,200 plus transatlantic flights) for four weeks of work within the same project. Members of this field school also tended to have less time off than the others, although under the circumstances this was appreciated as "more value for money." Nobody blamed anybody personally for these inequalities—as it was not anybody's personal fault or gain, and more to do with different traditions of educational and research funding—but it nevertheless contributed to erecting boundaries of sheer incomprehension on the one side and maybe some envy on the other. There were other inequalities too.

All students lived together under one roof (with the exception of some of the Italians who commuted from home), but they were often not able to spend their evenings, and especially weekends, together. The key scarce resource was the number of available seats in the cars that were used to shuttle students to the beaches or to undertake excursions to other destinations. Stanford students could draw on seemingly unlimited funds and even hire additional cars when needed, and NIU too was able to supply its paying students with sufficient space in vehicles, which they needed anyway to shuttle people during survey work. The Italians often spent their free time away from the project, but the Scandinavians had only limited funds for transport and that meant that far too often, some of their students had no access to the beach on weekday evenings or were left behind in the excavation house even during weekends. Short-term car hire in Salemi was not available, although students were even willing to pay with their own money. Everybody was aware of this problem and did their best to be as fair as possible, with elaborate booking systems and planning going on all week. The disadvantaged were often those with slightly lower status, who were a little less popular, more shy, or more tired than the others. This issue was the single biggest reason for frustration and friction among students, affecting the entire project. All these sentiments and experiences reflect what Michael Shanks (2004, 498) has called the "political economy" of a project—the existing social order that makes it work.

Effectively, the Monte Polizzo project became a social experiment, with important lessons (hopefully) to be learned and treasured by each participant. Arguably, these social experiences and specific lessons to be learned should be given far more attention by those running such projects. Rather than using cheap (or even lucrative) student labor for opening yet another trench or registering yet another bag of potsherds, the students' field experience might have been vastly improved by devoting as much attention to the time off work as to the time at work. This does not mean that every minute during a project's duration needs to be planned in advance or that there should not be room for spontaneity. But, to me, the Monte Polizzo experience illustrated that training excavations especially are not only about acquiring professional skills and experience but also about learning a professional culture (see also Moser forthcoming; Carman, chapter 8). What this culture will look like in the future depends a lot on how it is transmitted to new recruits. That transmission occurs on excursions and beach visits as much as during working hours.

TRAINING STUDENTS DURING FIELDWORK

But how successful was the Monte Polizzo project at teaching students valuable archaeological field skills to which everybody was committed? Despite all the best intentions of the project chiefs, most participants remained largely ignorant not only about the complex historical contexts of the site and the specific academic issues at stake but also about many of the specific methodologies employed to make new contributions to academic knowledge. When asked about the aims of the Monte Polizzo project, the respondents to my questionnaires tended to write in very general terms about learning about the ancient city of Monte Polizzo, about the ancient Elymians (who might once have occupied the site), and about the Iron Age and Bronze Age of Sicily. The senior project leaders did a lot to address this problem—we had weekly or twice-weekly seminars and regular academic lectures. But the problem could not be remedied during any single field season. Specific preparatory courses about the Sicilian past and the methods and techniques used in the project, as they took place in Göteborg in 1999 and as they (Ian Morris tells me) have now been introduced for all participating Stanford students too, are helping to empower all participants as full project members. There were also individual students in various teams who made their field research at Monte Polizzo the subject of their own research, in particular at the master's degree level. But these projects were relatively few and had the value of an added bonus rather than the educational core of the project.

At Monte Polizzo, as so often in archaeology, the site directors and their assistants (effectively the trainee or apprentice site directors) alone carried the burden of writing the all-decisive field reports (see, e.g., Morris et al. 2001; Prescott and Mühlenbock 2003). As principal investigators, they are responsible for the excavation and postexcavation work and can benefit from expert reports that come in long after the fieldwork itself—and therefore the involvement of most of the students—has ended. They carry forward the project from one season to the next and need to justify the progress made in each year to the institutions funding them, to the authorities providing permission, to the academy at large, and to themselves and their own academic careers. It is thus not surprising that, in 2000, one team director and his trusted apprentice regularly went back up the mountain while their students were resting or administering their finds during the hot afternoons. They used this undisturbed time to do much of the drawing and recording for the planned interim report and presumably subsequent publications. As student error and input concerning the emerging bigger picture are minimized, education is reduced to a favorable mix of labor camp and package holiday, with the accommodation and the served food belonging to one or the other, depending on whom you asked and when. The best students (best in what?) will later become chiefs themselves and perpetuate the system.

In this scheme of things, the large majority of students provide labor, which is largely used to generate primary data, and are given as pleasant an experience as is possible in return, while at the same time being initiated in the professional culture of archaeology, as discussed above. Although student satisfaction with both their own work and the project overall was high, a large majority of my 1999 sample would have appreciated additional teaching, both formal and hands on, about the various methodologies and approaches applied within the project. The extent to which inexperienced students can contribute to archaeological research might be limited, but that is not to say that the professional training outcome could not be improved. In 1999 and 2000, what the archaeological fieldwork at Monte Polizzo actually revealed about the past and the contribution it will make to academic scholarship was almost coincidental to how the project was experienced by many of those participating in it.

ARCHAEOLOGY AS AN ADVENTURE?

Archaeological fieldwork has traditionally had strong gendered associations and is often perceived as a masculine practice, affecting even recruitment and professional specialization (Woodall and Perricone 1981). Even now, women might occasionally feel pressure to act in more masculine ways on excavations, whereas feminine characteristics in men can be frowned upon (Moser forthcoming). The popular stereotype of the archaeologist is a male hero and adventurer wearing a khaki safari suit and a pith helmet, and carrying a gun. I remember the astonishment in the face of at least one male student who, early during the 2000 season, appeared on Monte Polizzo wearing various practical garments, some in khaki, when it turned out that his project director preferred clothes that had more in common with beachwear than with "suitable" expedition clothing.

I did not particularly focus on gender issues while working on Monte Polizzo but they can be inescapable (see also Avikunthak 2001). Some Italians found it incompatible with their own understanding of gender roles that women in the project were happily doing hard physical work such as deturfing with heavy tools. On the other hand, a few female students occasionally wore skimpy clothes that dazzled some men. Off work there was concern in 1999 about the behavior of young Sicilian men, including local police officers, toward some of our women when the women were walking alone in town. It was thus decreed that among the project participants every woman could request any man to be her escort.

The archaeological romance of eerie adventures in exotic locations, involving treasure hunting and fighting for a good cause, has become a widely applied stereotype of archaeology (Holtorf 2005, chapter 3). In the field, archaeology must be tough and include hardship and sacrifice, for archaeologists prefer to lead lives of exhaustion and earned rewards (see also Larsen et al. n.d.; Welinder 2000, 57–58). In its 2003 online poster, The Sicilian Archaeological Field School emphasized the word "discover," spelled in large letters. Students were then invited to "work and live in a small, medieval village near the Mediterranean" and to "explore ancient temples, ruins and monuments." This is archaeological romance writ large, and not even entirely fictitious. Our daily work involved exhausting physical labor on a mountaintop and a lot of sweating in the merciless midday summer sun of the southern Mediterranean. To compensate (and reward) ourselves we were drinking all sorts of tasty alcoholic drinks such as Zambouka and Limonello during the long and warm Sicilian summer evenings. Romance and discovery referred mostly to the ongoing search for the best local ice-cream parlor, the coolest pubs (Extra-Bar or Pacha-Bar?), the most beautiful beach (figure 7.2), and the most exciting sights in the region. We discovered the Carthaginian town on the small island of Mozia (once crossing over in hired kayaks) and went to explore the caves on the Isle of Lévanzo. We climbed up to the scenic temple of Segesta and walked through the impressively transformed ruins of Gibellina Vecchia. We enjoyed the atmosphere in the little Mediterranean tourist village of Marinella near the beach closest to Salemi and in the medieval town of Erice with the most amazing view

Figure 7.2. The fieldwork experience: Archaeologists at Scopello beach (Photo by Cornelius Holtorf)

over all of western Sicily. Having returned home, former participants often cultivate such memories from the field and revel in the possibility of returning during the following summer.

Some of the most fascinating and memorable discoveries and explorations of the fieldwork season took place both in the local town of Salemi and in the basement of the dig house itself. On the evening of July 9, 1999, for example, a large group of us walked to the ruined castle of Salemi, which we had always wanted to explore. The gate was closed, but adventurous as we were, being the archaeologists in town, we decided to have a look anyway. It was not difficult to climb over the fence and get a look at the entire site. On the way out, there were four people missing. We learned that the local police had detained them for trespassing. They were later released after answering some questions and stating their personal details. As archaeologists, it was said, they should have known that ruined castles can be dangerous to visit and respected that the site was closed. In retrospect, maybe we should not have gone. Our action was certainly never explicitly condoned by any project chief, and Ian Morris tells me now that "everyone currently involved in the project thinks that this was disgraceful behavior, and we deplore it." The episode affected the project's local status and proved embarrassing especially to another senior team member who had been caught in the act with the others. Apparently, even in 2002 when the castle reopened, the event was still remembered. It was an archaeological adventure that none of the involved parties will easily forget.

We also enjoyed exploring the deserted bottom floor of the building in the first and second floors of which we were accommodated. This large space was once used as a clinic and it had obviously not been cleaned up since its closure—only blocked off with bricks in a rudimentary fashion but insufficiently closed to stop us entering through the back door. Like contemporary urban explorers who explore the uncharted areas of our cities (e.g., infiltration.org), we could not resist finding out what lay underneath the floors we called home. We found a mess. One room was full of medical apparatus and papers spread out on the floor. In the center was what looked like a defunct X-ray machine, elsewhere a bone saw. In another room we found an old Italian flag and nearby a plow that was possibly still in occasional use, with access through a locked garage gate. There was much broken glass and other rubbish spread out all around; one room was full of sewage smelling appallingly—we wondered whether this came from our very own toilets. As one participant later remembered, we were living on top of "a classical horror film scenario." Unsurprisingly, one or two students subsequently experienced nightly spooks.

SO, WHAT HAVE WE LEARNED?

Enduring various psychological, physical, social, and cultural ordeals of fieldwork and the rewards one enjoys in compensation are crucial in the participants' experience of it. Within the Monte Polizzo project, there was a certain tension between the explicit archaeological aims of the project, including student training, and what the participants mainly learned and experienced. In effect, students were initiated or further promoted within their own professional culture, gaining social and cultural competency in how to act as an archaeologist and what to treasure in their collective memories. Certain norms, values, customs, and traditions were successfully transmitted to the novices. Exciting adventures were experienced, hardship endured, and pleasures enjoyed so that everybody felt they had proved themselves and been rewarded. All in all, no bad result. Arguably, it is results of precisely that kind that ultimately contribute more to the socialization of archaeologists than any mastered skills or available expertise regarding particular facts or objects found in the ground (Holtorf 2002; Moser forthcoming; cf. Van Reybrouck and Jacobs, chapter 3).

I have argued that emerging academic insights about the past are almost coincidental to what an excavation project is actually about (see also Avikunthak 2001; Shanks 2004; Larsen et al. n.d.). The really significant advances in knowledge are usually established and formulated by the project leaders long after the fieldwork has ended. Only one historic fact was learned by everybody during the excavations in 2000. It impressed some tremendously that Ian Morris, a professor at Stanford University, had in 1979 auditioned for the heavy-metal rock group Iron Maiden (unsuccessfully).

Archaeological fieldwork is not only the sum of applied methods and techniques but also an experience that is significant in many ways other than what it purports to be. I wish that this experience were much more strongly reflected not only in general assessments of what fieldwork is meant to achieve for archaeology but also in the design and evaluation of specific projects.

NOTE

1. For further details see these web pages: www.hf.uio.no/iakk/sicilia/; www.eoec.org; archaeology.stanford.edu/MountPolizzo/homepage.htm; and dig.anthro.niu.edu/sicily/sic_home.htm accessed July 17, 2005).

ACKNOWLEDGMENTS

Michael Shanks initially invited me to take part in the Monte Polizzo project in 1999, and I am grateful for this opportunity. I returned in 2000 due to support from the Norwegian project section and the University of Cambridge, where I was based at the time. For facilitating my work within the project I would like to thank Michael Shanks, Christopher Prescott, Ian Morris, all those project members who filled in my questionnaires, and all participants who de facto became my research subjects. Special thanks to Matthew Fitzjohn for translating questionnaire answers originally given in Italian. An earlier draft of this paper was widely circulated among project participants in 1999 and 2000 as well as some others, and I received valuable comments from Christel Andersson, Matt Edgeworth, Michael Kolb, Kristian Kristiansen, Ian Morris, Christian Mühlenbock, Ulla Rajala, and David Van Reybrouck. None of them necessarily agree with all or any of the views expressed in this chapter.

REFERENCES

Avikunthak, A. 2001. Rummaging for pasts: Excavating Sicily, digging Bombay. Video film. *Stanford Journal of Archaeology*, archaeology.stanford.edu/journal/newdraft/ashish/index.html (accessed July 17, 2005).

Becher, T. 1989. *Academic tribes and territories: Intellectual enquiry and the cultures of disciplines*. Milton Keynes: Open University Press.

Carman, J. 2004. Excavating excavation: A contribution to the social archaeology of archaeology. In *Digging in the dirt*, ed. G. Carver. BAR S1256. Oxford: Archaeopress.

Eibner, C., H. Fehr, and M. Nadler. 1996. *Baktrer Schnaps und Mammutschinken. Lieder von Archäologen für Archäologen*. Büchenbach, Germany: Dr. Faustus.

Gerholm, T. 1985. On tacit knowledge in academia. In *On communication 3*, ed. L. Gustavsson, 1–15. Selected papers from a seminar arranged by the Department of Communication Studies, May 1984. University of Linköping.

Hamilton, C. 2000. Faultlines: The construction of archaeological knowledge at Çatalhöyük. In *Towards reflexive method in archaeology: The example at Çatalhöyük*, ed. I. Hodder, 119–27. Cambridge, UK: McDonald Institute Monographs.

Holtorf, C. 2002. Notes on the life history of a pot sherd. *Journal of Material Culture* 7:49–71.

———. 2005. *From Stonehenge to Las Vegas: Archaeology as popular culture*. Walnut Creek, Calif.: Altamira Press.

Larsen, J., B. Olsen, A. Hesjedal, and I. Storli. n.d. *Camera archaeologica: Rapport fra et feltarbeid*. Tromsø museums skrifter 23.

Morris, I., T. Jackman, and E. Blake. 2001. Stanford University excavations on the acropolis of Monte Polizzo, Sicily, I: Preliminary report on the 2000 season. *Memoirs of the American Academy in Rome* 46:253–71.

Moser, S. Forthcoming. Gendered dimensions of archaeological practice: The stereotyping of archaeology as fieldwork. In *Practicing archaeology as a feminist*, ed. A. Wylie and M. Conkey. Santa Fe, N.Mex.: School of American Research.

Mühlenbock, C., and C. Prescott, eds. 2004. *The Scandinavian Sicilian Archaeological Project. Archaeological excavations at Monte Polizzo, Sicily. Reports 1998–2001*. Göteborg, Sweden: University of Göteborg, Department of Archaeology.

Pearson, M., and M. Shanks. 2001. *Theatre/Archaeology*. London: Routledge.

Prescott, C., and C. Mühlenbock. 2003. Mt. Polizzo, Sicily: Preliminary views on Elymians and ethnicity, landscape and identity. In *Scandinavian archaeological practice—in theory. Proceedings from the 6th Nordic TAG, Oslo 2001*, ed. J. Bergstøl, 26–37. Olso, Norway: University of Oslo, Department of Archaeology, Art History and Conservation.

Shanks, M. 2001–2003. Sicily—archaeological moments, metamedia.stanford.edu/traumwerk/index.php/Sicily - archaeological moments (accessed July 17, 2005).

———. 2004. Archaeology and Politics. In *A Companion to Archaeology*, ed. J. Bintliff, 490–508. Malden, Mass.: Blackwell.

Welinder, S. 2000. *Arkeologisk yrkesidentitet*. Tromsø, Norway: University of Tromsø, Institute of Archaeology.

Woodall, N., and P. Perricone. 1981. The archeologist as cowboy: The consequence of professional stereotype. *Journal of Field Archaeology* 8:506–9.

8

Digging the Dirt: Excavation as a Social Practice

John Carman

The "social archaeology of archaeology" (Carman 1996, 178; 2004) has been offered as a means toward the study of what archaeologists do. It has some affinity to the ethnography of archaeology (Edgeworth 1990, 2003), which is also concerned with what archaeologists do, but the concern of the ethnographer of archaeology is perhaps much more with how archaeologists go about what they do, starting from the premise that archaeology is in some sense a normal activity. The social archaeology of archaeology has more to do with what doing archaeology does in the world. It asks questions such as, Why archaeology at all? How did an archaeology like this develop—but not one like that? What do archaeologists make? What are the implications for wider society in having people who do archaeology and what they do in doing it? This kind of research derives from a particular approach to the world that takes little or nothing for granted: it is sometimes deliberately naive, perverse, and awkward. In conversation, Michel Foucault once commented that "People know what they do; they frequently know why they do what they do; but what they don't know is what they do does" (quoted in Dreyfus and Rabinow 1983, 187). We archaeologists know what we do. Archaeologists have a good idea why we do what we do. My challenge is that we do not know what we do *does*. Hence the need for a social archaeology of archaeology that inquires into archaeology itself as a set of material practices in the contemporary world.

As suggested elsewhere (Carman 1996, 178–83; 2004), the approach of a social archaeology of archaeology is to examine archaeological practices from three complementary perspectives: historical, contextual, and comparative. Here, however, the focus will be upon a comparative approach alone—not as advocated previously across territorial boundaries but rather to seek out parallels for archaeological behavior within the same cultural frame of reference. There is a close reliance on memory for the specific content of this chapter, gained over time at a number of different archaeological excavations, supplemented by the recollections of others and confirmed as part of wider experience in conversation. It cannot claim to be a definitive study of aspects of archaeological experience nor does it offer a very specific and replicable methodology. To a large extent, the truth of any statements made and generalizations drawn will be measured by the degree to which they accord with the experience of others and "ring bells" with readers. It is also hoped to encourage others to look at the particular practices of excavation in a new way, to reexamine assumptions, and to reassess so many of our shared taken-for-granted notions.

Other contributions to this book make valuable strides toward understanding professional archaeological practices in a specifically ethnographic manner. This chapter (and see also Carman 2004) is an attempt to generalize and especially to raise questions about the very material experience that is archaeological excavation as a set of specifically *social* practices. The focus here is upon the experience of the academic research excavation and the academic training excavation. Another kind of experience can be expected on a commercial, developer-funded excavation, where the objectives are different and the ethos that of the commercial workplace rather than the academy.

Archaeology is not done alone: arguably, because the function of archaeology is to contribute to our collective knowledge and understanding of the past, it cannot ever be a purely solitary pursuit. Accordingly, those aspects of excavation that we share will be the focus of this contribution. In taking this approach, we start from the position that wishing to spend time kneeling on the ground in the open air at all times of the year and in all kinds of weather, gently scraping at the surface with a very particular kind of tool, is a strange thing to want to do. Although taking a historical perspective is not one of the purposes of this paper, it is also worth bearing in mind that it is a very modern practice, with only a few decades of history behind it. Excavation involves the physical act of digging in the dirt (Carver 2004); this paper will dig in the dirt in another sense—by exposing to view some of the aspects of archaeological practice on-site usually unconsidered and certainly unpublished. In this respect, a number of aspects of the excavation as a social phenomenon spring to mind as taken-for-granted notions that are worthy of deeper thought: its location in relation to other activities, the process of induction for newcomers, and the social activities typical for a digging team.

LOCATION

The chosen location for any kind of archaeological activity is generally held (and assumed) to be the product of technical considerations deriving from the human use of space in the past. Especially in its contemporary form in the United Kingdom, the majority of locations for archaeological fieldwork are selected on the basis of mitigating the effects on buried archaeology of modern development projects (Cooper et al. 1995; Hunter and Ralston 1993). To that extent, they are chosen on exclusively practical grounds that owe nothing to peculiar disciplinary ideologies. At the same time, there are sound functional reasons for separating the site of excavation work from the surrounding area by barriers and hoardings: to keep out nighthawks and other possible despoilers; to prevent unauthorized access generally; and to minimize the possibility of accidental injury to people from equipment and deep excavation. Another reason for this separation—or possibly a consequence of it—is to mark the area as one where something unusual, special, and indeed interesting is taking place.

There is a well-established tradition (at least in urban England) of passersby taking time to watch construction work of any kind: conveniently placed slits are usually provided for this purpose in hoardings surrounding such work. Archaeological work is equally attractive and, of course, much of it looks to the untrained eye exactly like building operations. Separating out the area where such work is taking place marks it as special and different: a place apart from the rest of modern space. This separation of urban archaeology from its surroundings is not unlike the choice of location for so much academic research archaeology, especially the training excavation. These are most often well away from any institutional or other base, requiring the provision of transport to and from accommodation and other facilities, and frequently in isolated regions away from human habitation. Here, the idea of "the place apart" (from the rest of the world) is achieved by a direct physical separation from anywhere else. The effect is to create an isolated group of people with common aims and interest, out of effective communication with the rest of the world, and thrown onto their own devices for human warmth and mutual comfort.

This process of physical separation is integral to building a sense of common purpose and unity in an excavation team (the American term "digging crew" carries the same idea: the analogy is with the crew of a ship at sea, away from civilization). There is a close engagement with "the wild" involved here. Archaeological excavation is—perhaps above all else—a direct engagement between the intellect and the physical world. Among others, Ian Hodder has pointed out that excavation is a "bodily interpretation" (Hodder 1999, 92) involving the practical application of a tool to feel differences between archaeological structures and features, and he cites being handed a trowel by the excavator to feel for himself changes in soil on-site. The environment within which this takes place is equally material. Excavation sites might have—or at least are experienced as having—their own microclimate: one gazes out from the sun-illuminated trench to see rain falling elsewhere, or (and possibly more likely in the UK) from a sodden trench to see sunlight falling on a green distance. The sense of distance is crucial to an appreciation of the site where digging takes place: it must be away from other places, cut off from civilization, and remote as a desert island. Even when the site is in an urban or near-urban location, with a main road carrying heavy traffic only meters away, the sound of the outside world is softened by the placing of baulks and spoil heaps.

The sense of the place where the excavation is located is never part of the discourse of archaeology. The conventions are to locate sites in terms of plans, maps, and aerial photography (see, e.g., Barker 1982, 26–34) but not in terms of the experience of landscape and cultural meaning (for ideas see Bender 1993; Tilley 1994). As Christopher Tilley puts it:

> Looking at the two-dimensional plane of the modern topographic map with sites plotted on it, it is quite impossible to envisage the landscape in which these places are embedded. The representation fails, and cannot substitute for being there, being *in place*. [The] process of observation requires time and a feeling for the place. (75)

Experiences of place are always part of the excavation as a practice but, as Tilley suggests, are excluded from professional discourse. Cornelius Holtorf (2001) has particularly made this point in his discussion of the archaeological field trip, where he emphasizes the preponderance of "inward-looking" involved in site visits and a concomitant lack of "outward-looking" and urges instead a "focus on the sensual and bodily experiences which can be gained" from such educational activities (84). The same can be said for incorporating such experiences into our discourses of excavation.

ON-SITE TRAINING

The practice of excavation is central to archaeology for two linked reasons: it is a primary source of data for analysis and interpretation, and it is by doing excavation that archaeologists are made. Indeed, in many ways it is the exercise of the practical skills of the trowel-wielder that will determine position and status among other archaeologists. Within the context of a training excavation, a certain amount of incompetence in the specific technique being taught is allowed and even required on the part of trainees. In the context of a professional contracting unit, incompetence in what is deemed the appropriate technique will not be tolerated to the same extent. Volunteers working on-site alongside experienced excavators will be allowed a large measure of incompetence, partly for the sake of hospitality and partly in order to maintain the distinction between professional and amateur status. The specific social, political, economic, and professional context will need to be well appreciated in order to make sense of this apparently deliberate indulgence of below-standard working practice. The case of the dedicated training excavation (for which trainees might also be paying a fee and on which the majority will be new to the field) might be very specific, and approaches will vary. Where, however, newcomers are taken into a longer-term project, there is often a similar approach to their induction.

Very rarely will a newcomer join an established team and begin straight away scraping at the earth. Instead, he or she will often be placed among those responsible for processing finds. This has a number of functionally utilitarian aims: to introduce newcomers to the kinds of objects considered worthy of treating as finds; to give them a chance to get to know the daily and maybe weekly routine of the site; to become familiar with the site layout, health and safety procedures, and the locations of necessary facilities. It also has a strong socializing role since finds huts (or tents or vans) are places where virtually everyone on-site will be seen at some point of the day and might even provide the place where everyone convenes for protection from inclement weather. Working in the finds hut therefore allows newcomers an opportunity to meet and chat with all those involved in the project and—perhaps more importantly—for all those involved to meet and chat with newcomers. By the end of their time working on finds, newcomers will at once feel and be accepted as part of the larger team. As well as learning some of the valuable technical and professional aspects of this particular archaeological project, they will have integrated into the group that carries out the work, have given information about themselves and learned information about their fellows, and be familiar with the modes of address and topics of conversation habitual among the group members.

After a suitable period of such induction—long or short—the newcomer will be allowed to step beyond the baulk, onto the excavation itself: here is where excavating sheep are so often separated from burrowing goats. Usually in the company of a much more experienced mentor, the new excavator will be tested in various ways. Typically, newcomers will be assessed for their ability to deliver bucket- or wheelbarrow-loads of trowelled earth to the spoil heap with sufficient dispatch so as not to interfere with the speedy clearance of soil by the expert digger to whom they are attached. Failure to please could mean relegation always to less interesting parts of the site, while success could mean the acquisition of a near-permanent partner. At the same time they will be introduced to the sensory aspect of concepts so far grasped only in theory, such as the feel of different fills at the trowel head as well as their colors and shades, indicating stratigraphic relationships between features; the distinctive touch of worked stone; and the lightness of bone which betrays its nature even though it appears the same as neighboring stones.

Newcomers will also discover that references to the trowel as the main tool of excavation is a misleading simplification of a complex concept, in much the same way as references to the butcher's or the cook's knife; for all dedicated excavators, butchers, and cooks carry more than one such tool. Of course, excavation is carried out with more tools than the trowel—from mechanical diggers, picks, mattocks, and spades to the tiniest of dental tools and brushes. But there is more to the trowel itself, too. In the case of the archaeological excavator, an entire toolbox could become evident. Here will be trowels of such age and use that the head will be reduced to only a centimeter or less in length and breadth, and so blunt as to leave no mark on the softest surface and an entire range of others with heads of differing sizes, shapes, and degrees of sharpness—all available to cope with any kind of feature or soil type in any kind of climatic condition. These are, of course—like the tools of the cook or watchmaker or an expensive fountain pen—not to be shared or used by anyone other than the owner. They are an extension of the individual excavator's hand, and the shape and other qualities they have achieved through use reflect the peculiarities of grasp and wrist action of that particular person. Use by any other individual would inevitably lead to a change in the form of the trowel head that would be perceived by its owner and render it less usable by him. Or so at least he will believe, whether measurably demonstrable or not. Like the butcher, the cook, and the watchmaker, the novice excavator will look forward to the day when he too can show off his delicately bred collection of tools.

This direct engagement with materiality—of objects recovered from the site, of the soil to be dug, and the objects with which that digging is to be done—is a vital ingredient in the excavation experience. It is above all a physical and material experience—mediated by intellect but first and foremost a direct bodily contact with the material universe. This is perhaps one of the ways in which archaeology is distinguishable from other fields: it is a subject about material culture that employs the experience of materiality as its means of inculcating newcomers into the mystique of its practice.

CAMARADERIE: SOCIAL ACTIVITIES

No experience of excavation is complete without an appropriate social program. The act of separating the team from the rest of the world and embedding its members firmly in a material experience is one devoted to the creation of a sense of community. That community needs to express its oneness in ways other than work, and that is where purely recreational activity finds its role. Onsite, the work regime is hard and long hours are common, especially in summer. At the end of the working day, the immediate need is for the removal of accumulated grime and the provision of sustenance. Thereafter, since accommodation might be only of the most basic kind with minimal facilities, recreation takes place in the most convenient location dedicated to enjoyment, and (in the United Kingdom at least) the most available place is likely to be a hostelry. Here, beer is the most common choice to wash away the taste of soil. Beer has advantages: it is a relatively inexpensive alcoholic drink per unit of quantity, it quenches thirst effectively, it is par excellence the drink of the physical laborer, and it is easy to order. It can also make a useful topic of conversation in its own right, especially among those who claim detailed knowledge and expertise, which involves none of the complications that might arise from discussions of politics or religion. And, it loosens tongues. The typical conversation on any site and in the nearby pub, however, is of excavation itself. This is not usually of the current excavation but, instead, of other excavations elsewhere. Tales will be told of this or that famed archaeologist or site, of gross errors of practice or interpretation made, and of the peculiarities of particularly memorable personalities encountered. Such talk has two purposes: for speakers it confirms their right to discourse upon the practical aspects of fieldwork, since it serves to emphasize their breadth of experience and the professional contacts they have made; for novices, it acts as a device to broaden their vicarious knowledge and experience of fieldwork practice. Comparisons in such talk are usually odious, but where reasonably large quantities of beer have been drunk and the site director is well out of earshot, the talk may ultimately turn to the shortcomings of the leader of this particular enterprise as compared to others; of course, the shortcomings of those individuals so evident at the time will have been erased from memory.

Play on-site can be as hard as work, and here the physicality of archaeological practice is particularly emphasized. On-site parties (held perhaps to mark the departure of one team and the arrival of a new one, or to mark the end of the season's work) could be quite cheerfully ribald affairs. Aspects of the close physical intimacy of shared accommodation and heavy labor in close physical proximity, typical of this kind of work, can be drawn upon to be reflected in highly physical close-contact games: there might be much throwing of water, leaping over fires, and discarding of outer clothing. The formal hierarchy of the team might be challenged or inverted so that the (otherwise serious and responsible) site director emerges as the chief joker. Such activities can be related to the kinds of fun and games seen on, for instance, building sites, but the particular affinity of on-site jollification is also with those shipboard parties celebrating events such as crossing the line (of the equator), where those who have not done so before are treated to a range of trials to test their fitness for doing so. Again, the affinity with a shipborne crew separated from the rest of the world is evident. Archaeologists thus present themselves to each other as a band of siblings apart from the rest of the world—and privileged in being so.

CONCLUSION

The three elements considered here—physical isolation from the rest of the world, a focus on the task at hand to the exclusion of other concerns, and shared sociability—encourage among excavators a close tightness of community expressed in very material and indeed physical form. They all also lend to the practice of archaeological excavation a very particular style that can be related to other forms of contemporary activity, and part of the purpose of this chapter has been to identify some of these social correlates for archaeological activity. There is some affinity with the common practices of building work, and especially with the more craft-based types of labor. The close concern for tools and for the gradual introduction of newcomers to practice are typical of such work and are shared by archaeologists. The very particular kinds of social activity engaged in serve to emphasize the craft- (rather than intellect-) based nature of the work, and together these closely reflect the very material nature of engagement with the object of archaeological inquiry. Overall, archaeological excavation as practiced is a material engagement with a body of material: it serves to make archaeology and archaeologists what they are—and to emphasize their special character.

ACKNOWLEDGMENTS

Thanks are due to Geoff Carver for the inspiration for the title, which reflects that of his own *Digging in the Dirt* book: I hope this might act as a small advertisement for that publication. I am also grateful to all those with whom I have shared the experience of digging, both real and vicarious, and who I hope will not take anything I say here amiss.

REFERENCES

Barker, P. 1982. *Techniques of archaeological excavation*. 2nd ed. London: Batsford.
Bender, B. 1993. *Landscapes—politics and perspectives*. Oxford: Berg.
Carman, J. 1996. *Valuing ancient things: Archaeology and law*. London: Cassells.
———. 2004. Excavating excavation: A contribution to the social archaeology of archaeology. In *Digging in the dirt*, ed. G. Carver, BAR. 45–51. Oxford: Archaeopress.
Carver, G., ed. 2004. *Digging in the dirt*. BAR. Oxford: Archaeopress.
Cooper, M. A., A. Firth, J. Carman, and D. Wheatley, eds. 1995. *Managing archaeology*. London: Routledge.
Dreyfus, H. L., and P. Rabinow. 1983. *Beyond structuralism and hermeneutics*. Chicago: University of Chicago Press.
Edgeworth, M. 1990. Archaeology as practical reason: The perception of objects in excavation practice. *Archaeological Review from Cambridge* 9 (2):243–51.
———. 2003. *Acts of discovery: An ethnography of archaeological practice*. BAR (International Series) S1131. Oxford: Archaeopress.
Hodder, I. 1999. *The archaeological process*. Oxford: Blackwell.
Holtorf, C. 2001. Fieldtrip theory: Towards archaeological ways of seeing. In *Interrogating pedagogies: Archaeology in higher education*, ed. P. Rainbird and Y. Hammilakis. BAR (International Series) S948. Oxford: Archaeopress.
Hunter, J., and I. Ralston, eds. 1993. *Archaeological resource management in the UK: An introduction*. Stroud, UK: Sutton.
Tilley, C. 1994. *A phenomenology of landscape*. London: Berg.

9

Realisafiction: A Day of Work at Everybody-Knows-Land

Oğuz Erdur

Present experience has, I am afraid,
always found us "absent-minded."

—Friedrich Nietzsche

ONE DAY, BEFORE BREAKFAST

Work with a working mind. Otherwise, that feeling of "what on earth am I doing?" haunts you.

What makes thinking possible is *the lack*—the moment of closure of the
"mystic writing pad." The scrapings that have to be considered *nothing*, the soil
that's moved out of the way into the buckets. The "dust in the wind."

"You anthropologists have a way of making us say things we normally
wouldn't say," said *Chief-of-the-forked-mound* last night.

"Including, of course," I said, "this very thing you just said."

The reason I thought about this now, as I'm sitting around the "house,"
watching the *House-team* scrape and sweep and measure and record, is the fact
that I just asked *Boss-of-the-undead-house* whether what I watched yesterday
was a typical day of work.

"Typical?" she paused for a moment. "You could say that . . . though it was a
bit slow."

"You will, of course, want to see the hard copies of the unit sheets," she went
on, sensing a partially satiated appetite on my part. "People write stuff that ends
up not getting recorded into the database."

Figure 9.1.   A day of work at Everybody-Knows-Land (Photo by Jason Quinlan)

"Sure," I replied. "What others don't consider significant is often what's important to me. . . . I guess you already know: an anthropologist is someone who comes and listens to what you have to say and turns around and tells you what you *really* said!"

"Hah!" she exclaimed. "We'll see about that!"

Work under the tent began a short while ago. Apart from a few of us, the bench folk, they've already started habituating the house—staring into the ground at features and walls and various sheets of paper; murmuring, looking around, asking each other questions; taking the pink, purple, and blue buckets from here to over there and grabbing tools of various sorts in order to harass the soil.

Boss-of-the-undead-house calls on *Takes-pictures-when-called* and asks him to come and take a working shot of a feature that was partially excavated yesterday. (It's barely seven o'clock, yet the tent is already hot.) How does she know a "working shot" is needed, I wonder. She must have a certain scheme, a mental habit, the theory or purpose that precedes the observation, the baggage, or whatever else one might want to call it—but that *something*—with which she determines what these pictures, these unit sheets, these samples are accumulating toward—a certain principle as to how they will be used. Do these pictures—these artifacts created on the spot—have a life of their own? Or do they end up rather in the cyber version of what *Restoro-agitator* said yesterday about the bag after bag full of finds piled up in storage?

"Finds go to the museum," he said, "you know, the handsome ones. The rest—nobody really knows what to do with them. We keep them here because, what else really, we *have to* keep them—and also because this project has the money for storage like this. Some local excavations end up burying this kind of stuff back into the ground."

"Check this out! Isn't it pretty!" shouts *Red-tulip-of-many-a-pit* pointing at the ground, as she stands up from the spot she's just crouched into a minute ago.

(Everything blends into everything else here: basins, walls, the morning, ovens, my thoughts, yesterday, their words . . .)

"What did you find?" asks *Just-working-for-the-white-man-here*, closing in toward her.

"Not sure really . . . but I'm following it."

Boss-of-the-undead-house is careful not to get distracted, though she surely heard the conversation. She goes on explaining to *Bone-lady* how they need to understand the relationship between the wall this and the platform that. She coolly waits until her uttering comes to a natural end, turns casually toward *Red-tulip-of-many-a-pit*, takes a swift look at the ground in front of her and gives her the verdict: "You'll be happy to know perhaps that what you're digging is a basin!"

"Isn't that cute!" *Red-tulip-of-many-a-pit* giggles. "Don't you just love it? It's so easy to follow too!"

Street-cat-of-a-neighboring-land, who's been scraping the adjacent floor, gives her a sober look without saying anything. They then start talking about the relationship between the white basin and the brown surface right next to it.

Represents-the-land-and-sky has just come from his daily tour to the other side of the mound excavated by a team from *Land-of-solidarity*. "You've got to go see it!" he snorts as he eases into a spot next to me. "They all look like lobsters now—turned bright pink under the sun!"

"Really!" I smile hastily, as I keep taking notes, which, incidentally, nobody minds me doing anymore, while I keep talking to them at the same time.

The issue is that the *Solidarity-team* wanted to bring along a shelter to use and donate to the project. But the proper regulation for the procedure could not be found, so their shelter got stuck at customs. That's why they've been working directly under the blazing sun.

"Good luck waiting till we grow up!" says *Represents-the-land-and-sky*. "Who would be insane enough to deal with our bureaucracy?"

Boss-of-the-undead-house goes over to *Takes-pictures-when-called* and talks to him about the relationship between a photo number this and a photo number that. I have to ask her: What kind of a relationship are we after? Can it be anything but "this is later than that and that one is earlier than the other"?

She then turns toward me and asks whether I recognized how they incorporate the local language into their own.

I ask, "How?"

She explains: "When we decide a unit is unnecessary and gets to be cancelled, we say it is '*yok*-ed.'"

"What's that, again?"

"*Yok*-ed!" she says. "You know, as in *yok* for *gone* or *nonexistent* in your language."

"Oh, sorry, didn't get that the first time." I pause. "So you are keen, you mean—*On keeping the nothing foreign?*"

Kicks-walls-into-oblivion raises his head from his scraping, looks me in the eye for a short suspenseful while, making a soft "uuuu" sound, a gentle howl, during which *Boss-of-the-undead-house* laughs a disinterested laugh: "You just have to complicate everything, don't you, mister." Indeed, ma'am!—*that* is my job indeed. . . .

As I keep writing, it is *Just-working-for-the-white-man-here* this time who comes by to join me in the art of sitting. (*Represents-the-land-and-sky* is already bored and took off for the cool of the dig house.)

"Getting a lot of information there?"

"I am, yes. Though I hope all this really accumulates toward something. 'Cause honestly, I don't yet know what that something is."

"Good luck with that!" he smirks, making me paranoid as to whether he sees the game I've just started to play by myself: I've turned all mimetic here, doing in Rome as the Romans do—I record. Not only do I focus on minute relationships between things and words and questions, like they do, but I also ask them questions, the "answers" to which I wouldn't really consider *answers* in my real life. And, in the process, I surely become a feature of curiosity too. To them, my work is perhaps like what their work is to me: far from self-evident in terms of its—grounds of legitimacy? That indeed is what the annoyed look *Street-cat-of-a-neighboring-land* has just given to the sound of the shutter of my camera tells me.

Guards-mud-against-people, who in his own real life is a farmer from the local village, has just come into the tent. He shouted "hi" to all, got a few hellos back, and then, surprise, he came and sat next to me.

He asks me what it is that I'm doing. I tell him I'm not an archaeologist but an anthropologist and that I came here to see what it is that the archaeologists do. He asks me what my name is. He then tells me how he thought it was just the archaeologists who worked at the excavations, but that, he learned here, is clearly not the case. There are archaeologists, then there are micromorphologists and ethnobotanists and archaeozoologists, and many others like that. And now also the anthropologists, who don't even dig anything! They just hang out, talk to people, and write things. Even the archaeologists themselves have different kinds: "Classical . . ." He pauses.

"Prehistoric?" I interrupt.

"Yeah," he says. "That's the word I was looking for! I had to learn many things here, you know. Didn't really mean to. But what else really?"

Single attempts entail too many hazards. As *Guards-mud-against-people* left the tent, I went over to the pit in which the *Bone-lady* is working. "Any breakthroughs in science?" I asked her jokingly. I hadn't talked to her until that point and thought it was about time to break the ice. She shot back seriously and said something about multiple burials and that "though it's a small one, yes, it *is* a breakthrough indeed."

I felt I unintentionally offended her, as if I'm being cynical about the value of *her* work. I inadvertently pushed the "public secret" button, it seemed, of witnessing the nothing that is quite new under the sun and ended up being the self-aggrandizing fool who declares, "The King is naked!"—even though everybody here is very well learned about the intricacies of the dress code indeed!

So I simply had to write over that one hazardous moment and ask further questions. That was my only motive: to ask questions. But apparently I asked the right question by accident—about the mud curvature, which is where the skull was last year. We know from the data of *Said-paintings-faded-before-I-could-take-pictures*—the grand chief of the previous excavations here—that the north platforms are important. The Neolithic occupants of our house buried their dead under those, without knowing there already were burials down there, buried by earlier inhabitants. Or, they just didn't care. They took the bones out, buried new ones in—two people in the case of our specific pit—and put the bones they took out back in. Hence the jumble on top. Our working hypothesis was that there had to be identifiable individuals below the upper jumble, which indeed proved to be true.

Everybody's gone to breakfast. They've got to be wondering why I stayed behind and what it is that I keep writing at the expense of *sucuk*—the specialty sausage that tends to disappear immediately after it appears at the all-you-can-eat-without-appearing-too-greedy breakfast buffet. Its anti-*sucuk* function aside, my notebook surely works very effectively—as not just the trick that legitimizes my otherwise idle presence here but also as a source of mystery. Secrecy does magnify reality indeed! When would it be a good time to reveal my secret, I wonder—that I don't really have one?

SAME DAY, AFTER BREAKFAST

I'm two steps behind today—got up a little late. One needs a cognitive gap in order to organize perception. Here, it all is a big perception trip that longs for that gap. If only we could dig and think and live and experience like that—having access to the then and the now, living right now and, at the same time, two steps behind.

I talked to *Shoots-beams-out-of-the-machine* at breakfast. She's always been fascinated with "small stuff you don't see, which can actually kill you." She graduated and wants to go into genetics, forensics, or "some other stuff like that." But in the meantime, well, she's shooting beams out of the machine.

I also got to ask the *Old-waltz-master* what he's doing here. He said he's a volunteer and has been going to excavations for almost twenty years. He actually pays for coming here to work with the *House-team*. His father, you see, used to take him to the desert when he was a little boy and they used to search for finds. He simply never grew out of it. And some sixty years later, here he is, still searching for finds. (Too bad, I forgot to ask him which desert.)

I also talked briefly to *Farms-dead-plants* about this thing called "flotation," which apparently is a procedure of washing and rinsing the sampled soil in order to find something in what otherwise would be considered nothing. She said the women from the village—the *somethingers-out-of-nothing*—would come later in the week and I could talk to them too. Working here, they learned how to see, with their bare eyes, the tiny particles of charred plant and wood in the floated samples—the otherwise nothing, that is. The process is long, expensive, and requires many people. Apparently only here are samples taken from every unit, floated and analyzed, whereas almost any other dig will sample only particular contexts. Here, she explained, you can go into statistical comparisons, as you wish, of this pit with that one or that platform with this.

Work starts slowly after breakfast. There's a mellow music in the tent. *Takes-pictures-when-called* is waiting to be called to take a picture. I ask him what they do with all the pictures they take.

"We end up having way too many more pictures than we know what to do with!" he says and immediately realizes this didn't sound too good. He goes on telling me how they use special software to create cyber models of our house from the wide-angle pictures they take with a fisheye lens.

"*Thinks-the-tent-is-a-mountain* is all about going and getting what's new out there!" he explains, "you know, in terms of technology." *Boss-of-the-undead-house* and her boss, *Plaster-is-women-to-her*, are apparently all for this mode of preservation of knowledge—not for the sake of objectivity or any such bogus idea, of course, but for creating the possibilities of a subjective experience for anyone who'd like to go through the cyber version of our mud house.

I nod and smile and listen and make gestures. What kind of a relationship is it over here—the relationship between knowledge and its conditions of possibility? One of determination? Or of alienation? Or both? We know the things we know the way in which we know them—because those are the ways in which we actually *can* know them? What we end up knowing thus is not of real consequence for us in real life really but some sort of extension of our *technologies*? "They didn't really have to go to *Everybody-Knows-Land* in order to say most of what they say on *Everybody-Knows-Land*!" the famous native archaeologist *Sees-with-his-ears* had said mockingly, when I talked to him before coming here.

True enough, there's much envy about this project in archaeological circles and an accompanying mockery that goes around. I myself was scoffed at by an elderly archaeologist when she learned about my upcoming trip: "Oh dear! Why am I not surprised? Seems like everybody's going to *Everybody-Knows-Land* nowadays!"

Another was rather more subtle, regarding at least *my* quest: "That's no real archaeology over there, I'm telling you; it's more like a NASA camp. The money, the labs, the tools, the people . . . it's all surreal. We the locals could never even attempt something like that. Would we want to—that of course is another story."

Whatever else *Sees-with-his-ears* and others are saying out of envy or pomp or habit or whatever, are they also saying, knowingly or not, that there's an ontological break here—between discourse and practice (or between saying and doing, to be less pretentious)?

"Is this a tool or a flake?" asks *Street-cat-of-a-neighboring-land*, showing a small find to *Kicks-walls-into-oblivion*.

"I think it's a tool," replies the other, "but looks like it's broken."

I go over to the corner of the house where the EDM is set up and ask *Shoots-beams-out-of-the-machine* to explain to me, like she said she would, how the grid system works. The whole thing rests on a single datum point. Two stable points are needed to calculate the third. All coordinates on the mound can thus be mapped, using the magnetic north. If there's an error like they found out about yesterday, mappings of different seasons would not fit together, creating a sort of blur, as in the improperly juxtaposed color layers of a badly printed photograph in a newspaper.

There's an ideal-typical imagination at work here. All the layers, surfaces, features—minus the *nothing* that's scraped off—are mapped, abstracted, and transported into a Cartesian universe, making this endeavor fundamentally a—Cartesian science? Which would mean that, at its very best, it needs to operate with properly delineated and thus objectified objects—but it then goes around and talks about "interpretation"? How could this giant methodology machine allow for the kind of fluidity and relativity (and the implied nihilism) of hermeneutics—except when it fails to live up to its own *interpretensions*? And perhaps even more importantly, how could it account for the scraped off *nothing* that people experience all day, every day?

It's getting too hot in the tent. *Boss-of-the-undead-house* asks *Conscientious-ant-killer* to open one of the flaps, upon which the kitchen staff appears in the horizon. "The investigation team is here; you better behave yourselves!" shouts *Boss-of-the-undead-house*, as the three ladies from the local village, who cook and clean and wash and pretty much take care of the entire camp, come into our house for a visit.

As they move toward the burial pit in which *Bone-lady*, *Gnaws-on-old-teeth*, and a jumble of bones are all squished together, *Boss-of-the-undead-house* quickly tells me how these three and a couple of the *somethingers-out-of-nothing* also paid a visit last year. They stopped the dig and had the visitors go in, in order to see how they would "interpret" the house.

They immediately felt comfortable, she explained, saying "That's a place to sit, this is for that. . . ." The whole episode is apparently on film somewhere and translated. She also mentioned how they thought this was a big house; at least a dozen and a half people must have lived in it. I move over to the bone side of things and crouch by the three ladies looking into the burial pit.

"Look how thin our bones actually are. We all have a lot of fat!" says *Smiles-cookies*.

Cooks-food-in-blue is not amused: "God forbid, if you ever dug me up like this, I won't let go of my rights on you. I want to be left alone in my final sleep!"

Gnaws-on-old-teeth translates this for *Boss-of-the-undead-house* and *Bone-lady* at once, which creates a debate on the spot.

Boss-of-the-undead-house admits she wouldn't like the treatment either, though she doesn't sound too strong on that sentiment. The two in the pit immediately jump and say they wouldn't mind it at all, no! no! they wouldn't mind it at all. I say that theirs is a typical scientist's reaction and translate it all back to the three ladies.

"What's the big deal? We'll all end up like this, anyway," says *Her-daughter-is-a-bride*.

Gnaws-on-old-teeth then asks whether they are offended by their excavating these bones, gets the "no" she wants, and reassures the *Boss-of-the-undead-house* and *Bone-lady* that what they're doing is okay for "the locals."

Cooks-food-in-blue says the only reason she likes what they are doing is that, whoever they were, these people are at least remembered, and that's good. "But," she goes on repeating, "if you ever do that to me, I'll come back and haunt you!" The three then go over to the other end of the house and chat some with others.

Boss-of-the-undead-house suggests it might be interesting for me to look into the resemblance between this issue and the native burials in the New World and asks whether I'm familiar with the debate. I say I sure am, but the issue there has everything to do with how the natives, unlike the locals here, see the burials as their ancestral heritage.

"Exactly," says *Bone-lady*, as she keeps scratching the eye socket of the skull in front of her with a dental pick.

Boss-of-the-undead-house then asks whether the locals here might indeed be seeing these people as linked to themselves in some way. "Many consider *Everybody-Knows-Land* a part of their cultural heritage," she asserts.

"Those would be the urbanites," I react, "who understand heritage at a more abstract, national level. What *Cooks-food-in-blue* has just said, on the other hand, implies a clear otherization here, at the local level: these folks appear to see the burials as people unrelated to themselves, who lived here a long time ago."

"It has all to do with how the past is perceived, then," says *Boss-of-the-undead-house*. I concur.

As the three ladies say their good-byes, *Cooks-food-in-blue* turns to me: "See you," she says in foreign language. I laugh.

"Why do you laugh at me? That much of a foreign tongue, I too can speak!"

"I didn't laugh at you but laughed because you said that to *me*. Am I a foreigner, you reckon?"

"You tell me!" she smirks as she steps out. "You ain't exactly local either, are you?"

Gnaws-on-old-teeth, who apparently has still not gotten used to the aura of my notebook, cannot hold it anymore: "You wrote and wrote and still didn't get enough? What on earth do you keep writing?" I give her something of an explanation I make up on the spot, throw the words "thick description" in there and tell her how there's really nothing thick here to describe but only layer upon layer of thin stuff.

"Just like the platforms you guys keep scraping, you know: layer after layer of thin plaster."

More than half of the dozen and a half people in the house are on the other side of the tent, taking EDMs, filling out unit sheets, playing with tools, or climbing ropes for aerial shots, and posing quasi-self-consciously for the filmmakers from *Low-country*. Having arrived yesterday, these two have just come into the tent, set up, and started shooting, while the kitchen staff were doing their investigating.

"Would you just take a look at this?" *Boss-of-the-undead-house* raises her head and squeals, smiling in a kind of pretend frustration: "Only five of us in here are doing the digging; the rest are busy with their own very important things!"

SAME DAY, AFTER LUNCH

During lunch, *Gnaws-on-old-teeth* turned blatant, challenging what I do. I ended up talking about such things as the value of truth and politics of knowledge; how writing is contextual and thinking has preconditions that make it possible; and so forth. She agreed with pretty much nothing I said. And the problem was epistemology, as usual. Knowledge has obviously to be objective, according to her, literally, driven out of objects. And when it comes to ten-thousand-year-old teeth, whether one is local or foreign or a tramp or a woman is of no consequence: it is the teeth that do the speaking.

I had to think: the measure of silence one sometimes needs, in order just to speak.

On the way back from lunch, I asked *Boss-of-the-undead-house* about "relationships"—whether they are anything but temporal. "Yeah, basically what is earlier, what is later, what is contemporary . . . disappointed?"

"Not really," I said half-heartedly, "but it seems to me like there are many other kind of relationships going on here—in terms of this color to that feature, this surface to that person. . . . It seems like there's a deficiency of concepts and names to match what's going on."

"Yeah," she replied, in a manner I didn't know what to do with, "a lot of feelings involved . . ."

The afternoon shift is observably more lethargic than the morning; it is quite hard to stay alert as one gets broiled with food in stomach.

Chief-of-the-forked-mound comes to the tent and brings along *Draws-the-souls-of-stones*, who's just arrived at the camp today:

"Observing the natives in their natural environment?" he asks, as we are introduced.

"I am, indeed!"

"So," he teases on, "you're here to watch us watching you watch us watching you?"

"Exactly!" I laugh and play it down, "or something like that anyway."

"Does he really keep doing this all day?" chuckles *Chief-of-the-forked-mound*, looking at my notebook as if it's a sculpture I've made out of elephant dung.

"Oh dear," replies *Boss-of-the-undead-house* with bright eyes. "That's what they do in anthropology, don't you know!"

"You ain't seen nothin' yet!" I shouted to the laughing crowd, in a puny attempt at retaliation. "Just watch me chase you all around, day and night!"

Boss-of-the-undead-house has apparently not had enough pleasure out of mockery yet. Having found the collective attention suspended in the air for a moment, she turns to *Chief-of-the-forked-mound* and asks when, if ever, the big chief *Everybody-knows-him* will be coming to the camp this year.

"What's he up to, do you know? Is he busy writing yet another book? Let me take a guess: he'll call the next one *Archaeological Theory Tomorrow!*"

As the afternoon shift wavers toward its end, with my will to wakefulness following suit, I can't help but notice the long pause that has set in at the other end of the house, where *Kicks-walls-into-oblivion* and *Red-tulip-of-many-a-pit* seem to be having trouble: they apparently can't decide how to proceed with the remaining hour or so of work.

"What do you see?" he asks her.

"I don't see anything really. What do you see?"

"It looks round, this orangish thing . . . though it could be making a square too underneath. What do you think we should do?"

"Keep scraping till we know what we're doing. Or until three o'clock, anyway."

"What's that supposed to mean?"

"I mean, who cares whether it's here this big, or there that big? That ain't gonna change the interpretation of the Neolithic!"

Before cynicism gets out of hand, *Boss-of-the-undead-house* comes, takes a peek, and speaks in typically underdetermined language:

"This part seems to have collapsed in prehistory and . . . God knows what happened over there. . . . It's more or less certain that we won't be finding the shape of this thing for certain, which means we should remove something. What should we start with?"

"I think we need to clear this layer first," she goes on about what appears to me to be but a jumble, "'cause it seems to be sitting on that feature."

"This ain't no good," *Red-tulip-of-many-a-pit* turns all serious all of a sudden. "What if you are wrong? We won't be able to go the other way!"

"She looks like a magician to me anyway," I mutter, but they are too concerted to hear.

"C'mon," teases *Bone-lady* herself into what now is the major event in the house. "What's gonna happen when you grow up and graduate, *Red-tulip-of-many-a-pit*, when you can't decide . . . you just won't dig?"

"We know that won't do," responds *Boss-of-the-undead-house* as she grabs her trowel. "You just have to destroy a little sometimes—in order to see better."

SAME DAY, IN THE AFTERNOON

"What are you up to this afternoon?" I ask *Just-working-for-the-white-man-here*, as we sit under the veranda trying to cool down with tea and fruit.

"Nothing, really. I got nothing to do. And you can go ahead and quote me on this too: that's what archaeology is, my friend—a lot of nothing to do! . . . *Just-working-for-the-white-man-here*, personal communication, two thousand and one!"

"Yeah, dude! That's the spirit!" comes *Kicks-walls-into-oblivion* out of the kitchen with chocolate-spread biscuits in hand and joins what turns into a three-and-a-half-minute debate on what archaeology is. Despite the self-proclaimed uniqueness of this project, he insists that those who come from other camps for a visit—such as his own adviser—tend actually to like what they see. Beyond the lip service to theory and all that jazz, they think this is a scientifically well-operated dig.

Toward the end of our three and a half minutes, we even get to talk once again on my gig—how we anthropologists work in solitude, as opposed to the collective life over here: "Many in anthropology don't really believe in 'methodology' anymore," I assert. "And that has got everything to do with disillusionment—you know, with that thing called 'the correspondence theory of truth.'" How could we insist and pretend that our writing corresponds to documents and memory, to words and deeds, when we no longer believe in correspondence at a much more fundamental level? "All I can hope to do then," I conclude, "is to try and correspond *with* people."

Teatime is over. They go to their labs; I go take a cool shower.

10

Landscapes of Disciplinary Power: An Ethnography of Excavation and Survey at Leskernick

Michael Wilmore

Ethnography of archaeology is about the process of *doing* archaeology in a world where many such ways of doing coexist. It examines how such diversity affects archaeologists' participation in individual projects and the wider field of contemporary archaeology. Knowledge of specific situations illuminates our understanding of the wider discipline through a reflexive hermeneutic process that takes the multisited circumstances of this work into account (cf. Marcus 1995).

This chapter examines how the Leskernick project is embedded in the context of archaeology as practiced in the United Kingdom. It describes people's participation in this project, especially the desire to work in particular ways and the differentiations made between working practices considered acceptable or unacceptable. The project is analyzed sociologically in terms of the relative positions of participants within the wider context of archaeological organization. Such analysis offers one explanation for why participants favor some ideas and practices but reject others.

BACKGROUND

Between 1995 and 1999, Leskernick, a Bronze Age domestic and ritual site on the edge of Bodmin Moor (Cornwall, UK), was visited by researchers who came from the Institute of Archaeology and Department of Anthropology, University College, London (UCL) under the leadership of Barbara Bender, Sue Hamilton, and Chris Tilley. From 1996 to 1999 the project received financial support from the British Academy, supplemented by smaller grants from UCL. The project had several aims, including archaeological excavation and surface survey of the Bronze Age settlement, geological and environmental surveys of the area, production of landscape art, ethnographic study of the project, and experimentation with different approaches to fieldwork, analysis, and writing.[1]

The project's application of postprocessualist theories to the practice of a large-scale archaeological research project has excited interest; the preliminary report (Bender et al. 1997) is widely cited, both in publications and reading lists of archaeology courses. Statements the directors have made about the project arouse further interest:

> A further aim of the Leskernick project is to explore similarities and differences between the confined world of excavation and the large-scale settlement survey. What are the effects of differing research environments? . . . How do we "free-up" excavation while providing an acceptable empirical record? Who and what is the guardian of acceptability? . . . We want, during the Leskernick project, to try and create methodologies and ways of writing that more truthfully reflect the process of discovery, uncovery [*sic*], intuition, and interpretation. (Bender et al. 1997, 150-51)

I emphasize that this chapter makes no judgments about the validity of archaeological analysis of the Leskernick site. Questions about appropriate methodologies and interpretations in archaeology should be made within the boundaries of that discipline; other disciplines cannot provide answers to archaeological questions: we cannot perform some kind of alchemy whereby the lead of ethnography is turned into the gold of archaeological knowledge. Such claims have been made in the past, most notably with Durkheim's attempt to establish sociology as "an independent source of philosophical truth" (Gell 1992, 13). The problems of archaeology must be solved by archaeologists. Nevertheless, ethnographically informed sociological research might suggest areas that could repay careful consideration in relation to the practical conduct of archaeological research.

Fieldwork for my project was carried out during a five-week period of research at Leskernick in May and June 1997 and at various times both before and after this date when I visited Leskernick or interviewed project participants. Space limitations prohibit extensive quotation from evidence collected during fieldwork, but further information about my research methodology, in particular the use of material from participants' diaries kept as part of their involvement in fieldwork, can be found in Wilmore (2006). Following usual ethnographic conventions informants will be referred to anonymously or through the use of pseudonyms. The use of the project directors' real names where they occur in diary entries is an exception, as to change their names would make some diary entries difficult to understand. This decision may be contested by some of my informants, who have claimed that such practices deny their agency in relation to representation of the Leskernick project. Nevertheless, I feel that anonymous citation is warranted given that my project involves participants who have or might have an ongoing relationship within the discipline. I make full and grateful acknowledgment to all my informants by name at the end of this chapter.

AN ARCHAEOLOGICAL DIVISION OF LABOR

One sociological aspect of the project became apparent after I spoke to participants and read project diaries before the 1997 fieldwork season. This was a perceived distinction between excavators ("diggers") and surveyors ("settlement people").

> Sadly, we live in a split community. There is an absolute social divide between the diggers and the settlement people. The diggers created it from the outset and they maintain it. They are not part of the spirit and romance of Leskernick, only partially within the bubble of the hill.[2]

The project organization involved both vertical hierarchical authority (e.g., project directors, fieldwork supervisors, and student excavators) and a horizontal division of labor, the latter based upon a distinction between participants who were primarily excavators and those who were surveyors (cf. Bradley 2003). This horizontal distinction was the subject of anxiety and constantly referred to in participants' diaries. The distinction was used to explain the problems and tensions within the project. This discourse was part of the "common sense" of the project, a characteristic way of speaking that does not offer an explanation of the project's social dynamics, but is something that requires explanation.

Surveyors often contrasted the supposed dynamism of their work with the conservatism of excavation. Dichotomies used included stasis versus movement, an inward or downward focus of attention versus outward or upward focus, discovery versus nondiscovery, and the freedom to discuss methodology versus a prescribed methodology. Those involved in excavation tended, not surprisingly, to reverse these contrasts. For them, surface survey created only superficial understanding of the material remains of the past, whereas excavation, with its meticulous attention to detail, provided a clearer understanding of people's actions in the past. This understanding did not appear fully formed from the soil but was developed through discussion among the excavators carried out within the framework of their agreed techniques of archaeological excavation. The criticisms of excavation by the surveyors were, as the following diary excerpts show, often about aspects that could be seen as positive features; any lack of subjectivity or discussion was more apparent than real:

> I was somewhat bemused by the general reaction to the discussion after supper in Barbara's caravan last night. Carl was merely making the obvious point that none of us know why prehistoric people did what they did; all guesses are just guesses

unless they are tested against evidence, and most evidence can only be found by doing good excavation.[3]

At lunchtime Chris and Barbara came to see me about Debby's [an anthropology undergraduate] crystal from H23. Carl has refused to accept it as a small find. I could have predicted this since it is not a foreign stone and it is not a humanly produced artifact. For Carl it is technically no different to a mica fleck or a bracken root. During the morning Sally had recovered a similar but less attractive quartz crystal from topsoil of H39, and Todd had pointed out a granite block in the H39 tumble which incorporated several such crystals. After lunch I went over to H23. Shirley and Carl were the only people working there. I mentioned the quartz crystal to Carl. He determinedly refused to small find it, but in due course a compromise was negotiated, namely that it is a narrative find ("NF") which would be plotted on the plan as such, i.e., something that has contributed to trench discussion and consideration of the structure's interpretation.[4]

Comments about supposed distinctions were often balanced by statements that pointed out similarities in methodology:

The excavation was dominated by technical procedures, a rhetoric of recording. In the settlement [survey] work there was no obvious starting point or procedure to follow, no standard context sheets. But we rapidly tried to create standardisation in recording and got very concerned if things were not being done in the "right" way.[5]

While sitting on the cairn, smoking a roll-up before setting off with Chris and Sally, I observe an abundance of photocopied forms rustling in the wind, "HUT RECORDING FORM," and I begin to think that in striving for credibility the survey may be in danger of falling into the very traps which (I hope) we are trying to avoid.[6]

After lunch [I] talked to Barbara and Chris. They had been checking some of the settlement sketch-plans and have noted discrepancies . . . all very time consuming and casting some doubt on the completed sheets. Barbara said that we really needed "professional" trained sketch-planners which reminds me of my original plea for competent people on the excavation. The requirements of our separate methodologies are beginning to replicate each other.[7]

It is also obvious that participants' descriptions of each other's work seldom resembled actual practices. Surveying was carried out very systematically once the initial methodology had been refined in the first fieldwork seasons. Equally, excavation, portrayed by some as the rigid application of a set of inflexible rules, involves the practitioner in a continuous hermeneutic process, both in one's own relationship to the conditions of a particular archaeological environment and in discussions with other practitioners. Therefore, the maintenance of a discursive distinction between excavation and survey during the fieldwork cannot be explained in terms of essential differences in methodology (Bradley 2003). Nonetheless, for many participants such a difference was assumed to exist and was used to explain why cooperation between participants was often difficult to achieve in practice. This explanation must involve an examination of the role that the Leskernick project played in the life of the project members.

MAKING AN ARCHAEOLOGICAL WORKFORCE

Participation in the project is not simply the culmination of a series of past events but also a point in a participant's life history. Huddled together during a break inside the remains of a stone house that offers little protection from the elements, the participants might occupy the same space within the physical landscape, but each is located in very different points within their own biographical landscape. The clarity of participants' vision of this landscape was impressed upon me during fieldwork. Nearly all members of the excavation team had rejected a previous career path to pursue their interest in archaeology. They emphasized that their previous jobs had become routine, that there was little scope for career advancement now that they had reached a certain age, or that an office environment was restrictive. Working in archaeology was seen as an exciting change, and might also explain why they chose to work on a project that was widely acknowledged as different from the norm.[8]

Nevertheless, we should recognize that such career change involves considerable risk, because UK archaeology remains poorly paid with little job security. Participants pursue this career voluntarily, but the conditions of work that they subsequently encounter are not of their own making.

After a new legislative framework (*Planning and Policy Guidance* [PPG] *Note 16*) came into force in 1990, the principle of competitive tendering between excavation companies was introduced to field archaeology in the United Kingdom. This has created a situation where very few people are employed under permanent contract and the majority of archaeologists work within short-term contracts. Financial security, either in the present or in the future through pension provision, is rare (Chadwick 2000). Academic archaeology is hardly different, as there is intense competition for postgraduate, postdoctoral research grants and even short-term teaching contracts. Although archaeology is often described as a middle-class discipline in terms of the background of its participants (see conclusion), archaeological work cannot *necessarily* be considered in terms of the norms of bourgeois lifestyle. "How," asked one project director when reflecting on this point in an interview, "can anybody possibly have a relationship, a marriage, run a household, fund a pension when they are employed on the basis of short-term contracts? . . . Effectively people are disenfranchised from what people think are normal things."[9] Despite these problems, almost all participants regarded their involvement in archaeology as vocational and expressed a long-term commitment to the discipline.

Several participants also stressed the individuality of archaeologists. One told me that defining their identities in formal terms (using categories like ethnicity or marital status, for example) was problematic. Such normative questions would, according to this informant, be especially difficult to administer among archaeologists because they are all so different.[10] If I did a survey of bank clerks, he added, they would all be more or less the same. Comments such as this reveal two things. If we take them as a statement of statistical fact then it tells us something about the recruitment policies operating in the worlds of archaeology and banking, to use the contrast chosen by my informant. More accurately it would tell us something about the *absence* of a recruitment policy in archaeology. My informant was right to point out that, at least in terms of age and gender, the project participants were quite varied. It also reveals to us what at least one archaeologist believed to be the case about the discipline relative to his own self-identity. It is a location of relative freedom in the quotidian employment landscape that he perceived as valuing only employees' conformity. But this is a strange sort of freedom and bought at a price because field archaeology is not situated in a utopian location. It is situated "some-place" rather than "no-place" and is intimately *articulated* with the wider landscape of the United Kingdom's political economy (Chadwick 2003; Slack 1996).

Recent critiques of archaeological methodology emphasize hierarchical organization and adherence to tenets of empiricism in data collection (Hodder 1997; Shanks and Tilley 1992; Tilley 1989). Indeed, one of the primary inspirations of the Leskernick project was the directors' desire to explore reflexive methodologies that emphasized the process of archaeological knowledge creation. Some participants' identification of archaeology as a location of relative freedom in an otherwise constraining employment landscape would seem to be readily met through the aspirations of the project directors, who wanted to emphasize individual agency in the process of excavation rather than its tradition of collective discipline. The latter would appear to be the antithesis of the individualistic aspirations of the participants that I described above. And yet there was a significant degree of suspicion and occasionally opposition to the theoretical and methodological innovations introduced as part of this project. There were concomitant expressions of support for established excavation practices and organization from both students and excavation supervisors (although I do not wish to imply that individual members of the team always aligned themselves according to any crude, bipolar affiliation).

We can understand these apparent contradictions if we analyze excavation practices as an articulation by the fieldworkers of their position in a field that comprises both the Leskernick project and the wider field of employment in British archaeology. Here "field" is used in terms of Bourdieu's (1993) sociological sense of the word. What follows is necessarily only a summary of my argument. I use the terms "craft" and "objectivity" to stand for characteristics of excavation that are largely articulated nondiscursively through practical activity; these aspects of excavation are discussed but most forcefully demonstrated in the way that work is done, as opposed to the way people talk about their work.

When we talk of excavation as a craft we understand that the techniques of archaeological excavation are the accumulated product of many decades of work in the field. These techniques are the inheritance of all archaeologists and are passed on in the field from experienced masters of these techniques (the site supervisors and directors) to their apprentices (the students)—see Shanks and McGuire (1996). The senior project members tutor neophytes in fieldwork techniques. The craftiness of the archaeologist in recording is valued as highly as the ability to dig well, not to mention the manifest pleasure of students who are given the opportunity to record through drawing or photographing the results of their efforts (cf. the discussion of the role of stratigraphic matrices and context records in Chadwick 2000). It is a visible sign of the students' progress in the discipline because they are thereby shown to be trustworthy. As with most training excavations but unlike commercial archaeology, the entitlement to complete written records of what is discovered on this site usually remains the preserve of the site supervisor. As such, it indicates in practice the intermediate status of supervisors in mediating between students (who never write official records but dig a lot) and site directors (who write the final site report but may seldom dig)—see Wilmore (2006).

It is not coincidental that, apart from their common interest in archaeology, those members of the project who were most closely associated with the excavation were also characterized by an active engagement with music and other creative enterprises. They had a desire not just to listen but also to make music, not just to look at art but also to paint, or even to make beer as well as drink it so as "to enjoy the satisfaction of the process, especially when it turns out well."[11] It is not that they alone do these things, of course, but when my informants were confronted with the opportunity to offer a self-representation, these are the things they emphasized. Archaeology, as Michael Shanks (1992) has pointed out, remains a practical discipline with a strong craft ethos. As such it provides scope for active engagement with tangible objects of a worker's labor. This served as a focal point for making a contrast between my own work and that of the archaeologists when one participant, a mature undergraduate student, told me that "the archaeologists will be able to display their results," followed by the question, "What can you show?" The materiality and physicality of archaeology, especially when contrasted with work in the "information economy," becomes a resource through which participants can articulate a positive sense of self-identity.

Archaeologists who master accepted fieldwork techniques can also sell their labor in any place, as long as they are willing and able to relocate to other worksites. Adherence to objectivity in excavation is a manifestation of this because archaeologists who are not established in any fixed job or institution might regard methodological experimentation as conflicting with the need to seek employment elsewhere. Indeed, to recognize one's own subjectivity in this work might jeopardize employment prospects in a discipline that undertakes "unrepeatable experiments" (Barker 1982), the validity of which is based on trust in the practical skills of fellow workers.

As explained above, this is an essential consideration given the position of the excavator within the prevailing structures of the archaeological labor market both in the commercial and academic spheres, itself enmeshed within the wider political and economic structures of the contemporary nation-state (Hodder and Berggren 2003). Increasingly, the freedom from the constraints of the conventional workplace that my informants described is nostalgically associated with an era when research excavations were the norm and when the notions of production line work on a succession of barely distinguishable rescue excavations was unknown. Whether any such golden age of employment in field archaeology ever existed is debatable. Nevertheless, the ethos of excavation described here enables the fieldworker to survive within the landscape of the archaeological labor market, but also leads to an objectified form of knowledge that is subject to eventual appropriation by others who profit from their labor.

British industries have restructured their labor force to cope with the demands of the globalized economy (see Harvey 1989). Field archaeology, which might be perceived as a haven from these quotidian concerns, is no exception, having been rapidly transformed in its institutional structure and employment practices following PPG-16's introduction. Indeed, archaeology may even exemplify some of the principles of a flexible, post-Fordist labor market. Referring to traditional fieldwork practices may be a misnomer because many of these practices have been subject to considerable transformation in recent years, not least through the application of increasingly sophisticated data storage and analysis technologies (cf. Chadwick 2000). The term is used here as shorthand through which the distinction between objectives underlying traditional archaeological fieldwork can be distinguished from those of postprocessualist archaeology. We may debate the impact of postmodernity upon the theoretical development of archaeology in recent decades but must recognize that the working lives of many archaeologists could also be said to exemplify the material conditions of postmodernity.

CONCLUSION

It is interesting to note that while the list of the "nested identities" that are assumed to pertain to life at Leskernick in the Bronze Age includes "family, kin, community, age-set, [and] gender" (Bender et al. 1997), class is ignored. It is considered to be irrelevant to the analysis of "small-scale village-based societies without a market economy, cash, consumer goods, mass media, literacy, etc." (Leskernick Project 1999a). But the ethnographic analysis of the project was likewise described in terms of "first-hand study of the 'community' of archaeologists and anthropologists" (Leskernick Project 1999b) with the implication that participants in the project formed such a community in the first place. The aim of the project ethnography, according to one project director, was

> to know to what extent this artificial community in commas [*sic*] is extremely different to or apart from the rest of British society. I mean, we know most of them

are middle class and so on, but beyond those kinds of bland statement we don't actually know about beliefs or interests and lifestyles. And I think these are important elements in any research on the person, political beliefs, and so on, and so I hope that this sort of understanding will come out of it. And also understanding the way social relations on the project influence what happens, interactions and actions between people; the way they force the project in certain ways.[12]

As the foregoing analysis indicates, I fully concur with the latter part but believe that use of the term "community" (even in its ironic comma-ed form) and the bland statement that most of the participants are middle class create some analytical problems with regard to the ethnographic analysis of the project. Archaeology is a social field structured through the exchange of various species of capital, at once economic, cultural, and educational (Wilmore 2006; cf. Bourdieu 1993), and this means that differences between participants cannot be assigned only to "beliefs, interests, or lifestyles." The objective circumstances within which archaeologists live and work must be taken into account. Class might not be relevant to our understanding of Bronze Age society, but it is a vital component in our understanding of what occurs during archaeological research in the present day.

Academic archaeology maintains its prestigious position within the discipline through the crucial role that universities play in education (Hutson 1998), but the majority of archaeologists work in either the commercial sector or for national and local governments. Therefore, it is hardly surprising that the contradictory demands of fieldwork within these spheres are felt by archaeologists, including students who are learning to labor in the service of archaeology. The Leskernick project's laudable aim was the creation of a kind of Habermasian "ideal speech situation" within which the creation of knowledge of the prehistoric past could be shared by all the project participants (Bender et al. 1997; cf. Habermas 1992). However, Jürgen Habermas has been criticized for failing to take into account the full extent to which the bourgeois public sphere in early modern Europe operated through the exclusion of working-class participants, as well as women and other typically excluded minorities (Breckenridge 1995; MacGuigan 1996). Similarly, the situation of the Leskernick project in the wider contexts of archaeology as practiced in the United Kingdom placed limits upon participants' ability to enter into profitable discourse, because they were frequently dealing in nonequivalent currencies when it came to the exchange of knowledge or practical expertise.

During fieldwork all the participants in the project were aware not only of the relationships that they had to each other in that time and place but also of the relationships that they had to other agents within the wider archaeological landscape. In this sense the project was truly multidisciplinary and multisited because each participant—be they tenured academics, professional fieldworkers, postgraduate students, undergraduates, or volunteers seeking admission to programs in archaeological studies at university—experienced and expressed their agency as archaeologists differently, depending upon the particular constraints of their own position in this field. Academic critics of objectivity or empiricism in archaeological field research might be entirely warranted in their theoretical claims and counterclaims in support of alternative research methodologies. But we should recognize that traditional forms of fieldwork practice are not adopted out of intransigence or ignorance on the part of excavators. As Briggs (1996) observes:

> The politics of the "invention" literature [here referring to the broad field of constructivist studies of culture carried out within history and anthropology, of which the postprocessualist critique of "traditional" archaeology is one example] must be analyzed primarily not in terms of the epistemological value of opposing academic positions but in terms of the broad range of metadiscursive practices that constitute it, as well as those used by indigenous scholars and activists and by institutional authorities. (463)

The choices that face archaeologists concerning fieldwork methodology and the validity of different epistemological criteria are in this respect indigenous articulations of the desires of *all* those who strive to make a life for themselves as workers in the discipline of archaeology. This chapter has tried to understand how such disciplinary power is used and experienced by all those who work on the Leskernick project and within the landscape of British archaeology as a whole.

ACKNOWLEDGMENTS

I would like to thank everybody involved in the Leskernick project for contributing to my research, in particular those participants whose voices are heard in this chapter. They are, in alphabetical order, Angus, Ash, Barbara, Ceira, Ceri, Chris G., Chris T., Dan, Dave, Fay, Gary, Gill, Helen, Henry, Jane, Lesley, Mike, Penni, Steve, Stuart, Sue, and Wayne. I must offer special thanks for his invaluable support to Tony Williams, who was also working on the project ethnography in relation to the material culture of archaeological practice. I would like to thank Matt Edgeworth for his help and valuable discussion. Some portions of this chapter were presented in a slightly different form at the Material Culture Seminar, Department of Anthropology, UCL (December 1997), and I am grateful to all those who offered comments at that forum. I would like to thank the British Academy Grants Committee for the generous award of an Overseas Conference Grant, which greatly assisted my involvement in the 5th World Archaeology Conference. I am solely responsible for the opinions and content of this chapter.

NOTES

1. The website devoted to the project (www.ucl.ac.uk/leskernick/intro1.htm) gives further detail about the project and preliminary research findings. See also Bender et al. (1997) and Bender et al. (2006).

124 *Michael Wilmore*

2. Project director's diary entry June 14, 1996.
3. Scott, a volunteer excavator, diary entry June 3, 1996.
4. Sue, diary entry June 14, 1996.
5. Chris, diary entry (quoted in Bender et al. 1997, 165), undated.
6. Lance, diary entry June 12, 1996.
7. Sue, diary entry June 15, 1996.
8. We should note that the participants in the project are, therefore, a self-selected sample. Further research to examine the claims and argument advanced in this chapter using a wider sample or other projects for comparison is desirable but currently beyond the limits of this work.
9. Interviewed October 27, 1997.
10. Lenny, an undergraduate archaeologist, quoted in author's field notes, June 14, 1997.
11. Simon, response in follow-up interviews to fieldwork questionnaires (1997).
12. Interviewed October 16, 1997.

REFERENCES

Barker, P. 1982. *Techniques of archaeological excavation*. London: Batsford Books.
Bender, B., S. Hamilton, and C. Tilley. 1997. Leskernick: Stone worlds; alternative narratives; nested landscapes. *Proceedings of the Prehistoric Society* 63:147–78.
———. 2006. *Stone worlds: Narrative and reflexive approaches to landscape archaeology*. London: UCL Press.
———. n.d. The Leskernick project, www.ucl.ac.uk/leskernick/intro1.htm (accessed April 15, 2003).
Bourdieu, P. 1993. *The field of cultural production*. Cambridge, UK: Polity Press.
Bradley, R. 2003. Seeing things: Perception, experience and the constraints of excavation. *Journal of Social Archaeology* 3 (2):151–68.
Breckenridge, C., ed. 1995. *Consuming modernity: Public culture in a South Asian world*. Minneapolis: University of Minnesota Press.
Briggs, C. 1996. The politics of discursive authority in research on the "invention of tradition." *Cultural Anthropology* 11 (4):435–69.
Chadwick, A. 1997. Archaeology at the edge of chaos: Further towards reflexive excavation methodologies. *Assemblage* 3, www.shef.ac.uk/~assem/3/3chad.html (accessed April 15, 2003).
———. 2000. Taking English archaeology into the next millennium—a personal review of the state of the art. *Assemblage* 5, www.shef.ac.uk/assem/5/chad.html (accessed April 16, 2003).
———. 2003. Post-processualism, professionalization and archaeological methodologies: Towards reflective and radical practice. *Archaeological Dialogues* 10 (1):97–117.
Gell, A. 1992. *The anthropology of time*. Oxford: Berg.
Habermas, J. 1992. *The structural transformation of the public sphere: An inquiry into a category of bourgeois society*. Cambridge, UK: Polity Press.
Harvey, D. 1989. *The condition of postmodernity*. Oxford: Blackwell.
Hodder, I. 1997. Always momentary, fluid and flexible: Towards a reflexive excavation methodology. *Antiquity* 71:691–700.

Hodder, I., and A. Berggren. 2003. Social practice, method, and some problems of field archaeology. *American Antiquity* 68 (3):421–34.

Hutson, S. 1998. Strategies for the reproduction of prestige in archaeological discourse. *Assemblage* 4, www.shef.ac.uk/4/ (accessed April 16, 2003).

Leskernick Project. 1999a. Small-scale societies. Unpublished leaflet issued in conjunction with Stone Worlds Exhibition.

———. 1999b. Being on Leskernick today. Unpublished leaflet issued in conjunction with Stone Worlds Exhibition.

MacGuigan, J. 1996. *Culture and the public sphere.* London: Routledge.

Marcus, J. 1995. Ethnography in/of the world system: The emergence of multi-sited ethnography. *Annual Review of Anthropology* 24:95–117.

Shanks, M. 1992. *Experiencing the past.* London: Routledge.

Shanks, M., and R. H. McGuire. 1996. The craft of archaeology. *American Antiquity* 61 (1):75–88.

Shanks, M., and C. Tilley. 1992. *Re-constructing archaeology.* London: Routledge.

Slack, J. 1996. The theory and method of articulation in cultural studies. In *Stuart Hall: Critical dialogues in cultural studies*, ed. D. Morley and K-H. Chen, 112–27. London: Routledge.

Tilley, C. 1989. Excavation as theatre. *Antiquity* 63:275–80.

Wilmore, M. 2006. The book and the trowel: Archaeological practice and authority at the Leskernick project. In *Stone worlds: Narrative and reflexive approaches to landscape archaeology*, ed. B. Bender, S. Hamilton, and C. Tilley. London: UCL Press.

11

Histories, Identity, and Ownership: An Ethnographic Case Study in Archaeological Heritage Management in the Orkney Islands

Angela McClanahan

The use of ethnographic methods to examine the cultural values and beliefs attached to specific archaeological monuments by local communities and indigenous minorities has become routine in postcolonial countries with vocal social groups. Cultural ties between people and heritage sites, as well as cases where ownership of cultural properties is claimed and contested by Native American communities, are regularly examined in the United States by the government Bureau of Ethnology (Crespi 1999, 2001), for example. Similarly, public archaeology has become increasingly important in university curricula and a focus of conference sessions, edited volumes, and journal articles (see especially Merriman et al. 2004). The use of ethnography as a specific range of methodologies to examine the cultural value of archaeological remains in contemporary society, however, is still relatively rare in Britain and other parts of Europe (see Bender 1998 and Jones 2004 for notable exceptions).

This chapter contributes to wider discourse on the relationship between the use of ethnography in a variety of archaeological settings by focusing on a particular case study from Scotland in which ethnography was used to investigate the social and cultural values attached to a World Heritage Site in the Orkney Islands. It aims to do two things. First, it highlights the value of and need for the use of ethnographic methods as opposed to more quantitative approaches that have traditionally been used in relation to examining the role of archaeological heritage in contemporary society. Second, it contributes detailed findings on people's specific feelings toward the Orkney World Heritage Site, which can be compared to other historic sites in Orkney, as well as elsewhere in the world.

ETHNOGRAPHY VERSUS QUANTITATIVE METHODS
IN HERITAGE RESEARCH

Often, when surveys and questionnaires about how people feel toward the past and heritage are conducted, they tend to give overarching answers that lack specific detail about why people respond as they do. For example, English Heritage, the governmental body that manages England's historic and prehistoric heritage, recently commissioned the market research company MORI (Market and Opinion Research International) to undertake an extensive public survey of attitudes to heritage in England. The results, discussed in the publication *Power of Place* (English Heritage 2000), reveal statistics like "87% think it is right that there should be public funding to preserve [the historic environment]; 77% disagree that we preserve too much." These types of results do not, however, reveal details about how or why people think monuments and sites should be preserved.

Some heritage managers are calling into question whether these facts and figures alone present an adequate picture of how the heritage sites and monuments in their care are perceived (see Screven 1984, 1993). Many of these methods are market oriented and focus on heritage sites as commodities rather than tools that promote powerful cultural idioms about the past and provide the basis of group identities in the present. Areas of primary evaluation tend to focus on the assessment of the historic or environmental value of the site (Taplin, Scheld, and Low 2002) or financial aspects like entrance fees, cafés, shop sales, visitor satisfaction, and value for money.

Ethnographic assessment of people's understanding of and feelings toward heritage sites can provide much deeper, nuanced insights into a range of relationships between cultural groups, the sites themselves, and those who manage them.

ARCHAEOLOGY AND MANAGEMENT
IN THE ORKNEY ISLANDS

In 1999, a group of famous Neolithic monuments in the Orkney Islands, Scotland, were inscribed as a World Heritage Site by the United Nations Education Scientific and Cultural Organization (UNESCO). They include the Ring of Brodgar henge monument and its associated complex of cairns and smaller standing stones, the Stones of Stenness henge monument and adjacent stones, Maes Howe chambered tomb, and the settlement of Skara Brae. These monuments, which lie in specially designated Buffer Zones, are now collectively known as "The Heart of Neolithic Orkney" World Heritage Site. The sites were nominated for World Heritage Site status by Historic Scotland, the government agency responsible for Scotland's historic buildings and archaeological sites and monuments.

Figure 11.1.   Ring of Brodgar monument, Orkney (Photo by Angela McClanahan)

ORKNEY: THE ETHNOGRAPHIC CONTEXT

Sixteen of Orkney's ninety islands, islets, and skerries are currently inhabited, and the total population is just under 20,000. Orkney residents generally refer to the whole of the archipelago as "the County" and tend to divide the islands into three regions: the North Isles, the Southern Isles, and the Mainland. Apart from its own East/West divide, the Mainland is further separated into smaller districts and parishes, most of which, like each of the smaller islands, have their own community councils, village shops, and primary schools.

Agriculture, fishing, and tourism are the largest generators of income for the islands today (Orkney Islands Council 1996, 1998), and many residents have invested in small, niche-market industries like gourmet food, beer, and wine production, as well as arts and crafts like jewelry, textiles, and pottery. The transport industries, particularly the lifeline ferry services that operate between the Mainland and Caithness and between the islands within the archipelago, provide employment for many Orcadians. Cafés, newsagents, garages, and hotel restaurants exist in most villages and towns and these also provide services and employment for islanders.

With its wealth of archaeological monuments and Scandinavian connections, Orkney is often perceived as being remote and unusual in comparison to Scotland's Gaelic-speaking Highland and west coast island communities. Comprising one-half of Britain's Northern Isles, Orkney has only officially been recognized as "Scottish" for a little over five hundred years. Historians and heritage enthusiasts alike celebrate the fact that the islands were under Norse rule for hundreds of years prior to their often maligned "impignoration," or "pawning," to Scotland in 1468, one year before the same fate befell the neighboring Shetland Islands (Thomson 2001, 218). The Islands of Orkney came as a part of a package deal offered to Scotland as a dowry from a Danish king for the wedding of his daughter to James III (Thomson 2001, 218). Geographer and historian Ronald Miller refers to the Norsemen as the "founding fathers of Orkney" (Miller 1986, 268). Orkney is replete with Scandinavian place-names and material evidence of a Norse earldom. Later Christian settlements and earls' residences are plentiful in the landscape. During Norse rule in the Islands, vastly important historical accounts like the Orkneyingasaga were produced.

The transfer of Orkney to the Kingdom of Scotland is seen by many historians to be the most defining moment in the county's history (Rendall 2002). The Scottish earls installed in Orkney were widely despised as they practiced land reform, which resulted in the development of a feudal system engendering large-scale poverty and suffering among tenant farmers. The later establishment of the merchant laird system in the seventeenth century contributed to further economic decline and hardship for Orcadians. Property rent was increased while production capacities decreased, as the lairds refused to invest in modern technology that could have improved agricultural output (Rendall 2002). These particular periods, when Scottish rule was perceived as particularly cruel, are reviewed in the pages of hundreds of historical accounts and in histories of the Islands more generally (see Cluness 1951) and figure prominently in how Orcadians see themselves and their identity today.

Due to these histories, residents have mixed views about their identity, the place of heritage management in their community, and some reservations as to whether it is necessary to invest so much time and money in heritage development. As a result, the management of many of Orkney's well-known archaeological sites has become contested. On the one hand, Orkney is a modern community whose people are very much concerned with contemporary social and political issues and who consume forms of panglobal popular culture on a daily basis. On the other hand, Orkney's landscapes are brimming with historical and prehistoric monuments, their histories and identities are as much linked to Scandinavia as to Scotland, and there is certainly income to be generated from bringing in tourists to explore the natural and cultural features of the islands. Deciding how to prioritize the management of heritage is thus not always an easy or straightforward task. As one local councilor said at a meeting of the Economic Development Committee in one of Orkney's parishes, "Do we invest £200,000 to develop a heritage site for tourism, or do we spend it on the new retirement home we need in Dounby?"

AN "AUTHENTIC" CULTURE

The presentation of Orkney as an "authentic" culture, though seemingly in contrast to the tensions between investment in the present and the past as noted above, also extends to the manner in which Orcadian hosts treat their guests.

Five months of my time in Orkney was spent boarding at the Buttersquoy Farm, which is located in the parish of Stenness, about two miles form the Brodgar Rural Conservation area. My hosts, Jo-Anne and Charles, have owned Buttersquoy for over fifty years, from the time when Charles inherited the land. Buttersquoy is a beef farm, though some oats are also sown to feed the herds of cattle. Neeps and tatties are grown, but only enough so that the family can use them during the winter.

Thirty years ago, when their first adult child left home, Jo-Anne and Charles decided to convert part of their house into a bed-and-breakfast establishment to generate extra income from the tourist trade, which at that time was supplemental rather than integral to Orkney's economy. Two of the kitchen windows display a number of stickers visitors have sent to the couple from countries across the world, linking the distant homes of tourists with Orkney.

Jo-Anne, in her late sixties and very active, is a gracious hostess, bringing her guests biscuits and regularly topping up their teacups. She tends to their every need and asks them to think of Buttersquoy as their home while they are in Orkney. Charles is tall and physically fit. He charms guests with his broad Orkney accent, good looks, and penchant for telling stories. The couple understands what visitors expect from them and are well versed in delivering an authentic Orcadian farm experience.

Jo-Anne and I talked regularly in the enormous kitchen of the seven-bedroom farmhouse, which has a television, a sofa, and a table where she and her husband eat their meals. The space doubles as a sitting room during the summer, when guests use the more spacious dining room and lounge. This makes the kitchen the focal point for most of the social activity that takes place in the house. Between frequent visits from neighbors and meal times with family members, I asked her about Orkney history and archaeology. I asked what she thought about the sites in and around Stenness and whether she thought that World Heritage status had changed the way she and other community members felt about them.

"No, not really," she would say. "They're just the same as they were before." Her attitude to the monuments seemed to be a combination of ambivalent familiarity, mixed with a strong sense of place and identity. "The stones are something that are just there," she explained to me. "We just grew up with them, so to us, it seems like they've always been there, you know, part of the place. Sometimes, you don't even see them. But we are glad they're ours, though. Sometimes, we take visitors down so they can see the stones. We just sit in the car and wait so they can have their look around, you know."

Jo-Anne's comments, in many ways typical of numerous Orcadians I interviewed, indicate a seemingly contradictory practice of taking something for granted, while at the same time taking pride in it in terms of personal and/or community belonging. The ownership referent "ours" indicates the expression of a group sense of pride, also articulated, perhaps more explicitly, by Annabelle, who also grew up in the area. When I asked her what it was like growing up around the monuments, she said:

We didn't think it was anything marvelous; it was part of our lives, you know. We knew what it was. . . . We were children, you know; I couldn't have told you that this was even before Pictish times or anything. I couldn't have told you the exact history, but we knew it was old, historic, and *ours*.

Of course, such opinions are nuanced and differ from person to person. Annabelle offered a particularly articulate commentary on how and why she perceives the monuments and the landscape in the way she does:

One Sunday when I was about fourteen or fifteen there was to be an open-air service at the Ring of Brodgar, and Lord Birsay . . . took the service, he spoke, he gave the talk, and it was totally inspiring. He talked about Orkney, and the history and religion came all the way through his talk but he kept referring to what we had around us. . . . He talked about the stones and he turned and he stroked a stone and he said I feel that touch when I'm south . . . I feel that stone in my hand, and I just thought, wow! . . . I was there actually just a couple of weeks ago when my daughter was home and we had a most beautiful August night—sorry, September night—the most beautiful night, quite calm and cool and the two of us walked round the stones. . . . I think it was the atmosphere around the stones. It's very hard to put that into words, it's something you feel, you know; it's something you feel. I think it's a strange kind of security.

Although Annabelle invokes the same kind of language frequently used by visitors, for example, discussing the atmosphere of the Ring of Brodgar, she associates this with security and familiarity, whereas visitors I spoke with seemed to relate it to "otherness"—the remoteness of Orkney culture as well as the physical distance between the islands and mainland Britain. In the above quote, Annabelle considers a visit to Brodgar as a time and place where it is appropriate to reaffirm family ties (a visit with her daughter who has come home to Orkney from mainland Scotland) in which she associates the monument with home and a kind of belonging.

THE CONSULTATION GROUP

UNESCO recommends that the government agency responsible for nominating and maintaining a World Heritage Site consult with and inform interested parties in the local community about all proposed developments to the site. In accordance with this suggestion Historic Scotland sent invitations to those living in the immediate area of the Heart of Neolithic Orkney World Heritage Sites to form a Consultation Group. They also invited those who have particular interests in the monuments themselves, for example, tour guides and archaeologists, to attend regular meetings about World Heritage Site news.

My first encounter with the World Heritage Consultation Group involved going along to one of the early meetings in the summer of 2000. The meetings took place in a room in the Stenness Parish's Community School, which also functions as the village's community hall. For the Consultation Group meetings, rows of chairs were set up for attendees, and a slide projector and an overhead projector were placed at the front of the room for occasional presentations.

To my surprise, tempers flared, and the local residents seemed to disagree with almost every point being proposed by the presenter, a representative from the Orkney Islands Council, who was showing on an overhead projector various plans for car parks. Roadside signs designating when drivers were entering the World Heritage Area were also being proposed, and more contestations ensued. Concern was also expressed that inappropriate design could lead to "Disneyfication" of the area. Marker and gateway design must be sensitive to the local landscape and nonurban in character. At this time, discussion was mainly focused on how the objectives of the Management Plan relating to visitor access, interpretation, and traffic management could be taken forward. Despite such tensions, Consultation Group meetings have generated valuable discussion and ideas as to what people perceive about the management of the site. Nevertheless, it is useful to consider some of the sources of these tensions in more detail.

One of the issues is that of accountability and in particular the perception among some Consultation Group members that Historic Scotland, while dealing with difficult challenges, is somehow less accountable than, say, the local council. For instance, Rose, who has been involved in the Consultation Group from the beginning, provided the following justification of her feelings about the way the site is managed and the function of the group.

> I just wish people would say, well, they don't really know [what the monuments mean]. I just find it worrying that everything has got to have an explanation. . . . I've been [to the Consultation Group] sometimes when people have been looking at that and heated arguments . . . about it and people have said, "oh, that's not necessarily so." And [it's] the Council I feel sorry for because the Council get batted by everybody. . . . I think they're trying to manage a juggling act which is almost impossible because they're sort of where everybody comes to, they're the ones who have got to sort of give out the planning permission, they've got to listen to everybody's arguments. I don't agree with everything they do and every decision they make, but they're the only ones who are actually accountable. I really wish that they would have more say [in the management of the World Heritage Sites] 'cause they would have to listen to local people more.

Throughout the research, particularly in ethnographic interviews, many Orkney residents claimed to perceive World Heritage Status to be a pleasant, symbolic gesture, but they are not quite sure of the benefits it will really bring. Although this topic has been discussed at length by Historic Scotland officials during meetings of the Consultation Group in Stenness, the perceived philosophical meaning of the term "World Heritage Site" is still somewhat vague. Interestingly, some of the comments people made about the accolade stemmed from issues closely associated with the feeling that Orcadians as a community didn't need officials from the outside world to tell them their monuments are special.

This research has shown that issues of ownership, for example, as raised by Jo-Anne and Annabelle above, are of particular importance with respect to the development of the World Heritage Sites. Will the inscription of the place as a World Heritage Site make people view the landscapes in which they grew up and presently dwell differently? All of the native Orcadians I questioned directly about this suggested it would have little impact. For instance:

CHLOE: No it doesn't change. I think that it makes you . . . think that other people are going to be made more aware of it; I mean we've always been aware of it, but you know other people maybe don't pay that much attention to that kind of thing. . . . I mean I could tell you somebody in Stenness who's never been at the Ring [of Brodgar].

WILLIAM: Well, does it make much difference? I don't think so. It certainly offers some protection but you might say over the top in a sense.

HUGH: No, it's still the same place to me. I mean, all this World Heritage carry on . . . we need to stop being so concerned with the dead and the things they made. They're in the past . . . gone. It's the living people we need to take care of.

These comments illustrate that in many ways people view the World Heritage Status in a mundane way in relation to their daily practices. Their conceptions of any new kind of boundaries—for example, buffer zones—do not bear on their experience of the monuments and the landscape in practice in the same way that it resonates with those involved in the management and development of the World Heritage Sites. Native Orcadians' and Orkney residents' engagement with the monuments differs from visitors' experiences in terms of their familiarity with the place, particularly the daily recognition of the landscape as home. This type of engagement is not necessarily as intentional as a purposeful visit to a monument (though in certain contexts local residents also make such visits) but is no less important in terms of the sense of place they provide. Furthermore, despite local residents' assertions that the management of the monuments has little impact on the ways that they perceive them, other conversations reveal a more profound impact.

I asked Maggie, a lifelong Stenness resident, if the landscape in and around Stenness has changed since she grew up. She paused to consider what to say, looked down at her own coffee, then out the window, and said, "When you've been with a place and seen it as it was, things are different, you know. But I suppose you have to change with the times." There was no tone of sadness or nostalgia in her voice; rather, her comments were pointed and exhibited a matter-of-fact practicality that reveals a clear concern with the present.

As the conversation unfolded, she frequently related to me how she felt about the management of some of the individual monuments of the World Heritage Sites. She talked about how, in the past, Historic Scotland erected signs and fences around Maes Howe and tried to have "unpleasantries," like black, plastic-covered hay bales removed from the area. She talked about how using official stewards formalized the experience of the monument, perhaps giving people a false impression of Orkney.

> All this talk about World Heritage . . . I mean, it's an honor, but as Orcadians, we've always known the value of our landscape. Folk come here because they've heard about it and wanted to come and see it—not because it's a World Heritage Site. Not one of my guests has said that's why they came here. Do you know when all the World Heritage tourists are going to come? We don't want it to become a Disneyland either. . . . Folk need to see that Orkney is on the cutting edge of agriculture, just as modern as any farm down South.

Such comments reveal seemingly contradictory feelings about the influence of outside rules and regulations on Orkney culture, but also demonstrate a need to show outsiders that Orkney culture is equal to other societies in terms of its technologies and ways of life. On the one hand, Maggie's comments are indicative that memories of other events, which are in some cases conflated, possibly slightly erroneous, and not necessarily connected to current efforts, can often influence how people engage with and perceive organizations and their activities. On the other hand, memories can also be connected to events or relationships that did take place but might have been perceived differently by representatives of management groups and organizations who did not realize the extent or nature of their impact.

CONCLUSION

We have seen that a small part of the Orkney landscape, which has been branded as a World Heritage Site, is both a physical and conceptual terrain "across which sites of power [are] mapped" (Daniels and Cosgrove 1988). Through everyday, mundane action, the landscape of Stenness and Brodgar is lived and politicized, with many interest groups (referred to as stakeholders by heritage and tourist agencies) negotiating different aspects of their identities and needs and with the landscape being used as both an explicit and implicit tool. Beliefs about archaeological remains and the management of them have always been inextricably linked with the circumstances of history and influenced by sociocultural factors such as class, economic structure, and most recently, the global market forces of tourism. From early explorations and rifling of the tombs to amateur antiquarian excavations and the inscription of the Heart of Neolithic Orkney World Heritage Sites, the social values placed on the material evidence of the past are clearly affected by historic events and trends.

Communication problems arise between groups when management organizations see themselves as helping local communities by introducing international (or simply outside) values in the form of any type of designation of renown. In the case of the Orkney World Heritage Sites, this has caused some people in the Stenness community to feel that their choices (or lack thereof) and voices are being impinged upon, if not completely ignored by the state and "highbrow" outside research interests. Knowledge of historical repression in Orkney, particularly episodes in history like the poor conditions in which Orcadians lived under the merchant laird system, probably contribute to negative feelings toward outside authority. As one interviewee commented, "We don't really speak up to authority figures when we should because we've been told we shouldn't in the past. I know that's not an excuse, but it's our way, sometimes. We don't put ourselves forward enough."

Issues of encroachment by outside influence, whether perceived by outsiders or not, also enter into feelings of loss with respect to Orkney customs and traditions, especially in terms of the large numbers of incomers entering Orkney since World War II, and particularly since the 1970s (Forsythe 1982). Similarly, Orcadians' feelings toward investment in the present rather than the past (and the contexts in which this subject was often raised during my fieldwork) are not always explicitly linked to feelings toward heritage agencies and their employees. Rather, it seems that the general topic of the inscription of the "Heart of Neolithic Orkney" as a World Heritage Site stirs feelings for some that are embedded in broader issues like social change and the perceived encroachment of outside values on Orcadian culture.

Fear of widespread change causes some to perceive that traditional Orkney life has collapsed in the face of changing values, work ethics, and access to information and outsiders coming into the landscape. In many ways, the introduction of World Heritage Status has exacerbated such feelings among some Orcadians in that it represents outside organizations coming in to assert power over the community. As many people said to me, "We don't mind incomers coming up to live, as long as they don't try to change it."

One of the recommendations generated by this research, resulting from feelings and attitudes like those expressed in the above two paragraphs, would be to approach communities in a different fashion. Historic Scotland's image is a corporate one, which is reflected in documents and management style, as well as surface appearances. In many ways, such symbols can become barriers in terms of how individuals and groups from the agency are perceived by a community with which they wish to communicate. Such insights can be gleaned from ethnographic methods, which can have a positive influence on heritage management policy as it relates to local communities and visitors of archaeological sites.

ACKNOWLEDGMENTS

Many thanks are due to Siân Jones and Sally Foster, both of whom have commented extensively on texts produced as a result of this project. Thanks also to the informants who took the time to answer my questions about Orkney life and heritage.

REFERENCES

Bender, B. 1998. *Stonehenge: Making space.* Oxford: Berg.

Cluness, A. T. 1951. *The Shetland Isles.* London: R. Hale.

Crespi, M. 1999. *A brief ethnography of magnolia plantation: Planning for Cane River Creole National Historical Park* (draft). Denver: National Park Service.

———. 2001. Seeking inclusiveness. In *Common ground: Archaeology and ethnography in the public interest. Stewards of the human landscape.* Washington, D.C: National Park Service.

Daniels, S., and D. Cosgrove. 1988. Introduction: Iconography and landscape. In *The iconography of landscape,* ed. D. Cosgrove and S. Daniels. Cambridge: Cambridge University Press.

English Heritage. 2000. *Power of place: The future of the historic environment.*

Forsythe, D. 1982. *Urban-rural migration: Change and conflict in an Orkney Island community.* London: Social Science Research Council.

Jones, S. 2004. *Early medieval sculpture and the production of meaning, value and place: The case of Hilton of Cadboll.* Edinburgh: Historic Scotland.

Merriman, N., ed. 2004. *Public archaeology.* London: Routledge.

Miller, R. 1986. Who are the Orcadians? In *The people of Orkney,* ed. R. Berry and H. Firth, 268–75. Kirkwall: The Orkney Press.

Orkney Islands Council. 1996. *Orkney economic review.* Kirkwall: Orkney Islands Council.

———. 1998. *Orkney economic review.* Kirkwall: Orkney Islands Council.

Rendall, J. 2002. *A jar of seed-corn: Portrait of an island farm.* Kirkwall: The Orcadian Limited.

Screven, C. G. 1984. Educational evaluation and research in museums and public exhibits: A bibliography. *Curator* 27 (2):147–65.

———. 1993. Visitor studies in the U.S. *Museum* 178 (2).

Serrell, B. 1998. *Paying attention: Visitors and museum exhibitions.* Professional Practice Series. Washington, D.C.: American Association of Museums.

Taplin, D., S. Scheld, and S. Low. 2002. Rapid ethnographic assessment in urban parks: A case study of Independence National Historical Park. *Human Organization* 61 (1):80–93.

Thomson, W. 2001. *The New History of Orkney.* Edinburgh: Mercat Press.

12

Among Totem Poles and Clan Power in Tanum, Sweden: An Ethnographic Perspective on Communicative Artifacts of Heritage Management

Håkan Karlsson and Anders Gustafsson

When we use an ethnographic approach, turning inward our outward-looking gaze and re-encountering our everyday activities, it becomes obvious that archaeology contains its fair share of unusual rituals and social activities. These not only produce material culture (artifacts) in various forms but also create specific forms of social relationships between different actors. During the last fifteen years various aspects of these socially and culturally embedded archaeological activities and their material remains have been studied within the framework of a number of reflexive approaches. Such approaches have a common ground in ethnographic ideas and methods, even if this is not explicitly stated in all cases (cf. Olsen 1993; Gero 1994, 1996; Goodwin 1994; Hodder 2000; Shankland 1997; Holtorf 2002; Edgeworth 2003; Gustafsson and Karlsson 2004a).

If one views the rock carvings in Tanum today with the eyes of an ethnographer, the everyday activities carried out by contemporary heritage management practitioners can seem very strange. If we look at these practices only as archaeologists, we run the risk of becoming culturally and contextually blinded, as well as questioned by our colleagues. Some activities have been carried out in the same way for decades, and within the archaeological culture one is socialized to view them as completely natural. However, leaving the well-trodden and traditional paths of archaeology, we are convinced that an ethnographic approach and the application of ethnographic methods to archaeology can teach us something about ourselves and about archaeology as a social, cultural, and existential activity carried out in the present. Such an approach can provoke and shock our thoughts and let them run in new directions. The familiar activities of archaeology and our fixed social role within the discipline can no longer be taken as self-evident. Ethnography enables us to consider archaeology as a specific social and cultural activity carried out within particular historical, ideological, and sociopolitical contexts. Even if an ethnographic perspective primarily focuses on the culture of contemporary archaeology, its activities, and material culture, this does not mean that the past and its peoples are ignored; rather, it is the other way around. Such a standpoint lets us view archaeology and its material culture as a cultural phenomenon and enables us to study it in the same way as we archaeologists study past (and in some cases, present) societies and their material culture. This can lead to new ways of looking at and understanding the past through the recognition that archaeological interpretations of the past are always embedded in the contextually and socially dependent archaeological processes of the present.

The purpose of this chapter is to contribute to debate concerning the benefits of using ethnographic approaches and methods in archaeology. This is done through (1) a brief discussion of the history of ritualized communicative artifacts such as signposts and information boards within Swedish heritage management and (2) a more specific presentation and discussion detailing ethnographic reflections on the content and symbolism of such artifacts at the World Heritage listed site of rock carvings in Tanum, Sweden.

SIGNPOSTS AND INFORMATION BOARDS AS TOTEM POLES

When discussing the communicative relationship between Swedish heritage management and the public, there is a broad spectrum of activities, artifacts, and methods that could be chosen as a starting point. Here the example is restricted to the content and symbolism of signposts (at the roadside) and information boards (adjacent to monuments/sites). These artifacts are the principal means through which Swedish heritage management has communicated with the public during the last eighty years.

Signposts and information boards represent a form of culturally embedded artifacts that signify a specific symbolic meaning. They have their origin in the cultural practices of heritage management. In most cases, they provide the only guidance that a visitor to a prehistoric monument or site receives. It is therefore important to realize that it is the content and embedded symbolism of these artifacts that contribute to the visitor's experience and understanding of a monument or site. At the same time, via their symbolism, they communicate the grounds for the relationship between the culture of heritage management and the public. This argument can be taken even further, and it can be said that for some people these artifacts, their texts, and inherent symbolism are the first and sometimes the only information received about the past and the role of heritage management (Räf 1995, 27).

The placement of signposts and information boards at monuments and sites is just one of a range of possible methods of communication, but it is a method

Figure 12.1.   1940s signpost at stone circle in Åbrott, Kville parish, Bohuslän

that during the twentieth century has had tremendous success in the context of Swedish heritage management practice. This success is so profound that the methodological and pedagogical advantages and disadvantages of these artifacts no longer seem to be discussed. That is, the use of the signpost and information board has become an axiomatic and ritualized method. Of course, there are discussions about the content of the signposts and information boards and their technical design (cf. Bergdahl Bulukin 1984; Dunér et al. 1996; af Geijerstam 1998, 97–100), but the question of whether their use represents a good methodological approach or not is seldom discussed (cf. Sörenson 1989; af Geijerstam 1998; Gustafsson and Karlsson 2004b). Their implicit symbolism as power markers or totem poles for the culture of heritage management has hitherto been discussed only in a few texts (Gustafsson and Karlsson 2004a). So the questions of what epistemological viewpoint underlies this ritualized method and how it developed are neglected within the contemporary context of heritage management.

At first glance, and from a traditional archaeological viewpoint, it might seem peculiar to discuss the question of how and why the use of artifacts such as signposts and information boards adjacent to monuments or sites has become the prevailing method of communication—or to ask what these artifacts symbolize with regard to the relationship between heritage management and the public.

However, from an ethnographic standpoint an even more peculiar thing is that today the use of signposts as communicative artifacts is so natural and ritualized that they are not viewed as the outcome of a deliberate methodological choice. Like all methods of communication, this one does have a specific history—a history intimately connected to epistemological, symbolical, and sociopolitical considerations, as well as to trends in the wider society. At a general level the use of signposts in the context of heritage management follows the overall trend of signing, which different sectors of Swedish society have seen throughout the twentieth century. Signing as a heritage management practice has an unbroken continuity from the 1920s on (cf. Dunér et al. 1996; Curman 1927, 1928, 1929). Of course, the technical design as well as the content of signposts has changed during these eighty years and we have argued elsewhere that these artifacts can be divided into four types or generations: (1) admonition and adult education (1925–1950); (2) adult education and tourism (1950–1970); (3) quantification and mass production (1979–1990); and (4) flexibility and individuality (1990 onward) (Gustafsson and Karlsson 2004a, 2004c). The main symbolism of these artifacts has not changed. They all, despite different content and technical design, communicate a clear dichotomy between experts (the heritage management) and amateurs (the public). In doing so they also communicate clearly to the latter who is in charge when it comes to the interpretation of the past and its sites and monuments. Thus, these artifacts stand as totem poles, signaling territorial rights and boundaries (not just geographically but also intellectually) on behalf of the Heritage Management Clan.

Let us now turn toward a specific case study where we can see how this symbolism works in practice—at the signposts and information boards that can be found close to the World Heritage listed rock carvings in Tanum, Bohuslän.

TOTEM POLES PUT INTO PRACTICE

The information boards near the rock carvings in Tanum were erected in the mid-1990s as part of the public information theme "The rock-carving journey" (*Hällristningsresan*). They function on three levels of information (Bengtsson 2002). The first level consists of trisected metal boards that are placed at the four classic rock-carving sites of Aspeberget, Fossum, Litsleby, and Vitlycke. The second level consists of two-sided metal boards in the form of an open book, placed at the main areas of carvings at the different sites. This is the kind of information board, for example, that the visitor finds near the famous carvings at Vitlycke. The third level consists of one-sided metal boards that present specific carvings.

In providing the first information that the visitor sees, level 1 boards give a general background to the carvings through a presentation of their chronology and unique character. There are also some admonishing passages of text telling the visitor that the carvings are protected by law.

One of the main themes presented in the texts carried by information boards at Aspeberget and Vitlycke is that the carvings are seriously threatened. The threat is primarily in the form of air pollution and trampling. On the first-level board at Aspeberget (figure 12.2), for instance, are the following words:

A THREATENED WORLD HERITAGE. The existence of the rock carvings is threatened by environmental pollution. They are carved in granite and have resisted the influence of the weather and the wind for 3,000 years. Now the air of Europe is saturated with sulfur from factories and cars, and different minerals in the granite are starting to break up. When the rocks start to weather they lose their resistance to night frost, changes in temperature, and trampling feet. (our translation)

This threatening statement is further strengthened by the picture that frames the text on the board of the second level (figure 12.3).

THE ROCK CARVINGS ARE WEATHERING. The rain and the air are saturated with sulfur and nitrogen from cars, factories, and oil heating. The pollution settles in the rock's mineral granules, which weather and absorb water. Salts in the water increase in volume and break up the mineral granules from the surface of the rock. This process can during a few decades destroy the mysterious pictures that have survived about 3,000 years of natural influence from strong sunshine, frost, and lichens. On the surface of the rocks that are breaking up in this way, however, these natural influences become devastating. (our translation)

Figure 12.2.   Information board, level 1: Aspeberget

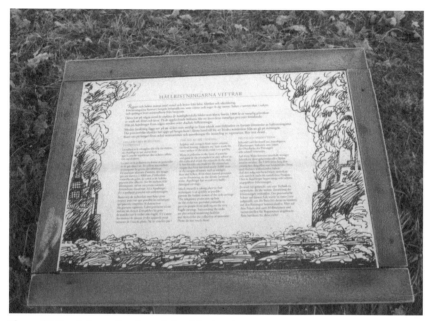

Figure 12.3.   Information board, level 2: Aspeberget

As seen in figure 12.3, this text is also framed by belching chimneys, myriads of cars, and threatening—probably sulfur-saturated—clouds.

When the visitor has passed these fateful texts and, via a stair, arrived at the first rock-carving surface at Aspeberget—stopping to view the carvings and the third-level information board (figure 12.4)—the logical crescendo is presented.

> THIS HUGE ROCK CARVING IS COVERED. The deeply carved pictures have weathered greatly during the last few years, and many details are obliterated. The protective cover shields the rock carvings from air pollution, salts, and variations in humidity and temperature. Here the surface is illustrated in its entirety. (our translation)

Perhaps the most suitable word is "anticlimax." The visitor can see only the rock carving on the illustration (at least during low season). This is a recurrent situation at Aspeberget, since a number of other rock surfaces with carvings along the prepared pathway are also covered. Some of the carvings are covered permanently, and at one of these the visitor can read:

> HERE A ROCK CARVING IS PUT TO FINAL REST. Here we have been forced to bury a seriously damaged carving. It is one of the most interesting in the area, and it now lies under a protective cover consisting of earth and sand. (Aspeberget, information board, level 3; our translation)

The question is, what sort of impressions and memories will visitors take with them from their encounter with the rock carvings at Aspeberget and Vitlycke,

Figure 12.4.   The anticlimax. Information board, level 3: Aspeberget

against the background of the information board's content and symbolism? The primary impression no doubt consists of thoughts concerning how sensitive and threatened these fantastic and unique rock carvings are and that it is the modern industrial society that threatens the remains from our prehistory—forcing heritage management to cover some of the carvings permanently. Another impression is probably linked to the fact that there are a number of admonitions in the information board text, in the form of sentences such as: "do not walk on the rock-carvings," "forbidden," "absolutely forbidden," and "do not touch anything." That is, the carvings are protected from the public, for the public.

Heritage management is thus admonishing the public not to approach or touch their cultural heritage physically. At the same time heritage managers are presented almost as physicians or shamans working on a cure that will heal the sick rock carvings and, on a preventive level, offer the carvings not yet affected a profound resistance against their sulfur allergy. Everything seems to be so clear concerning the interpretation of the rock carvings. There are no unanswered questions and no mention of earlier interpretations or popular beliefs. The visitor's general impression of archaeology/heritage management is thus one of a criticizing teacher—an expert with shamanic qualities and absolute knowledge. Another impression could be based on the fact that the texts can be seen as a political argument in the contemporary environmental debate. Is it the case that the weathering of the rock carvings is being used here in the service of a specific political standpoint concerning industrial society's relation to its environment? Such a standpoint has clear similarities with older theological arguments, which see civilization degenerating in the direction of Armageddon. It is ironic, then, that contemporary heritage management seems to be completely blinded by a belief in the ability of the natural sciences to care for the rock carvings. Even more ironic is that this has led to the partial destruction of some carvings by means of various chemical and technical experiments (Gustafsson and Karlsson 2004a, 2004b).

It could be argued that the content of the information boards presents a form of (positivistic) narration that is based upon clear dichotomies between past and present, and between experts and amateurs. Since there is no room for alternative interpretations concerning the rock carvings, the information boards can be seen as authoritarian decrees coming from above, that is, from the Heritage Management Clan. This means that the actual narration is not just creating obstacles for the public's physical approach to the rock carvings but also to the public's cognitive and reflexive approach to them. What can be pondered about the rock carvings when the experts seem so clear and certain about everything? One can also argue that, where the rock carvings have been covered (symbolically killed), the information boards have come to replace the carvings themselves. This means that the signifier stands literally in the place of the signified, in the same way as a gravestone signifies the former existence of and stands in the place of a person who was once alive. Thus, the main symbolism is that the Heritage Management Clan is in charge when it comes to the interpretation and understanding of the past and its material remains, as well as when it comes to the protection of our common heritage. The signposts and information boards thus serve as totem poles symbolizing that this is the geographical and intellectual territory of the Heritage Management Clan—a clan that has the shamanic power to decide over the life and death of rock carvings.

CONCLUSION

We have briefly presented above, from a Swedish perspective, the history and use of ritualized communicative artifacts such as signposts and information boards in Swedish heritage management. We have also discussed the role that ethnographic fieldwork might play in approaching the content and symbolism of these communicative artifacts near the World Heritage listed rock carvings in Tanum, Sweden.

On a general level it is obvious that the ritualized use of signposts contradicts all forms of dialogue and openness. This method of communication has a closed structure in the sense that it requires active senders (heritage managers) and passive receivers (the public). In this structure the communicative relationship between heritage managers and the public necessarily has the form of a monologue. It can be argued that the actual methodology is constructed upon an authoritarian epistemological view where there exist, among other things, clear dichotomies between experts and amateurs, subject and object, interpreter and interpreted, science and society, and not least between past and present. We would like to stress that, even if the purpose of these artifacts (at least officially) is to mediate information about the rock carvings to the public, the main symbolism, both in the information presented and in the artifacts themselves, is that the heritage management is in charge when it comes to the interpretation and understanding of the past and its material remains. When it comes to the protection of our common heritage, the message is that the rock carvings are the geographical and intellectual territory of the Heritage Management Clan. The symbolism, then, is mainly about power and authority, that is, the power and authority of heritage management over the past and over the public. It is a power that works both on the disciplinary and the personal level. If heritage managers do not show the society that they are indispensable experts, they risk losing both economical support and their employment.

The narration presented by the Swedish heritage management at Tanum has little to do with the past; rather, most of it is a contemporary construction of the past put together within the cultural framework of heritage management's longing for power.

Thus, it can be concluded that, as archaeologists, we are not used to approaching our own subject from an ethnographic point of view. Yet if we take this step and approach our own discipline as a specific culture fixed in a historical, ideological, and sociopolitical context, we will find that it has much to teach us about our subject, about ourselves, and perhaps also about the past. It has undoubtedly helped us to move beyond the conventional ways of viewing the world, which are a consequence of our own archaeological socialization, in order to bring to light these strange examples of contemporary heritage management culture. There are many reasons—not least ethical and democratic ones— why this culture and its rituals should be examined even further from an ethnographic point of departure. The next step in our own research is to observe how members of the public move around and interact with the artifacts discussed in this text at various places in Bohuslän (Andersson and Persson forthcoming).

ACKNOWLEDGMENTS

This chapter was written within the framework of the project "Cultural Heritage as Societal Dialogue" that we carried out during the period 2002–2004, with financial support from the National Heritage Board.

REFERENCES

Andersson, L., and M. Persson. Forthcoming. Att följa stigen. En publikundersökning kring besökarens rörelsemönster och agerande vid Blomsholms fornlämningsområde. In situ 2004.

Bengtsson, L., curator. 2002. Oral communication. Tanum, Sweden: Vitlycke Museum.

Bergdahl Bulukin, E. 1984. *Fornvård i Göteborgs och Bohus län: Information från länsstyrelsen 1984.* Länsstyrelsen i Göteborgs och Bohus län.

Curman, S. 1927. Riksantikvariens årsberättelse för år 1926. In *KVHAA Årsbok 1927*, 1–58. Stockholm, Sweden: KVHAA.

———. 1928. Riksantikvariens årsberättelse för år 1927. In *KVHAA Årsbok 1928*, 1–149. Stockholm, Sweden: KVHAA.

———. 1929. Riksantikvariens årsberättelse för år 1928. In *KVHAA Årsbok 1929*, 1–90. Stockholm, Sweden: KVHAA.

Dunér, M., E. Rosander, and O. Tulin. 1996. *Skyltar för svenska kulturmiljöer.* Stockholm, Sweden: Riksantikvarieämbetet.

Edgeworth, M. 2003. *Acts of discovery: An ethnography of archaeological practice.* BAR International Series 1131. Oxford: Archaeopress.

Geijerstam, J. af. 1998. *Miljön som minne. Att göra historien levande i kulturlandskapet.* Stockholm, Sweden: Riksantikvarieämbetet.

Gero, J. 1994. Gender division of labor in the construction of archaeological knowledge in the United States. In *Social construction of the past: Representation as power*, ed. G. Bond and A. Gilliam. London: Routledge.

———. 1996. Archaeological practice and gendered encounters with field data. In *Engendering archaeology: Women and prehistory*, ed. J. Gero and M. Conkey, 251–80. Philadelphia: University of Pennsylvania Press.

Goodwin, C. 1994. Professional vision. *American Anthropologist* 96 (3):606–33.

Gustafsson, A., and H. Karlsson. 2002. Kulturarv som samhällsdialog. *Humanistdagboken* 15:105–16.

———. 2004a. *Plats på scen. Kring beskrivning och förmedling av Bohusläns fasta fornlämningar genom tiderna.* Uddevalla, Sweden: Bohusläns museum, Riksantikvarieämbetet.

———. 2004b. Solid as a Rock? An ethnographical study of the management of Rockcarvings. *Current Swedish Archaeology* 12:23–42.

———. 2004c. *Kulturarv som samhällsdialog? En betraktelse av kulturarvsförmedling.* Stockholm, Sweden: Riksantikvarieämbetet.

Hodder, I., ed. 2000. *Towards reflexive method in archaeology: The example at Çatalhöyük.* Cambridge, UK: McDonald Institute Monographs.

Holtorf, C. 2002. Notes on the life history of a pot sherd. *Journal of Material Culture* 7:49–71.

Olsen, B. 1993. *Camera archaeologica: Rapport fra et feltarbeid.* Tromsø, Norway: Tromsø museums skrifter 23.

Räf, E. 1995. Varför var det så ont om folk förr? In *Arkeologi och förmedling*, ed. E. Andersson, M. Dahlgren, and K. Jennbert, Report Series No. 54, 27–32. Lund, Sweden: University of Lund, Institute of Archaeology.

Shankland, D. 1997. The anthropology of an archaeological presence. In *On the surface: The re-opening of Çatalhöyük*, ed. I. Hodder, 186–202. Cambridge, UK: McDonald Institute Monographs.

Sörenson, U. 1989. *Resan till sevärdheten.* Stockholm, Sweden: STFs förlag.

13

Amazonian Archaeology and Local Identities

Denise Maria Cavalcante Gomes

The aim of this chapter is to describe social interactions between an archaeological research project and the Parauá, a traditional community located one hundred kilometers south of Santarém, in Amazonia, Brazil. It focuses reflexively on how these interactions influence the production of archaeological knowledge on the one hand and the construction of local identities on the other. Even though the chapter is written from the personal point of view of an archaeologist, a kind of ethnography of archaeology emerges (Edgeworth 2003).

Aspects of the construction of archaeological knowledge, it is argued here, are made possible through the participation of local workers in fieldwork. At the same time, the interface between local people and the archaeological project has political dimensions, and the role of archaeology in the process of construction of contemporary identities is also an important topic for discussion. For this reason, contextual information about the local population and the area of research is provided.

During fieldwork, participation of workers in the research led to a better understanding of the environment, the location of resources, and the relationship of these with local cosmologies. Involvement of the community was highlighted by processes of constant negotiation of access to some research areas and appropriation of aspects of archaeological discourse by political leaderships in the construction of local identities.

Since the beginning of the research project, archaeology proved to be a source of conflict. Local people were suspicious of the archaeological work. The lack of familiarity of some members of the Parauá community with archaeological investigation in general, and archaeological surveys in particular (which involved the opening of transects across their territory), led to the emergence of political opposition as well as to sympathizers who helped and supported the research.

As Layton (1994) suggests, the only solution to conflicts of interest between researchers and local communities is to facilitate partial control by the latter over access to their own past. This implies a reflexive archaeological practice of a sociopolitical nature (Allen et al. 2002; Ardren 2002; Clarke 2002, 250; Rodriguez 2001).

In Brazil, as in other Latin American countries, consideration of ethnic issues and the rights of indigenous and traditional populations in relation to management of their sites and cultural heritage is relatively recent. Funari (2001, 241) points out that some recent initiatives in Brazil indicate an involvement with indigenous populations and demonstrate a commitment to a more ethical archaeological practice. In Amazonia, however, there have been very few such research projects (Green et al. 2003).

Brazilian archaeologists have not previously been prepared to deal with local communities, or to face situations of conflict that might put projects at risk. For some, fieldwork in remote areas of Brazil is still seen as a romantic adventure. But I believe that this report of my own experience, giving an account of the cultural differences and political interfaces that occur between archaeologists and local communities, can stimulate other archaeologists to think about their own experiences in similar fieldwork situations.

THE ARCHAEOLOGICAL CONTEXT OF THE AREA OF STUDY

Santarém (1000–1500 A.D.) has been considered a setting for the emergence of complex societies in the lower Amazon before the arrival of Europeans. According to Roosevelt's interpretative model (based on ethnohistorical accounts, former archaeological research, and recent excavations), there was intensive agriculture, social and political hierarchy, territorial concentration, an increase and expansion of war, large-scale organization of labor, and the presence of specialists—the latter exemplified by the development of elaborately designed ceramics (Roosevelt 1992, 1999). Recent studies of stylistic variation of ceramics in museum collections, in terms of both decoration and technology, point to the existence of a regional style, possibly shared by other communities surrounding Santarém (Gomes 2001, 2002).

As part of my PhD research, I wanted to test hypotheses about the establishment of the boundaries of Santarém society, the distribution of a regional style, and the possible inclusion of ecologically peripheral areas in the same political system. The area occupied by the Parauá community on the lower Tapajós River, one hundred kilometers south of Santarém, was chosen as a suitable location (figure 13.1). Previous research in the area, carried out in the 1920s (Nimuendajú 1949), indicated that communities belonging to the same culture

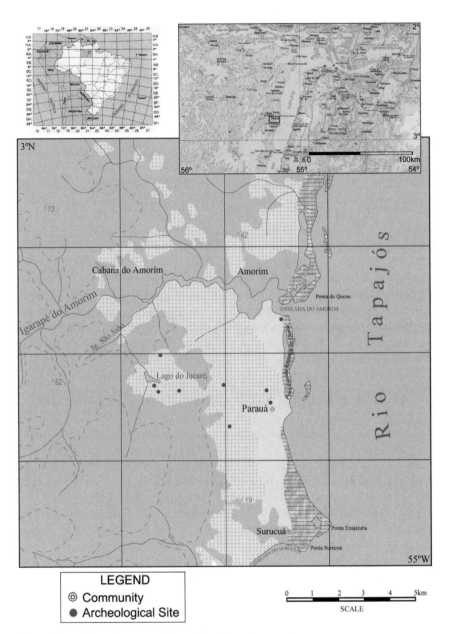

Figure 13.1.   Location map of Parauá territory, Amazonia

might have occupied the right bank of the Tapajós River. The expectation, therefore, was to find Santarém settlements in this area, located on the left bank. However, that was not what happened. The archaeological survey found ten archaeological sites within an area of forty square kilometers, corresponding to the current territory of the Parauá community. Nine of these sites were related to precolonial occupations of ancient Formative societies—their ceramics being associated with the Amazon Incised Rim tradition (Meggers and Evans 1961). This ceramic complex, dating from about 3800 to 1000 B.P., is representative of the inception of the first horticulturalists in this area and in its later phase is partly contemporary with the beginning of Santarém chiefdoms.

CONTEMPORARY COMMUNITIES IN AMAZONIA

Traditional riverside communities in Amazonia, also known as Amazon *caboclos*, are mixed-blood populations resulting from marriages between Indians and Portuguese colonizers—and, to a lesser extent, northeastern Brazilians who came to work in the area during the period of the Rubber Cycle (Parker 1989, 251). Although historically and culturally related to Indian populations that occupied the Amazon lowlands at the time of European contact, *caboclos* are distinct from current indigenous Amazonian societies. They represent a specific social historic formation created by Portuguese colonization between 1615 and 1800, which homogenized the existing diversity of former indigenous groups (Arenz 2000).

In the process of construction of *caboclo* identities, their subsistence strategies, residential patterns, technologies, perception of resources, and forms of management of environmental resources (Adams 1994; Balée 1989, 1998; Roosevelt 1989) are clear evidence of an indigenous heritage. So too are their religious practices and their cosmological beliefs about the forest and spirits of the river; these were incorporated and combined into Iberian traditions (Arenz 2000; Vaz 1996; Wagley 1957). A partial explanation of observed patterns arises from the persistence of a regional economy, based on the extraction of natural resources (Parker 1989, 255). An important point, however, is that although some of the Parauá recognize their indigenous cultural heritage, they do not consider themselves to be Indians and vehemently refuse to be classified as Indians.

The Parauá are a community of five hundred inhabitants, who live off manioc subsistence farming, collecting, and fishing. Most families are directly involved in these activities, either for their own consumption or for commercial enterprise. Local commerce is restricted to three small stores. Other paid activities are related to occupations in the two schools. There is a health center, a church, and an ambulance launch that transports urgent medical cases to Santarém, but there is no electric light and no sanitation. Generally speaking, monetary circulation is low and is supplemented by more traditional forms of exchange.

Houses of the community are situated along two streets, creating two neighborhoods separated by the Mangal *igarapé* (stream), which serves as a meeting point as well as a landmark. Most homes house nuclear families, though some have extended families with couples, children, old-age people, and newlywed sons and daughters. Traditional structures called flour houses, used for the making of flour and other subproducts of manioc, are present in the majority of homes, which also have modern radios and an occasional television set, powered by a community generator.

As well as an elected president, there are community leaders who gain power by virtue of their prestige among the inhabitants. However, the constitution of political groups is not homogenous, being directly related to clashes of interest associated with distinct political tendencies based in Santarém. The configuration of these groups greatly influenced the conflict that arose in relation to the development of my archaeological research.

THE ARCHAEOLOGICAL RESEARCH: CONFLICT, COOPERATION, AND THE CONSTRUCTION OF IDENTITIES

Friendly contact with the president of the community and with one of the political leaders, established months before the beginning of fieldwork in 2001, was not enough to prevent one of the divergent factions from filing a report to IBAMA (Brazilian Institute of the Environment)—linking the archaeological research to biopiracy activities. This led to an initial standstill in research and resulted in my physical removal from the location by agents of the institution until the situation was cleared up with the help of IPHAN (National Institute of Historical and Artistic Heritage).

The motive behind the accusation of biopiracy derived firstly from the general insecurity felt by riverside communities regarding ownership of their lands, which in turn resulted from the transformation of the area into an Extractivist Reserve (an area of nature conservation managed by IBAMA). Secondly, it derived from the lack of familiarity with archaeological investigation and the general suspicion of archaeological fieldwork this gives rise to. Some Amazonian riverside communities perceive the archaeologist to be someone who seeks mineral riches, who will sell the artifacts and take financial advantage of any excavations. This is quite similar to views of archaeologists held by Canadian Inuits, as reported by Bielawski (1994, 231). It is also close to the view of Mayan populations in the Yucatán area of Mexico, some of whom consider archaeologists to be invaders of their land (Rodriguez 2001).

Here I must acknowledge my own naïveté in conceiving of research in Amazonia to be nonproblematic with regard to access to land, sites, and artifacts, and also with regard to the implications of archaeological research on the identities of the local inhabitants. But the troubled beginning I have outlined marked the start of a relationship built on dialogue and based on constant ne-

Figure 13.2.   Archaeologist and members of the Parauá community (Photo by Denise Gomes)

gotiation, close cooperation, friendship, and reciprocity during three years of working together.

From the very beginning of the project, the decision was made to establish the research team's base in the community in order to achieve a greater closeness with the inhabitants and their way of life. During fieldwork, the team (made up of me and occasional archaeologist colleagues willing to collaborate) was based mainly in a small house that remained empty most of the rest of the time, being used by the priest only when he came from Santarém to hold his services in the community. Sometimes we stayed in the house of a local inhabitant. Here we put up our hammocks in the open air, protected by a straw covering. The team's meals were prepared by a cook and at the end of the afternoon baths were taken in the Mangal stream, together with a crowd of children and young people.

A decisive factor in dispersing initial distrust was my participation in social events. I attended birthday parties, funerals, watched soccer tournaments, had lunch with neighbors, spent weekends at the beach, made bicycle trips to visit other communities, and accompanied processions and parties for saints, with celebrations that lasted for ten days. I learned how to dance local rhythms, to the delight of the older women and children who had a lot of fun with my lack of ability. The hiring of local workers, who played an active participatory role in the process of investigation, led to information about the project being disseminated in the community; this also contributed to the elimination of distrust.

As part of the strategy to disseminate information, meetings were held in the community school with a view to presenting results of the archaeological research. Students, parents, teachers, and political leaders attended these meetings. In my last field season, a brochure was produced and distributed among the audience especially to deal with the subject of illegal trade of archaeological antiquities in the area. Generally speaking, the people listened with interest to my statements on the archaeological work but felt too intimidated to participate more actively in the discussions (although they tended to do so on less formal occasions). A certain time seems to be necessary before information is digested and taken up again in informal conversations or teachers' meetings.

There is, then, an apparent indifference to the archaeological heritage. But even though local people see little connection with their past, some leaders have found a way of appropriating archaeological discourse in order to reinforce the community identity. The refusal of the Parauá community to self-identify as Indians is quite different from the actions of neighboring communities, who have recently chosen the alternative political option of recreating some Indian traditions, even though their connections with any indigenous group are harder to verify. This suggests a process of construction of contrastive local identities. Lack of direct historical continuity between precolonial occupations and the contemporary community, a subject that was constantly discussed during public assemblages, was considered a positive aspect in this particular context. It is an argument taken from my talks on archaeological fieldwork that is being used to help support a self-image of the population as modern Brazilian citizens.

THE FIELDWORK

Logistical difficulties encountered in carrying out fieldwork in Amazonia include lack of surface visibility and limited access to the terrain, brought about by dense vegetation. In this sense, the hiring of local workers was of great importance. Their labor made possible the opening of the transects, which served as access routes for the team to move around within the secondary forest, as well as the conducting of subsurface tests during archaeological surveys and site delimitation.

A team of six workers was initially involved with activities such as cutting down vegetation, putting up numbered stakes along the transects, and carrying out shovel tests at regular intervals. Another task they accomplished was the reconnaissance of plant species in archaeological sites. For the next stage of work, a smaller group was trained to sieve soil and dig test pits before joining archaeologists in the excavation of larger units (figure 13.3).

Those workers who could read and write were encouraged to register notes on the archaeological evidence and to draw profiles, with the help of students and archaeologists. At this point they started to feel a bit like archaeologists and to suggest interpretations of intrasite distributions, identifying different areas of

Figure 13.3.   Students and local workers excavating at the Lago do Jacaré site (Photo by Denise Gomes)

concentration of archaeological refuse and patterns of settlements that might be represented by the sites observed during the survey. Some of their ideas were quite appropriate, for example, the way they perceive the relationship between larger residential sites, fish camps, and other sites of specific purpose.

Findings of highly decorated artifacts were met with surprise. But the workers immediately recognized artifacts that were part of the paraphernalia for processing manioc because these could be related to practices of subsistence, which they themselves were familiar with. However, the excavation of a funerary urn containing calcinated human bones was the discovery that caused the greatest commotion. The urn was excavated by all with the greatest care and interest. Each detail of the artifact—its form, dimensions, surface properties, and use marks—was closely observed in the field. On the initiative of the workers themselves, the spot was never left unattended, even during mealtimes, until the process was concluded, as they feared that other people might disturb the excavation.

As this was an individual PhD project not attached to a larger academic project, the team's composition was itinerant and varied according to each phase of work. In fact, the only constant members were the workers and I. As a woman and director of the project, I have come to realize that hierarchical relations acquire different shades due to cultural and gender inequalities (Gero 1996) in the context of a traditional society.

In relation to social inequalities, I tried to minimize existing differences by offering democratic access to information and strengthening social ties with the workers. This might have helped to develop the team spirit and group cohesion manifested on many different occasions, especially in situations involving conflict. Lastly, it is important to realize the extent to which the hired workers became involved with the archaeological work, their commitment not solely motivated by economic gain. There was an interest in fulfilling responsibilities and carrying out each task competently. Although most research is still carried out within the myth of objective data collection, we know that scientific practice is guided socially and politically (Shanks and Tilley 1987, 1989; Gero 1994). In this case, interaction with the Parauá community allowed access to different perspectives and interpretations, and we should recognize their active participation in the construction of archaeological knowledge.

One example of the active role of the local community in archaeological practice is connected to their cosmological beliefs and tales, especially those about supernatural beings. These cosmological schemes are part of the everyday cognition of the riverside populations in Amazonia (Vaz 1996, 59). Learning about them altered my perception of how the *caboclos* manage and interact with the environment through the medium of forces that act as guardians of natural resources, and which therefore are widely valued by the population. Archaeological sites are permeated by a complex relationship with beings from different cosmological levels, as are the different ecosystems crossed during the archaeological survey.

According to oral information, the community area is inhabited by spirits, good and bad, that make certain places, such as the *igapó* forests, Jacaré Lake, the *igarapés* (streams), and rocks situated on the banks of the Tapajós River dangerous to go to if certain rules are not observed. The *igapó* forests consist of a kind of swamp that floods periodically, having big trees with exposed roots and a great quantity of snakes. These are not only places of refuge for some species of fish during the flood season but also the home of dangerous creatures believed to be the owners of the *igarapé*—two great snakes with women's heads, slanted eyes, and bodies covered with yellow scales.

The rocks on the banks of the Tapajós River delimit the home of the freshwater dolphins, which are said to charm people who come too close and to carry them away to their submerged world at the bottom of the river—the enchanted land. As for Jacaré Lake, a place that contains various archaeological sites, this houses other enchanted beings besides the spirits of the ancient inhabitants. It is only through a dialogue held with these spirits and supernatural beings by one of the workers (a man who also acts as shaman for the community) that the archaeological team was allowed access to those locations and the bad spirits dissipated.

CONCLUSION

For me a significant problem in explaining *caboclos* identities is the idea of historical continuity between past and present populations. As an archaeologist I should plainly state that there are no historical continuities between ancient formative societies and present *caboclos* in Parauá. Various historical processes related to the European colonization, specifically religious missions, have destroyed the cultural, social, and political organization of several former indigenous groups in the Lower Amazon.

Caboclos are a new population arising from drastic changes that affected the cultural diversity of native societies (different languages, forms of social organization, rituals, etc.). That diversity was replaced by another language (first Tupiguarani and then Portuguese), another religion, and a new way of life, creating a "generic Indian" with a cultural heritage that is part Iberian and part indigenous, with additional cultural contributions from other groups (Arenz 2000; Ribeiro 1997, 319–20).

This is not particular to the people of Parauá. It can be generalized for much of Brazilian Amazonia. Today, the historical peasants known as *caboclos* are considered by some scholars as the inheritors of the ecological knowledge of Amazonian natives (Murrieta and WinklerPrins 2003, 35). From an archaeological perspective, what they really have in common with formative Amazonian societies are agricultural and management practices related to the manipulation of natural resources and also food technologies associated with the preparation of manioc, their main staple food.

What is particular to Parauá *caboclos* is not their history but the way they present that history in the construction of identities. As a socially marginalized population, in the context of class divisions of the national society, the *caboclos* want to emphasize their cultural identities. This can be done in different ways, depending on the advantages they think they could obtain. The first option is to state that they are modern citizens, denying any connection with the past. The second option is to identify with an indigenous heritage.

As an archaeologist who has worked at Parauá for three years, I have come to understand, in practice, just how fluid the process of construction of modern identities is. Populations can do whatever they want with information provided by archaeologists. And this group from Parauá has chosen the first alternative— that is, they have chosen to use the results of the archaeological work to help support their statement that they are modern citizens.

It would be easy to assume that the Parauá community was being manipulated or that the results of the archaeological work would somehow undermine identities. This is not what I see in this situation. Instead, these people are actively appropriating something that at first sight they did not agree with and considered dangerous (the archaeological work) for their own benefit.

Their chosen option was to emphasize and self-identify as modern citizens, in contrast with neighboring communities that have chosen the alternative strategy of emphasizing the links with their indigenous cultural heritage. This is an example of self-empowerment of members of the community, expressing their partial control over the contents of archaeological research and incorporating it into the historical process of the construction of cultural identities.

There are clearly ethical aspects to the way the results of the archaeological research are presented to the community. Since the beginning of the project we decided to concentrate all the discussions at the local school, as a way of identifying the archaeological research as a scientific and not an economic project. As part of the same strategy, we tried to deliver information neutrally and without stressing any particular aspect. The choices made by political leaders stem from a dynamic process of formation of identities in this part of the Lower Tapajós.

It can be concluded that archaeological practices developed together with the Parauá community—and all our social interactions and engagements with them—are inevitably political in character, attached to a continual process of construction of fluid and polymorphous identities (Jones 1997), constantly negotiated in the face of different demands of local communities.

This chapter has been written from the point of view of an archaeological fieldworker and not that of an ethnographer as such. But rather than just present objective knowledge about the archaeology of the region, I have also tried to include an account of the role of local people in the production of archaeological knowledge, as well as the role of archaeology in the construction of local identities. What has emerged, I would argue, is a kind of ethnography of archaeology, which enables us to glimpse at least something of the complex social interface that can develop between archaeologists and local communities.

ACKNOWLEDGMENTS

This chapter was originally presented at the session on Ethnography of Archaeology at WAC5, organized by Matt Edgeworth and me in June 2003. It was revised as a result of comments during the session itself and afterwards. In this context, I would like to thank Matt Edgeworth for sharing with me this memorable opportunity. I am also indebted to Joan Gero and Meg Conkey for the support received during my participation in WAC5. Matt Edgeworth, Pedro Paulo Funari, and José Oliver have made comments and valued suggestions. Susan Pyne was responsible for the chapter's translation into English. The fieldwork was supported by Fapesp, and my trip to Washington, D.C., was kindly financed by Women-to-WAC.

REFERENCES

Adams, C. 1994. As Florestas Virgens Manejadas. *Revista do Museu Paraense Emílio Goeldi, Série Antropológica* 10 (1):3–20.

Allen, H., D. Johns, C. Phillips, K. Day, T. O'Brien, and N. Mutunga. 2002. Wahingaro (the lost portion): Strengthening relationship between people and wetlands in north Taranaki, New Zealand. *World Archaeology* 34 (2):315–29.

Ardren, T. 2002. Conversations about the production of archaeological knowledge and community museums at Chunchucmil and Kochol, Yucatán, México. *World Archaeology* 34 (2):379–400.

Arenz, K. H. 2000. *Filhos e Filhas do Beiradão: A formação sócio-histórica dos ribeirinhos da Amazônia*, Santarém, Faculdades Integradas do Tapajós—FIT.

Balée, W. 1989. The culture of Amazonian forests. *Advances in Economic Botany* 7:1–21.

———. 1998. Historical ecology: Premises and postulates. In *Advances in Historical Ecology*, ed. W. Balée, 13–29. New York: Academic Press.

Bielawski, E. 1994. Dual perceptions of the past: Archaeology and Inuit culture. In *Conflict in the Archaeology of Living Traditions*, ed. R. Layton, 228–36. London: Routledge.

Clarke, A. 2002. The ideal and the real: Cultural and personal transformations of archaeological research on Groote Eylandt, Northern Australia. *World Archaeology* 34 (2):249–64.

Edgeworth, M. 2003. *Acts of discovery: An ethnography of archaeological practice*, BAR International Series 1131. Oxford: Archaeopress.

Funari, P. P. A. 2001. Public archaeology from a Latin American perspective. *Public Archaeology* 1:239–43.

Gero, J. 1994. Gender division of labour in the construction of archaeological knowledge in the United States. In *Social construction of the past: Representation as power*, ed. G. C. Bond and A. Gilliam, 144–53. London: Routledge.

———. 1996. Archaeological practice and gendered encounters with field data. In *Engendering archaeology: Women and prehistory*, ed. J. Gero and M. Conkey, 251–80. Philadelphia: University of Pennsylvania Press.

Gomes, D. M. C. 2001. Santarém: Symbolism and power in the tropical forest. In *Unknown Amazon*, ed. C. McEwam, C. Barreto, and E. Neves, 134–55. London: The British Museum Press.

———. 2002. *Cerâmica Arqueológica da Amazônia: Vasilhas da Coleção Tapajônica MAE-USP*, São Paulo, Edusp, Fapesp, Imprensa Oficial.

Green, L. F., D. R. Green, and E. Neves. 2003. Indigenous knowledge and archaeological science: The challenges of public archaeology in the Reserva Uaçá. *Journal of Social Archaeology* 3 (3):366–97.

Jones, S. 1997. *The archaeology of ethnicity: Constructing archaeology in the past and present*. London: Routledge.

Layton, R. 1994. Introduction. In *Conflict in the archaeology of living traditions*, ed. R. Layton, 1–21. London: Routledge.

Meggers, B., and C. Evans. 1961. An experimental formulation of horizon styles in tropical forest of South America. In *Essays in precolumbian art and archaeology*, ed. S. Lothrop, 372–88. Cambridge, Mass.: Harvard University Press.

Murrieta, R. S. S., and A. M. G. A. WinklerPrins. 2003. Flowers of water: Homegardens and gender roles in a riverine Caboclo community in the Lower Amazon, Brazil. *Culture & Agriculture* 25 (1):35–47.

Nimuendajú, C. 1949. Os Tapajó. *Boletim do Museu Paraense Emílio Goeldi* 10:93–106.

Parker, E. 1989. A neglected human resource in Amazonia: The Amazon Caboclo. *Advances in Economic Botany* 7:249–59.

Ribeiro, D. 1997. *O Povo Brasileiro: A formação e o sentido do Brasil*. São Paulo, Brazil: Companhia das Letras.

160   *Denise Maria Cavalcante Gomes*

Rodriguez, T. 2001. Maya perception of ancestral remains: Multiple places in a local space. *Berkeley McNair Research Journal* 9.

Roosevelt, A. 1989. Resource management in Amazonia before the conquest: Beyond ethnographic projection. *Advances in Economic Botany* 7:30–62.

———. 1992. Arqueologia Amazônica. In *História dos Índios do Brasil*, ed. M. Carneiro da Cunha, 53–86. Editora Cia. das Letras. São Paulo, Brazil: Companhia das Letras.

———. 1999. The development of prehistoric complex societies: Amazonia, a tropical forest. In *Complex polities in the ancient tropical world*, ed. E. A. Bacus and L. J. Lecero, 13–33. Arlington, Va.: American Anthropological Association.

Shanks, M., and C. Tilley. 1987. *Re-constructing archaeology*. Cambridge: Cambridge University Press.

———. 1989. Archaeology into the 1990s. *Norwegian Archaeological Review* 22 (1):1–11.

Vaz, F. 1996. Ribeirinhos da Amazonia: Identidade e Magia na Floresta. *Cultura Vozes* 2:47–65.

Wagley, C. 1957. *Uma Comunidade Amazônia: Estudo do homem nos Trópicos*. São Paulo, Brazil: Companhia Editora Nacional.

14

Conjunctures in the Making of an Ancient Maya Archaeological Site

Timoteo Rodriguez

A farmer hired as an archaeological laborer unearths an obsidian blade and then asks, "How much do you sell this obsidian for?"

The archaeologist replies, "We do not sell them. It is illegal to sell artifacts because they are the patrimony of Mexico. . . . We do this archaeological research to study and produce knowledge about the past."

The farmer then asks, "So how much is the knowledge worth?"

ETHOS, PLACE, AND HISTORIES

This chapter discusses a situation in Kochol, Yucatán, Mexico, where a Yucatec Maya farming community[1] and a North American archaeological project share a landscape embedded with remains of an ancient city known today as the Chunchucmil archaeological zone.[2] Findings suggest that the peak population twelve hundred years ago could have been thirty to fifty thousand inhabitants (Dahlin 2000). Today, Kochol's population is 1,270 (INEGI 2000). Archaeologists conduct research on this landscape and hire Kochol farmers as archaeological laborers. Simultaneously, the local community uses this same land to raise cattle, hunt, and farm—often directly over the ruins. This chapter shows how a difference of understandings arose between local farmers and foreign scholars, constituting different perceptions of the same space through their different practices. Furthermore, since "space" is a social construction produced through an engaging gaze of a social actor—a farmer, archaeologist, or ethnographer—the shared landscape in question becomes materially and symbolically contested.

In February 2002, the Kochol community prevented the project from conducting research on the communal farmland. Over the course of three field visits, I experienced the emergence of this conflict by working as an archaeologist with the project and by conducting independent ethnographic research. My line of inquiry proceeds through mediated experiences, which contribute to a process of self-formation and thus a perspective that has been referred to as an attitude or an ethos (Rabinow 2003). Researchers negotiate their ethos as they come to terms with understanding the conditions of the inquiries. Paul Rabinow reminds us that "understanding is a conceptual, political, and ethical practice" (3). Thus, I do not want either to essentialize or to pretend to be a voice for the people of this study. Instead, I position my voice in conversation with others.

This chapter examines two points as to why this situation occurred. First, the conflict is over multiple places in a local space (Rodriguez 2001). I use the term "space" as a conceptual tool to describe various social facts, not all of which are spatial in any constant sense. Since "space" through words, images, or material forms can refer to ways of orienting and representing things like a built environment, nature, or productive land, this implies that "space is socially constituted just as profoundly as is discourse and its agents" (Hanks 2000, 2001). If we understand the landscape of Kochol as a multidimensional space composed of multiple positions, then we can understand space as a social field of practice (Bourdieu 1993).

The social construction of space compels a further distinction of "place making" as a material and symbolic reconfiguration of a position (de Certeau 1984) that occurs in a field of practice. Therefore, what we have on the land of Kochol are multiple fields of practice (archaeology, farming, and ethnography), each continuously defining its own "place," all of which coincide on a single landscape. Additionally, since a field of practice is not bound by location, I depart from Michel de Certeau (1984, 117) by inquiring how these multiple places materially and symbolically overlap in this particular land expanse. Given the permeability of place, and by rethinking George Marcus's (1995) argument for multisited ethnography (see also Bartu 2000), we find that these multiple places can also be considered different "sites" of cultural production in a local space. Furthermore, a global aspect of this local landscape is "an emergent dimension of arguing about the connection among [these multiple and overlapping] sites" (Marcus 1995, 99).

Empirically following the thread of social processes that binds this research, we find that this land is in fact understood, constructed, operated upon, and historically located in very distinct ways by different groups of people: (1) the farming community for whom this is farmland that they inhabit and make their livelihood through subsistence and cash crop farming; (2) archaeologists for whom this land is an exceptionally rich and a largely unreconstructed archaeological site, which promises a tremendous yield of knowledge from which to produce academic capital by writing papers, earning degrees, and making a livelihood in the academy (Bourdieu 1988); and (3) ethnographers who also acquire academic capital but are less reliant on the materiality of the landscape than on its social environment. Though there is disparity of dependence, both academics and farmers depend on the same land.

My second point is that there is an underlying difference of attitude and practice within this material-symbolic landscape, which rests on structures of interests that grant values to different histories. Social actors have an unequal or nonmutual access to an array of positions or possibilities developed through a modern/colonial world system (Quijano and Wallerstein 1992; Mignolo 2000). Thus, what shapes the sense of possibilities for an actor cannot just be local: it is transnational and transcultural. But to say that these opinions and practices are rooted historically and in a larger space than the local is not to say that they are fixed. On the contrary, the processes that have shaped the positions and possibilities for actors in contemporary Yucatán are continuously emergent and linked translocally and transtemporally. What we see in the present is actually a product of long and multiple histories. Hence, the case study will show that archaeologists and farmers act upon different senses of history that accord different weights of importance to notions of the physical landscape and the types of practices associated with it.

GENEALOGY OF CONFLICT

Every field season the archaeological project meets with the community of Kochol in a town meeting called an *asamblea*. Archaeologists go to the *asambleas* to greet and inform the community of research being conducted by showing maps, videos, and artifacts excavated from the communal farmland. The communal land system is an outcome of the 1910 Revolution, which was largely an uprising of peasants that sought to overthrow the debt-peonage enslavement of the Hacienda system. The 1937 Agrarian Land Reform from Article 27 of the Mexican Constitution appropriated the oppressive plantations from the Hispanic patrons, establishing the land as a communal *ejido* and repositioning subjugated people of the Hacienda system into communal landholders, or *ejidatarios*. The political organization of *ejido* communities is based on the practice of *Asamblea General*, where the *ejidatarios* discuss and vote on matters related to the community and the communal land. Although much of the *ejido* of Kochol has been divided into parcels of individual ownership, the land continues to be managed communally (Rodriguez 2001). Furthermore, in Kochol the titles of individual ownership seem to reinforce the attitudes toward communal land rights. One farmer declared "if the community agreed then we would sell our land, but I do not think that will ever happen." Another farmer told me that "the value of the land is priceless."

I was a participant at the May 2001 field season *asamblea* where about a dozen archaeologists and approximately two dozen male farmers convened. At this meeting the project proposed the idea of an archaeological tourist museum on the *ejido* and the organization of a local committee (rather than solely the federal agency, the Instituto Nacional de Antropología e Historia, or INAH) to administer the museum. An archaeologist stated, "We want to help your community through archaeology. We can open a museum to be owned and operated by the people of Kochol. We can plant trees on the site to provide shade for tourists. These are the same trees that your ancestors planted." Another member of the project wrote in an article, "The Kochol community museum will become another ongoing and evolving experience through which members of the local community and staff archaeologists can share in the production of archaeological knowledge" (Ardren 2002, 390).

The project wanted to include the community in order that it should get lasting economic benefits from archaeology. The archaeological zone in Kochol would probably never be of the same caliber as other archaeological museums like Tulum, Chichén Itzá, or Uxmal (see Castañeda 1996; Juárez 2002). But even at these sites, despite infrastructure improvements in tourist areas, economic benefits have been minimal for local communities. Hotel ownership and control is confined to large-scale Mexican chains and foreign investors (Castañeda 1996; Clancy 1999; Ardren 2001). Rather than reproducing a similar scenario in Kochol, the project was proposing a community-operated museum where locals could gain long-term benefits from archaeology by managing the site, giving guided tours, and selling novelties. The museum in Kochol would be shaped out of the area of farmland with the highest concentration of ancient monumental architecture, which I will refer to as zone 1.

The archaeologists view the *ejido* of Kochol as part of an ancient Maya archaeological site, which today encompasses five *ejidos*.[3] The site is conceptualized roughly in three concentric rings: the rural part of the ancient city where mounds are scattered in all directions with no distinct boundaries, the ancient residential area, and the ancient downtown (zone 1). These last two rings are approximately fifteen square kilometers of very dense ancient urban residential ruins. The size of the mounds ranges from two to eighteen meters high. An archaeologist described the selection of zone 1 as the location of the community museum in the following way: "We had selected an area that we would like to protect as an archaeological site. We theoretically delineated a small area. Mainly the site center is what we considered could be attractive for tourists." Viewed from a global economy of knowledge production (Joyce 2002), this museum proposal comes from a specific epistemological and historical location (Mignolo 1995).

The museum proposal developed from a paradigm that put great value on archaeological science and ancient Maya history rather than alternative forms of knowledge and subsequent histories. What became apparent at the *asamblea* was the project's vision of "place" in relation to the local physical landscape and their sense of history as exemplified in this statement: "People from all over the world want to see where and how your ancestors lived." When the archaeologist said "your ancestors," the lineages of local farmers and the ancient history of the Maya were collapsed into a single continuum. Throughout Yucatán, most farmers self-identify as Mestizo—not Maya (Hervik 2002). Furthermore, many do not necessarily consider their ancestors to be the builders of the pyramids. Rather, in Kochol most people told me that the builders of the mounds were a different generation, a different race, and of a different epoch. Some people said giants built the mounds, but a majority of people told me the Alux (dwarfs) were the ancient builders. Throughout Yucatán, there are well-documented narratives of this sort (see Tozzer 1907; Villa Rojas 1945; Rodriguez 2001). Still other *Kocholeños* told me that ancient Mayans built the ruins, but as one said, "In this [current] epoch, we are different. We do not speak Maya language in the same way because it is mixed with Spanish. It is not pure Maya like the ancestors spoke."

At the *asamblea* in Kochol, the archaeologists' proposal might not have seemed confrontational. They were attempting to share a vision of a museum that would generate income, but an underlying assumption was that *Kocholeños* would view the ruins as their ancestral heritage and therefore desire to preserve the archaeological site. Many farmers view the *ejido* as their patrimony but not because of its potential as an archaeological site. This was evident when a farmer responded to the museum proposal with this question: "Is [INAH] going to put a fence around the whole area like in Oxkintok?" This question illustrates that the farmers are not operating with the same sense of local space, nor in the same continuum of history as the archaeologists. It is rather the case that the farmers operate in a physical landscape and a social history that pertains to communal land rights. Furthermore, this farmer was acutely aware how other sites operated and he knew that fencing in part of the *ejido* would exclude access to farming practices.

Another farmer asked, "If we do not accept this from you, then what will happen?" An archaeologist replied, "One day INAH will come and open a museum here, and you guys will not have control of the land." Laura Nader (1997) reminds us that controlling processes are about clusters of beliefs that restrict alternative conceptions of reality, offer narrow options, and foreclose different futures. The archaeologists' position in wanting to help the community created a sense of inevitability that foreclosed on alternate futures. The archaeologist's statement does not express an intentional deception toward the community but does indicate a disconnection between archaeologists and farmers as they operate in different notions of place in the same landscape. An archaeologist reflected on the comment made at the *asamblea*: "We neglected to mention that INAH may never make [zone 1] an archaeological museum."

The different languages (Maya, English, and Spanish) spoken at the *asamblea* facilitated multiple interpretations. The project director spoke in English, which was translated to Spanish. The *Kocholeños* heard it in Spanish and discussed it in Maya, then a farmer responded in Spanish and it was translated back to English. Thus, there was plenty of room for divergent understandings. As one archaeologist stated in reflection, "We have such different perspectives.

Our words were perceived in a very different way—I mean quite different from the way that we were giving it meaning." Similarly, Paul Sullivan (1989) illustrates how, in the 1930s, there was a series of miscommunications between rebel Mayas of Tusik and a foreign archaeologist at Chichén Itzá about the intentions of scholarship in relation to Maya interests. He wrote, "Each encounter between Maya and foreigners was an extraordinary experiment in cross-communication . . . they did not speak each other's language very well; had different senses of place, time, causality; and different knowledge of what had gone on before." Sullivan's account reflects what transpired in Kochol. First there was a communicative breakdown of understanding with regard to the intentions of the messages being conveyed. Secondly, and more importantly, different and almost incommensurable sets of values were being attributed to the same terrain (compare Lipe 1984, 4).

The combination of miscommunications and different symbolic values of the land was the genesis of conflict between farmers and the archaeologists. The result of the *asamblea* was that rumors spread throughout the community of Kochol that the land was going to be closed by gringos (Anglo-Americans or foreigners). One farmer who did not attend the *asamblea* said, "We heard that the gringos wanted to plant trees and build a fence around the area [of zone 1]." A few weeks after the *asamblea*, the symbolic value of the farmers' land materialized into an act of resistance toward archaeology. Farmers cleared vegetation to make a papaya parcel in zone 1 near the largest pyramids. Up to that time only maize had been cultivated in this area. The eldest of these farmers, whom I will call Don A, spoke to me of his passion for farming and referred to the soil in zone 1 in the Maya language as *cacab*—very fertile terrain (see Redfield and Villa Rojas 1962, 43; Hanks 1990). Additionally, numerous Kochol farmers told me that zone 1 contains the best areas of the *ejido* to cultivate. This is explained by the accumulation of rich soil and moisture between the crumbled stones of the ruins. In this particular region of Yucatán, topsoil is extremely thin and bedrock is often fully exposed. Recall that zone 1 is the area of ruins of the ancient urban downtown; thus, the healthiest crops grow out of a dense area of mounds. Alfonso Villa Rojas (1945) noted, "Of primary importance is the selection of a good piece of land for *milpa* [maize]. The farmer knows that the black land (*ek-luum*) is more fertile . . . because they are supposed to be the sites of ancient villages. Wells, cenotes, and little mounds containing archaeological remains are frequently found in such places" (56).

Since no Kochol farmer had ever planted papaya in zone 1 before, some archaeologists became quite alarmed. One archaeologist said, "We were taken a back by this action because papaya is more destructive [to the site than maize] and this could be the first episode in a trend that we want to avoid, [namely,] more people utilizing the very center of the site [zone 1]." Some archaeologists, then, considered the papaya parcel to be a move of opposition to archaeological practice and went to speak with Don A about the matter.

The project's field season ended, but I returned to Kochol a few months later. It turned out that the papaya parcel was never completed. According to Don A, the archaeologists told him that he was prohibited from working in zone 1. Don A said, "I asked [the archaeologists] how could I be prohibited if this is my *ejido*? I have my agrarian rights." Don A's value of land stems from the history and practice of an *ejidatario*—not that of a descendant of the ancient Maya. As Don A put it, "I do not ask for work. I do not have employment or study, and I do not answer to any patron. . . . We make this land fruitful with our labor . . . and we will not let the archaeologists close the land . . . because for us it is the patrimony of our children." His threat of a papaya parcel in zone 1 was definitely a move to counter the archaeological work on his *ejido*.

In February 2002, which was the beginning of the next archaeological field season, the project went to the *asamblea* of Kochol. An archaeologist recounted, "We did not want to address the museum issue. So, I finished talking, it was translated into Maya, and then it got pretty animated. One of the first questions that came out was, "Are you going to take our land away from us?" I explained that we are not here to take the land away. We just want to investigate some of the things in the land and we want to do it with your collaboration. A farmer responded, "We heard that you want to take our land away from us and so we do not want you to work here."

The result of this *asamblea* was that the project was prevented from working on the land of Kochol for over two months. There were a few town meetings to debate the issue of the archaeologists conducting research on the *ejido*—one in which the community requested a representative from INAH to explain the legal status of the project in relation to the land.

Finally the *comisarios* (elected officials of the community) went to the project stating, "We have decided that we want you to sign a letter (*acta*) that says you will not take our land away, and then, once we have that document in hand we are going to vote to see if you guys can work." The project actively engaged with the community leaders to work out this incident just as other challenges within a trajectory of encounters had previously been worked out. The *comisarios* took the version of the archaeologist's letter to the director of INI (Insituto Nacional Indigenista), who revised it to include national Mexican constitution laws and international labor/indigenous rights. The *comisario* read the *acta* to the *ejidatrios* at the *asamblea*. It stated, "[The project] has no legal or moral capacity under any concept or title to the land of Kochol without previous agreement and consent of the legitimate owners who are the *ejidatarios*." The community finally voted and allowed the archaeologists to commence research on the *ejido*. This *acta* clearly demonstrates that the conflict was grounded in the different sets of values that *ejidatarios* and archaeologists had in relation to the landscape. For many in Kochol, the land is materially and symbolically valuable as a local communal farm rather than a World Heritage archaeological site or museum.

But, just as there are no typical farmers, there are no typical archaeologists. Some members of the project were more interested in conducting archaeological research than in a collaborative development of a museum. Furthermore, there were some *Kocholeños*, particularly women and younger farmers, who told me that a museum would benefit the community. A woman stated, "There are different opinions in Kochol about a museum. There are a few people who . . . want to have a museum . . . like Oxkintok." A younger farmer told me, "Kochol needs a museum so we can learn about the ancient Maya." Additionally, most locals agreed that the relatively high wages paid by the project for labor are truly beneficial. An elderly *ejidatario* stated, "We pray to God that the project gets funds to return next year so we can work because the community really benefits in this time when things are very difficult." In contrast, Don A said, "What good is the pay if it ultimately leads to our land being closed to us?" Still, the project attempted to challenge usual archaeological practice by offering more than just wage labor. As one archaeologist put it, "We wanted to find a way to help the community and we thought that the museum would be a way. Now when I think back to the *asamblea*, we were very naive. We definitely did it with good intentions, but we created more trouble for ourselves and for the community."

CONCEPTS, POLITICS, AND DILEMMAS

This multifaceted study demonstrates that the different sets of values ascribed to the same landscape actually correspond to different fields of practice (archaeology, farming, or ethnography), each defining its own place. Conflict arose because multiple places overlap in a single space. Don A's attempt to plant a papaya parcel in zone 1 and the archaeologists' hypothetical delineation of zone 1 as a proposed museum are both moves to transform a symbolic notion of the landscape into a materialization of place. In this study, place making has to do with human engagement as an activity, which is an interplay of labor, residency, and rights of ownership. Through this interplay of engagement, we might then grasp how these deeply embedded notions cause *ejidatarios* to believe that archaeologists are attempting to close the land. The transformation of the land by archaeological labor into an archaeological site leads to a very different notion of place from that which the farmers have. When a mound is excavated, federal law requires that the excavated edifices be consolidated with cement. Thus the landscape is physically and permanently altered. It is this material-symbolic transformation that some farmers resist. As one told me, "I have been to Uxmal and Lol Tun. Those are archaeological sites, but this land here is not a site. This land is to farm."

The construction of lived space by Maya farmers cannot be understood in isolation from their agricultural practices (Hanks 1990). A Kochol elder explained, "Who does the land belong to? God says this: the land belongs to the one that works it. And the one that does not work it, it is not his. And so, what happens? With our agrarian rights, the land is ours. If we tell people that they cannot enter our land, it is because we are the owners." This statement connects the notion of place making to a social history of agrarian law in which *ejidatarios* own the land that they inhabit and cultivate. Additionally, the semantics of the Maya language illustrate notions of labor, residence, and ownership. As William Hanks (1990) noted, "Regardless of its configuration, every kind of space has a *yuumil* (lord, owner) to whom it belongs." The language also illustrates place making by way of the terms *iknal* or (one's) place.

The notions of *iknal* and *yuumil* are useful tools in considering the conflict in Kochol. Here the land has been transformed by two different kinds of labor. But working the land (whether agriculturally or archaeologically) is not necessarily enough to lay a special claim. Rather, a more profound connection of an enduring inhabitance of a space links the notions of *iknal* and *yuumil*, and consequently links Maya farmers to the land. Furthermore, there are significant social histories from which these practices of labor and notions of ownership emerge.

The problem that arose in Kochol is actually rooted in another struggle, which is a conflict over different values of history. The place making that we see in this situation is a product of multiple histories that have created competing claims to the same land. The project's politics appeared inclusive toward the farming community in that it attempted to involve the community in archaeological discourse. But, given the archaeological "locus of enunciation" (Mignolo 1995) in the hierarchy of global economy of knowledge production, the epistemic position of the museum proposal was actually exclusionary to *ejidatarios*: first because it entailed the privileging of archaeological and thus a Westernized conceptual framework and second because it would have set into motion a series of events that would have created very different kinds of relations between farmers and their land. Some *Kocholeños* who were adamantly against the proposal clearly understood this potential for change. Furthermore, it is the archaeologists who regard the ancient Maya histories as the most pertinent to their practice and understandings of local space. Many farmers, on the other hand, do not necessarily consider the builders of the pyramids their ancestors but instead view the ruins as important because they hold *cacab*—fertile soil to grow crops. The farmers focus on a more recent past, that of colonial and revolutionary histories. These social histories produced the notions of land rights for the farmers and thus the right to prevent or allow archaeological work on their *ejido*.

In Yucatan I have come to understand how problematic it is to conduct a study that involves investigating other people's lives and work. Through my own trials and errors in this field research, I realize the difficulties of not only responsibly portraying other people but also attempting to conduct research that truly benefits the people involved or affected. As researchers, our focus on academic objectives might become blurred to other realities that seem beyond the scope of our inquiries. In archaeological practice, "part of our problem rests with the illusion that the subjects of our research are dead and buried, literally, and that our 'scientific' research goals are paramount" (Meskell 2002). But living people are affected by archaeology. This chapter demonstrates that there are multiple enactments of a landscape through differences of social histories, and therefore, it is vital to recognize disparities in power relations embedded in research practices. An overarching conundrum is posed by Rosemary Joyce (2002): "Archaeologists have long offered examples of how our research will benefit descendant [or local] communities; how often do we ask what harm we might do?" This query calls for questioning the hierarchy of the global economy of archaeological knowledge production "by studying up as well as down . . . studying the colonizer rather than [just] the colonized" (Nader 1972).

An anthropological moral dilemma is posed by the practice of ethnography of archaeology. First, the object of study departs from the traditional subjects: it is, in part, a translocal community of archaeologists that become the *ethnos*. Archaeologists must not be singled out as the sole subject of study; we should also consider an ethnography of ethnographers. Second, since part of the task is never to construct an exoticized or essentialized object of study, we (researchers and scholars) should consider ethnography of archaeology as the critical ontology of ourselves. According to Michel Foucault (2003), "The critical ontology of ourselves must not be considered as a theory, doctrine, nor even a permanent body of knowledge that is accumulating. It must be conceived as an attitude, an ethos, a philosophical life in which the critique of what we are is the historical analysis of the limits imposed on us [and reproduced by us]. Simultaneously, the critical ontology of ourselves must be considered an experiment with the possibility of going beyond those limits" (56). Thus, the object of this sort of study is not merely a community of farmers, archaeologists, or ethnographers—nor is it solely concerned with the competitive status of their material-symbolic stakes. The focus of this type of inquiry is the problematization of an attitude that we bring to the field of archaeology.

NOTES

1. By using the term "Maya" I refer to the people of Kochol as primarily Yucatec Maya language speakers. The people of Kochol do not self-identify as Maya but as Mestizo.
2. The archaeological zone takes its name from the neighboring town of Chunchucmil, which is a problem for the people of Kochol since the largest pyramids are in Kochol.
3. These include Kochol, Chunchucmil, San Mateo, Halacho, and Coahuila.

ACKNOWLEDGMENTS

Although this chapter does not necessarily reflect all the feedback given, I am deeply grateful to Valentina Rizzo, Scott Hutson, Traci Ardren, Aline Magnoni,

Bruce Dahlin, William F. Hanks, Rosemary A. Joyce, Laura Nader, William Taylor, Juan Cocom, Quetzil Castañeda, Lisa Breglia, and Matt Edgeworth.

REFERENCES

Andrews, A. P. 2001. Notes on the history of Chunchucmil, Yucatan, and Venezia, Camp. Unpublished.

Ardren, T. 2001. Where are the Maya in ancient Maya archaeological tourism: Advertising and the appropriation of culture. Paper presented at the 100th Annual Meeting of the American Anthropological Association, Washington, D.C.

———. 2002. Conversations about the production of knowledge and community museums at Chunchucmil and Kochol, Yucatan Mexico. *World Archaeology* 34 (2):379–400.

Baños Ramirez, O. 1989. *Yucatán: Ejidos sin Campesinos*. Universidad Autónoma de Yucatán, Mérida.

Bartu, A. 2000. Where is Çatalhöyük? Multiple sites in the construction of an archaeological site. In *Towards reflexive method in archaeology: The example at Çatalhöyük*, ed. I. Hodder, 101–9. Cambridge, UK: McDonald Institute Monographs.

Bourdieu, P. 1988. *Homo academicus*. Trans. P. Collier. Stanford: Stanford University Press.

———. 1993. *The field of cultural production*. New York: Columbia University Press.

Casey, E. 1997. *The fate of place*. Berkeley: University of California Press.

Castañeda, Q. E. 1996. *In the museum of Maya culture*. Minneapolis: University of Minnesota Press.

Certeau, M. de. 1984. *The practice of everyday life*. Berkeley: University of California Press.

Clancy, M. J. 1999. Tourism and development: Evidence from Mexico. *Annals of Tourism Research* 26:1–20.

Dahlin, B. H. 2000. The barricade and abandonment of Chunchucmil. *Latin American Antiquity* 11 (3):283–98.

Foucault, M. 2003. What is enlightenment? In *The essential Foucault: Selections from essential works of Foucault, 1954–1984*, ed. P. Rabinow and N. Rose. New York: New Press.

Hanks, W. F. 1990. *Referential practice*. Chicago: University of Chicago Press.

———. 2000. *Intertexts: Writings on language, utterance, and context*. Lanham, Md.: Rowman & Littlefield.

———. 2001. Reducción and the remaking of the social landscape in colonial Yucatan. Paper presented at the 100th Annual Meeting of the American Anthropological Association, Washington, D.C.

Hervik, P. 2002. *Mayan people: Within and beyond boundaries*. New York: Routledge.

Instituto Nacional de Estadística, Geografía e Informática. 2002. Census. Aguascalientes, Mexico.

Joyce, R. A. 2002. Academic freedom, stewardship, and cultural heritage: Weighing the interests of stakeholders in crafting repatriation approaches. In *The dead and their possessions*, ed. C. Fforde, J. Hubert, and P. Turnball, 99–107. London: Routledge.

Juárez, A. M. 2002. Ongoing struggles: Mayas and immigrants in tourist Era Tulum. *Journal of Latin American Anthropology* 7 (1):34–67.

Lipe, W. D. 1984. Value and meaning in cultural resources. In *Approaches to the archaeological heritage*, ed. H. Cleere, 1–11. Cambridge: Cambridge University Press.

Magnoni, A. 2002. Doing archaeology in a post-colonial world: Archaeological research in an ancient landscape inhabited by modern people. Unpublished manuscript.

Marcus, G. 1995. Ethnography in/of the world system: The emergence of multi-sited ethnography. *Annual Review of Anthropology* 24:95–117.

Meskell, L. 2002. The intersections of identity and politics in archaeology. *Annual Review of Anthropology* 31:279–301.

Mignolo, W. D. 1995. *The darker side of the renaissance*. Ann Arbor: University of Michigan Press.

———. 2000. *Local histories/global designs*. Princeton, N.J.: Princeton University Press.

Millet Carmara, L. 1994. *Mirador Campechano*. Universidad Autónoma de Campeche, Mexico.

Nader, L. 1972. Up the anthropologists. In *Reinventing Anthropology*, ed. D. Hymes, 284–311. New York, Pantheon Books.

———. 1997. Controlling processes: Tracing the dynamic components of power. *Current Anthropology* 38 (5):711–23.

Quijano, A., and I. Wallerstein. 1992. Americanity as a concept: The Americas in the modern world system. *International Social Sciences Journal* 134.

Rabinow, P. 2003. *Anthropos today: Reflections on modern equipment*. Princeton, N.J.: Princeton University Press.

Redfield, R., and A. Villa Rojas. 1962. *Chan Kom: A Maya village*. Chicago: University of Chicago Press.

Rodriguez, Timoteo. 2001. Maya perceptions of ancestral remains: Multiple places in a local space. *Berkeley McNair Research Journal* 9:21–45.

Sullivan, P. 1989. *Unfinished conversations: Mayas and foreigners between two wars*. New York: Alfred A. Knopf.

Tozzer, A. 1907. *A comparative study of the Mayas and Lacandones*. New York: Macmillan.

Villa Rojas, A. 1945. *The Maya of East Central Quintana Roo*. Washington, D.C: Carnegie Institution.

15

Complicit Agendas: Ethnography of Archaeology as Ethical Research Practice

Lisa Breglia

This chapter explores the role of ethnographic research in archaeological excavation projects, questioning how ethnographers and archaeologists might create and enact collaborative research agendas within a shared site of fieldwork. I base this discussion on my own experiences as an ethnographer working at a Maya archaeological site (Breglia 2003, in press), which I briefly describe in the first section. During the course of more than two years of visiting and conducting ethnographic research in and around archaeological sites throughout Mexico's Yucatán Peninsula, I realized a need for engaging with both archaeologists and the discourse of their discipline in a serious, responsible, and engaged manner—not only on an intellectual level but also in terms of ethics. It is this latter level of engagement, ethics, upon which I focus this discussion. While archaeology and ethnography are anthropological kin, so to speak, their methods, conceptions of data, and field research processes are quite different. But one very real similarity I have observed, particularly among foreign archaeological projects working in Mexico, is a shared commitment to cultivate relationships with local communities. While ethnographers have long relied upon communities as their loci of research, archaeological practice is only beginning to account for local beliefs, needs, and desires in any systematic sense.

Taking into account the disciplinary differences and similarities between ethnography and archaeology, especially those that shape local community relations, I believe that the two fields can work together—and together, work with local communities—to develop intellectually cogent and socially responsible research agendas. The second section of this chapter outlines four key concepts as a set of parameters for defining field research situated at the interface of ethnography and archaeology, in the interstices of what all of these disciplines typically conceive of as their objects of study. Each of these four concepts redefines how local people—often uncritically assumed to be descendant communities—are culturally, politically, ethnically, and otherwise positioned by history, anthropology, and ideologies of development. At the same time, each serves to highlight the tension that exists between the practical and ethical levels of engagement between researchers and local communities. In sum, this chapter offers a provisional definition of ethnography of archaeology as an eminently ethical engagement between archaeologists, ethnographers, and local communities.

SETTING THE SITE OF RESEARCH

Archaeologists, mostly from U.S. institutions, have been working at the site of Chunchucmil, Yucatán, for several years. The site has proven to be a challenge for researchers, not just in an intellectual sense but also in the everyday organizing and carrying out of excavations and other on-site work. The project's relationships with surrounding communities who hold communal farming rights to the land upon which the archaeological zone sits have been, particularly in the case of one community, Kochol, strained and tense. To their consternation (and to their credit), members of the project have spent immeasurable amounts of time and energy in working with community residents of surrounding pueblos to figure out rotations of work schedules, fair wages and hours, and the like. In the Chunchucmil project, directors, assistants, and students are highly interested in connecting the project to its surrounding communities, disseminating information in the pueblos regarding work at the site, and giving tours of the site to local children and adults. In general, the project has made great efforts to do what they feel is right, to practice an ethical archaeology. This approach or attitude is, in part, indicative of a reflexive turn within the human and social sciences, as researchers have begun to feel their ethical obligation to "describe the ways in which moral positions and norms take shape in diverse, broad, and conflicted spaces of social life" (Marcus 1999, 20). Indeed, archaeologists find themselves dealing with ethical questions in the field regarding the handling of human remains, ownership or custodianship of artifacts, looting, and site preservation and responsibility to future generations. Outside of the field site, ethical issues move into a concern with the social contexts and audiences of research practice and knowledge production.

I developed an association with the Chunchucmil archaeological project as the project codirector was looking for an ethnographer to join her team to work in the communities surrounding the project's excavation site. The project desired the involvement of an ethnographer for several reasons, most connected with the increasingly complex political and economic negotiations between the project and members of local communities. The first involves questions of the legal rights as well as the ethics of the archaeologists excavating on the communally held agricultural lands of the site's neighboring communities. In the initial couple of years of mapping, excavation, and clearing of the site some misunderstandings had occurred between the archaeologists and community residents. The most crucial of these came about due to the complexity of the land tenure situation: the land, coterminous with the zone, was shared by five different communities according to the Mexican land-grant (*ejido*) distributions of the 1930s. In order to successfully carry out their work, archaeologists had to first unravel the disputed *ejido* boundaries and, second, implement a fair and equitable manner of hiring local laborers from among the different communities of landholders. Alongside this logistical issue was another that archaeologists felt that an ethnographer could help with. As part of their commitment to a public or community archaeology approach, the project was initiating an agenda for tourism development in and around the site. This agenda featured ambitious plans for an artifact museum to be located in the town of Chunchucmil and a living museum (loosely based on Colonial Williamsburg—in which local community residents would move out of their towns into the archaeological zone to demonstrate daily life practices of the ancient Maya) in the excavated Kochol *ejido* land. Through personal communication, public assembly, and wildfire rumor, the archaeological project quickly planted seeds of both hope and suspicion among local residents.

During the spring and summer of 2001 I carried out ethnographic research in the excavation site of the archaeological zone of Chunchucmil as one part of a more extensive comparative study of the politics of cultural patrimony in Yucatán. The majority of informants I worked with were from the Maya community of Kochol located approximately four kilometers away from the site center. Given my lack of training in archaeology and my hybrid disciplinary status, I spent the majority of my time in the excavation sites working alongside the laborers from Kochol, carrying out the same tasks to which they were assigned. During these weeks, I lived with other project members in the Casa Principal of the former hacienda of Chunchucmil. After an hour or so of language study each morning, usually in consultation with the archaeologists' cook and maid, I would bike to the excavation sites (often two or three in proximity to each other). I usually timed my arrival with the workers' morning rest. I typically spent the break time with the workers conversing, teaching English, or practicing Maya.

When each break was over, I joined in their work, either digging, hauling rocks, or looking for ceramic, bone, and obsidian fragments at the sifting table a few meters from the excavation area. With a tape recorder in a pocket and my notebook in the back of my pants, I used the time I spent working alongside the excavators to conduct conversations and interviews. Though my work as an ethnographer was tied in some very obvious ways to the archaeological project, the openness and sensitivity of my informants enabled them to view my heterodox position with a careful discernment of both my role vis-à-vis other project

members and the directors, as well as the discipline of cultural anthropology and
its methods and subject matter. They knew that I wasn't an archaeologist. Yet
they were quite aware that I, too, was conducting an investigation in the area,
the parameters of which were articulated in mutually intelligible terms as "history" and "culture." "History" in this case referred to the henequen era of the late
nineteenth through early twentieth century, and "culture" signified the local
imagination of the traditional Maya beliefs and lifeways. Both of these terms
carry a heavy, ironic weight in the everyday lives of the Maya residents of these
contemporary communities as both refer to a sense of loss or dispossession. For
"history" invokes the time that northwestern Yucatán was nearly exclusively
dominated by the hacienda system: the concentration of large tracts of land in
the hands of a wealthy, white Yucatec minority. Chunchucmil and Kochol, like
many neighboring communities, were established in order to concentrate the
Maya population into labor centers to support the intensive monocrop cultivation of henequen—a sisal-like plant processed into a fiber for making rope. It is
to this particular historical context that, for many local residents, a loss of culture
is attributed. As multiple generations of the Maya people of this region were literally not free to practice cultural traditions (many of these agricultural), these
lifeways were forced into disuse and relegated to the memories of only the old-
est of contemporary community residents.[1]

Residents to this day, many of whom are regularly employed on a rotating
basis by the archaeological project, lament the devastating effects of the
highly disciplinary–forced, labor-system haciendas on generations of Yucatec
Maya. "It robbed us of our strength," Don Celso, a resident of Kochol, tells
me as he takes a break from planting his small plot of corn within eyeshot of
a group of excavators working around the mounds that dot the community's
federal land grant. His comment is powerful in its double meaning: not only
has the back breaking work of henequen cultivation debilitated the physical
body, so has it weakened the community's ability to make heritage claims on
both the tangible and intangible cultural properties in their midst. Historically
positioned as they have been, and far from the busy routes of Yucatán's
tourism network, these communities had hardly been reached by the dominant discourse of cultural heritage until archaeologists arrived. In stark contrast to local Mayas at the World Heritage site of Chichén Itzá, for example,
residents around the Chunchucmil site had neither the language nor the tools
for incorporating the ruins in their midst into a properly modern site of ancient Maya culture (see, for example, Breglia 2003, in press; Castañeda 1996).
In other words, strategically distanced by not only land and labor regimes but
also through a host of other arts of the Mexican state from the privileged archaeological, touristy, and governmentalistic discourses on ancient Maya civilization, local Maya at Chunchucmil had come to explicitly not position
themselves as descendants of the ancient Maya. Nor did they immediately
embrace the economic development potentiated by the archaeological work
at the site. For many *ejidatarios* (landholding farmers), excavation work at

Chunchucmil represented a kind of invasion of their land. For many, this land was eminently valuable and historically hard won.

An obvious explanation for this attitude lies within the physical context of Don Celso's above statement: a profoundly ironic landscape. Before the Spanish conquest, Chunchucmil was a site of flourishing trade. Later it became a site of de facto enslavement of Maya people on the henequen haciendas. Now, only a few decades after the local indigenous population was granted free access to the land through the Mexican federal *ejido* system in the late 1930s, the site has become reterritorialized by archaeological development. The sound of picks and shovels striking the landscape's abundant stone outcroppings echoing across Kochol's *ejido* might be new, but the signal it carries—the introduction of yet another mode of production in which locals are far from self-determining—has been oft repeated throughout history.

Local sentiments that authentic Maya culture has been violently stripped away by the hacienda system has left a door open, so to speak, for the entrance of archaeological discourse of Maya heritage in these communities.[2] Most significantly, archaeologists have begun a public dialogue about the ancient Maya, a civilization to which residents previously felt little connection. As a consequence, the meaning and indeed the value—both cultural and economic—of the land upon which the unexcavated and unrestored monuments sit has begun what might be a slow, and possibly rocky, transformation. This transformation was still nascent when I first arrived in Chunchucmil and Kochol. I quickly realized that the project codirector Traci Ardren is, in a certain sense, quite right when she claims, "Archaeology changes everything." Yet this change was difficult to account within preexisting theoretical and methodological constructs. Because of their own research obligations, archaeologists (even the most publicly committed among them) could not devote themselves toward the creation of an ethnographic description of the situation. At the same time, an ethnographer would have to tread lightly on the turf of their disciplinary kin, the archaeologists, while taking the necessary step of including the excavation sites with the mise-en-scène of ethnographic inquiry. I had never felt so committed to a task that made me so uneasy.

As I came to understand the social, cultural, economic, and political changes wrought by the spatial transformation of this land (hacienda, *ejido*, archaeological site), I began to realize the need for a new methodology. The provisional goal of my own research was to create an ethnographic account articulating the procedures of archaeology within the social, cultural, and economic landscape in which the Chunchucmil project had announced itself and was subsequently gaining momentum. Rather than producing an ethnography of archaeology enclosed within the parameters of workaday archaeological practice, I sought to produce an ethnography of archaeology that foregrounds archaeological practice as a culturally and historically contingent activity. Thus, while neither archaeological data nor its scientific methods of investigation figure in any way in my own research, the activities of archaeology, particularly as they relate to the local communities, serve as a springboard for much of my ethnography. In pre-vious research at the Maya archaeological site Chichén Itzá (located some one hundred kilometers distant), I had found that over a hundred years of archaeo-logical work at the site—which led to its becoming a major international tourism destination—had greatly influenced local conceptions of what Maya heritage is and how the site is inflected with varying understandings of the ar-ticulation of the ancient Maya to the contemporary world. In multiple ways, lo-cal residents utilize the site to make claims to the cultural patrimony that is si-multaneously theirs and that of the Mexican state. Would this phenomenon express itself differently around the site of Chunchucmil after only five years of archaeological work? Unlike other conceptions of ethnography of archaeology (see, for example, Shankland 1997; Bartu 2000; Rodríguez 2001), I did not re-strict my investigation only to the local communities' perceptions of the mounds, archaeology, the future of heritage development, or a combination of the three. Instead, the archaeological project was only an occasion upon which other local histories were narrated, political ideologies were espoused, and hopes and fears about the past, present, and future were expressed.

KEY CONCEPTS FOR AN ETHNOGRAPHY OF ARCHAEOLOGY

My experiences in working with an archaeological project prompted the gen-eration of a series of ideas—methodological, theoretical, and practical—leading me to develop my own sense of ethnography of archaeology. In other words, it was only after the completion of my fieldwork in Yucatán that I became more familiar with how different impulses in the discipline of archaeology have forged linkages (at least nominally) with ethnography. I am referring not only to ethnoarchaeology and reflexive archaeology but also to the field of social ar-chaeology, where researchers are producing archaeological ethnographies as they find resonance between the enterprises of ethnography and archaeology through both theoretical frameworks and interpretive schemata (Robin and Rothschild 2002). However, most of these movements are situated exclusively within the realm of archaeology itself and are primarily concerned with layer-ing ethnographic method onto the interpretation of material culture. Not typi-cally taken into consideration are the complexities of ethnographic research and knowledge and the rich contribution that ethnography, done by ethnogra-phers, can make to understand the social, political, cultural, and economic con-texts, both historical and contemporary, of archaeological fieldwork.

In defining my particular understanding of the ethnography of archaeology, it is important to trace its development within the context of (1) postprocessual archaeology and (2) new ethnography, as it emerges out of the 1980s writing culture critique.[3] Ethnography of archaeology, as I understand it in its nascence, does not refer to a traditional ethnographic object of study.[4] Also, marked by a commitment to reflexivity and multivocality, it does not anchor itself within the realm of workaday archaeology. With the realization that ethnography of archaeology is referring to a theoretically and methodologically specialized area within each discipline, we may begin to set the parameters for the in situ collaboration between ethnography and archaeology. I thus offer the following four elements as contributions to our provisional definitions of ethnography of archaeology: complicity, explicitness, collaboration, and intervention. These four guiding concepts cut across disciplinary boundaries between business-as-usual ethnography and archaeology, calling attention to the distinctions and linkages between multiple social actors.

Complicity

Rather than referring to participants in an unscrupulous plot, I, following George Marcus (1998), use complicity as a synonym for complexity. This particular use of the term carries with it, significantly for our purposes here, the notion of involvement, or implication. In a complicit ethnography of archaeology, two entities are complicit through their relationship to a third party. According to this scheme, archaeology and ethnography may be complicit, or complexly involved, in their relationship to a research agenda, a community, or both. The researchers might be complicit with local communities in the investigation of archeological effects in a given or emergent context. Within the complicit agenda, the needs and interests, as well as subject positions, of each party are reflexively implicated in one another.

Explicitness

Considering research engagements and the production of knowledge, explicitness refers to that which is developed in detail and, hence, clear or definite. Explicitness thus refers to the disclosure of situated knowledge and the conditions of the production of that knowledge. In the case of Chunchucmil, I feel that the project is obligated to be explicit about how the ideology of development (namely, the development of tourism potential in an archaeological site) plays a key role in its agendas.

Collaboration

As opposed to the historically accepted mode of the lone ethnographer in the field, archaeological fieldwork is predicated upon the need for not only multiple researchers but also a good deal of labor from both skilled and unskilled local workers. An ethnography of archaeology requires not only that the ethnographer break out of the classic lone ethnographer mode but also that archaeologists realize the conditions of labor wrought within an excavation project. Thus, the concept of collaboration highlights the role of labor and cooperation in research endeavors. In a field site where multiple social actors are engaged (archaeologists,

ethnographers, state officials, and local communities, whose members might or
might not be involved with or even interested in the activities at the archaeological site), all parties are, in a strong sense, co-laborers. As diverse social actors
bring their own specialized skills, methods, and knowledge to the project at
hand, it should be considered that these contributions are not equal, and that outside influences, pressures, and commitments shape the particular mise-en-scène
of research.

Intervention

The multiple actions of archaeology within landscapes both ancient and contemporary are interventions in the daily lives of local residents, in the land
tenure regimes of areas targeted for excavation, as well as in the local, regional,
and national politics of heritage, development, and tourism. Indeed, "doing archaeology changes things" (Ardren et al. 2000). The nature of these "things" and
the spatio-temporal effects of the changes they suggest must be considered
within their proper cultural and historical context. Further, the disclosure of the
forms of intervention precipitated by excavation projects must be supplemented by the extra-archaeological context of the local landscape.

These concepts—by no means exhaustive—offer some important points of
departure in the construction of an ethnography of archaeology. Each has two
layers of significance. The first is methodological, referring to the goals of an investigation; in other words, how research gets done. This is the "insider"
sphere, which is generally concerned with researchers' relationships among
themselves and the project at hand. Each concept carries another layer of significance: the act of bringing the "outside" into the context of archaeological
practice. The "outside" is composed of everything otherwise thought to be ex-
traneous to the scientific project of archaeology such as local beliefs about the
ancient past, the identity politics of descendant communities, de jure and de
facto land use and ownership regimes, and general political economy. The inside and outside of the archaeological fieldwork project can also be described
as practical versus ethical research engagements. Practical refers to straight archaeological investigation while attention to the ethical opens the parameters
of the anthropological project to include the contingencies of fieldwork.

The distinction between these two different kinds of engagements is played
out through the spatialization of landscape into disciplinary turfs, so to speak.
While the excavation site is the realm of archaeology, ethnographers are expected to claim their stake in the living community. Just as ethnographers now
realize the fluidness of community (i.e., not always coterminous with geographical boundaries), newer currents in archaeological practice are particularly cognizant of the social and cultural politics of the field—not only in excavation work but also in the wider arena of knowledge production. However,
recognition of the importance of local relationships beyond obvious pragmatic
needs has not been a point of reflection in the discipline's mainstream dis-

course. Local populations are the communities from which projects draw their labor pools, in which they might live themselves for many months of the year. Yet what are the ethics of these pragmatic engagements?

Today, many archaeologists recognize that the field extends beyond the borders of officially recognized archaeological sites or zones. Indeed, this is what Bartu (2000) appropriately calls the recognition of "multiple sites of the archaeological site." In the interest of promoting ethical engagements, archaeologists associated with various forms of indigenous archaeologies, archaeology in the public interest, and social archaeology have moved their gaze beyond excavation sites toward local communities. What are the ethical implications in this site (or sight) shift? Does the local community become archaeologized, or subordinated to the goals and practices of archaeology? How do archaeologists distinguish pragmatic or logistical engagements with local communities from ethical engagements? Do fair hiring practices, decent wages, public disclosure of development plans, and so on, indicate ethical practice, or are they merely the logistics ultimately supporting archaeology's interest in furthering the data bank of scientific discovery? Indeed, this is troubling territory. Are ethical practices really just logistics in disguise?

During my time as a researcher in and around the Chunchucmil site, I observed archaeologists becoming increasingly involved with local community members. Certain assumptions on the part of archaeologists made me distinctly uncomfortable; namely, the assumption that archaeological development is both necessary and good and that residents of Kochol and Chunchucmil should embrace their ancient heritage. The cultural and political complexities of the production and reception of these assumptions, I believe, are tied to the confusion between the ethical desire to give back to local communities and the pragmatic need to meet the disciplinary mandate of getting the (archaeological) work done. An ethnography of archaeology begins by acknowledging this deep and often frustrating problem of how to carry out archaeology that meets both the standards of the discipline as well as the cultural context of the local community. What I thus offer in conclusion below is a series of suggestions for how ethnography of archaeology can aid in building a locally meaningful, ethical context for fieldwork.

CONCLUSION: AN ETHICAL
ETHNOGRAPHY OF ARCHAEOLOGY

An ethnography of archaeology can offer a detailed, historically and culturally specific context to aid in bridging the problem of conceptions of the local communities involved in and affected by archaeological projects. Rather than proceeding from situational ethics, in which no outside measures are brought in by which to set standards or judge a particular ethical interaction, these research agendas are based within what I term in situ ethics. The site that both forms and informs in situ ethics is a polyvalent assemblage of discourses and practices: historical and contemporary, local and global, inside and outside. From my own perspective, the baseline context for developing an in situ ethical engagement is the political economy of an archaeological site. That is, the contemporary and recent historical political economy of spaces that have become modern-day archaeological zones. An example of this from my own research involves the historical study (using property titles and *ejido* records, see Breglia 2003) of the transformations in land tenure and use and the ways in which current archaeological investigations promote an array of new kinds of land use. A second factor to consider is the degree of involvement by both governmental and nongovernmental organizations in the site or region. Is the community already a target of other governmental social programs or private sector development schemes? Is the community actively seeking development projects? Of what kind? Is the project sustainable by the community itself?

Via negativa, I will present a few points that move toward establishing some guidelines for what I believe ethnography of archaeology is *not*. First and foremost, ethnography of archaeology should not immediately be cast under the same rubric as applied anthropology. Second, in the collaborative undertaking, ethnography should not be seen as in the employ of archaeology: it should not be seen as a set of tasks and pieces of information that facilitate a business-as-usual attitude by an archaeological project. My third concern is with locations and objects of study: an ethnography of archaeology should not presume that the excavation site is the archaeologist's realm, and the "village" is the exclusive domain of the ethnographer. Neither is mutually exclusive. Bring the practice of ethnography to the archaeological site, and bring archaeology to the communities. And last but certainly not least, the ethnography of archaeology should not be entirely caught up in a closed hermeneutics of disciplinary self-reflexivity. It should always look to the outsides, to the unexplored disciplinary interstices: ethnography of archaeology thus has the challenging task of comprehending a continuously deterritorializing object of study. Finally, I suggest that we explore ethnography of archaeology not at its newly forming center but at its limits. By its limits I by no means suggest a task of identifying and enumerating its possible limitations. Instead, I am referring to working precisely in those decolonized areas viable-yet-hidden in the disciplinary interstices of ethnography and archaeology.

Can two very different sets of social actors work within an agenda in which they are ethically complicit? Can two disciplines work within an academic and social reality to mutually support an ethical research agenda that treats local community members as autonomous yet participatory agents within these agendas? Researchers, whether ethnographers or archaeologists, have an ethical commitment before they approach a field site and how they imagine this field site in relation to the living communities that share its space. The intention of this chapter is to further the possibilities of collaboration between archaeologists and ethnographers in the site of research itself, hoping that this can make for more ethical practice vis-à-vis those to whom our research is so important—the communities with whom we work.

NOTES

1. For an extended discussion of the effects of the henequen haciendas on these communities and its significance in terms of contemporary archaeological development, see Breglia (in press).

2. For a detailed discussion of a similar situation, see Castañeda's (1996) discussion of "zero degree culture" in relation to the Maya town of Pisté, located in close proximity to the archaeological site of Chichén Itzá.

3. In the years just following the linguistic turn in ethnography, marked by the publication of *Anthropology as Cultural Critique* (Marcus and Fischer 1986) and *Writing Culture* (Clifford and Marcus 1986), archaeology began to consider the possibilities of reflexive disciplinary practice, as well as the emergent context of the contingencies of archaeological interpretation. On the heels of ethnography's crisis of representation followed archaeologists such as Ian Hodder, Michael Shanks (1992), and Christopher Tilley (1993), who by the late 1980s–early 1990s were beginning to define a postprocessual archaeology based in a self-conscious reflexive, multivocal archaeological text.

4. However, it has interesting connections to the anthropology of science.

ACKNOWLEDGMENTS

I am particularly indebted to those members of the Pakbeh team who facilitated my research, especially Traci Ardren, Aline Magnoni, Scott Hutson, and Travis Stanton. Portions of this chapter were presented at the 5th World Archaeological Congress for the session "Ethnography of Archaeology." I thank organizers Matt Edgeworth and Denise Gomes for their invitation to participate.

REFERENCES

Ardren, T. 2002. Conversations about the production of archaeological knowledge and community museums at Chunchucmil and Kochol, Yucatán. *World Archaeology* 34 (2):379–400.

Ardren, T., et al. 2000. Archaeology and the Maya landscape at Chunchucmil, Yucatán, Mexico. Paper presented at the meetings of the American Anthropological Association, San Francisco.

Bartu, A. 2000. Where is Çatalhöyük? Multiple sites in the construction of an archaeological site. In *Towards a reflexive method in archaeology: The example at Çatalhöyük*, ed. I. Hodder, 101–10. Cambridge, UK: McDonald Institute Monographs.

Breglia, L. 2002a. In situ collaboration: Ethnographers and archaeologists in the field. Paper presented at Symposium on Ethics and the Practice of Archaeology, University of Pennsylvania Museum, Philadelphia.

———. 2002b. The temporality of stone: Monumental ambivalence in an archaeologized landscape. Paper presented at the meetings of the American Anthropological Association, New Orleans.

———. 2003. Docile descendants and illegitimate heirs: Privatization of cultural patrimony in Mexico. PhD diss., Rice University.

———. In press. *Monumental ambivalence: The politics of heritage.* Austin: University of Texas Press.

Castañeda, Q. 1996. *In the museum of Maya culture: Touring Chichén Itzá.* Minneapolis: University of Minnesota Press.

Clifford, J. 1997. *Routes: Travel and translation in the late twentieth century.* Cambridge, Mass.: Harvard University Press.

Clifford, J., and G. Marcus, eds. 1986. *Writing culture.* Berkeley: University of California Press.

Gupta, A., and J. Ferguson. 1997. *Anthropological locations: Boundaries and grounds of a field science.* Berkeley: University of California Press.

Hodder, I. 1983. *The present past: An introduction to anthropology for archaeologists.* New York: Pica Press.

———, ed. 1996. *On the Surface: Çatalhöyük 1993–95.* Cambridge, UK: McDonald Institute Monographs.

———. 1997. Always momentary, fluid and flexible: Towards a reflexive excavation methodology. *Antiquity* 71:691–700.

———. 1998. The past as passion and play: Çatalhöyük as a site of conflict in the construction of multiple pasts. In *Archaeology under fire: Nationalism, politics and heritage in the Eastern Mediterranean and Middle East,* ed. L. Meskell, 124–39. London: Routledge.

———. 2000. *Towards a reflexive method in archaeology: The example at Çatalhöyük.* Cambridge, UK: McDonald Institute Monographs.

Marcus, G. 1998. *Ethnography through thick and thin.* Princeton, N.J.: Princeton University Press.

Marcus, G., ed. 1999. Critical anthropology now: An introduction. In *Critical anthropology now.* Santa Fe: School of American Research.

Marcus, G., and M. Fischer. 1986. *Anthropology as cultural critique.* Chicago: University of Chicago Press.

Robin, C., and N. A. Rothschild. 2002. Archaeological ethnographies: Social dynamics of an outdoor space. *Journal of Social Archaeology* 2 (2):159–72.

Rodriguez, T. 2001. Maya perception of ancestral remains: Multiple places in a local space. *Berkeley McNair Research Journal* 9.

Shankland, D. 1997. The anthropology of an archaeological presence. In *On the surface: The re-opening of Çatalhöyük,* ed. I. Hodder, 186–202. Cambridge, UK: McDonald Institute Monographs.

Shankland, D. 1999a. Ethno-archaeology at Küçükköy. *Anatolian Archaeology* 5:23–24.

———. 1999b. Integrating the past: Folklore, mounds and people at Çatalhöyük. In *Archaeology and folklore,* ed. A. Gazin-Schwartz and C. Holtorf, 139–57. London: Routledge.

Shanks, M. 1992. *Experiencing archaeology.* London: Routledge.

Tilley, C. 1993. Interpretation and a poetics of the past. In *Interpretative Archaeology,* ed. C. Tilley, 1–27. Oxford: Berg.

Index

About the Contributors

Jonathan Bateman is information officer of the Council for British Archaeology. His main research interest lies in the relationship between archaeology and the images the discipline uses and creates, with a particular focus on photography both as a subject and as a tool for illustrating practice. His relevant publications include "Immediate Realities: An Anthropology of Computer Visualization in Archaeology" in *Internet Archaeology* 8 (2000) and "Wearing Juninho's Shirt: Record and Negotiation in Excavation Photographs" in *Envisioning the Past: Archaeology and the Image* (edited by Sam Smiles and Stephanie Moser, 2004).

Lisa Breglia is a cultural anthropologist who currently teaches at Wesleyan University in Connecticut. She has conducted extensive ethnographic and historical research in and around archaeological sites in Yucatán, Mexico. Full results of this fieldwork will be published in 2006 as *Monumental Ambivalence: The Politics of Heritage*. Her current research and writing projects focus on cultural and intellectual property policy in the context of globalization. As a key site for this study, she examines a Switzerland-based nongovernmental organization's worldwide project to name the New 7 Wonders of the World. This investigation details tensions between the international community's desire to promote a universal ethos of "the common heritage of Humankind" and the local significance of these monumental heritage sites.

John Carman has recently been appointed Research Fellow in Heritage Valuation at Birmingham University in the United Kingdom. His particular research interests include ideas about value and categorization of the archaeological heritage, and how ideas about ownership affect the management of objects, sites, and landscapes. He is also codirector with Patricia Carman of the Bloody Meadows Project on historic battlefields. His books include *Valuing Ancient Things: Archaeology and Law* (1996), *Ancient Warfare: Archaeological Perspectives* (coedited with Anthony Harding, 1999), and *Archaeology and Heritage: An Introduction* (2002). The first volume of results from the Bloody Meadows Project will be published in 2006.

Matt Edgeworth directs and manages archaeological projects in a commercial environment. Currently working as site director for Cambrian Archaeological Projects Ltd in the United Kingdom, he has a doctorate in archaeology and social anthropology from the University of Durham, UK, and is author of numerous excavation reports, urban surveys, and so forth. His ethnography of an archaeological excavation in England was recently published as *Acts of Discovery* (2003).

Oğuz Erdur has a BA in economics and an MS in environmental sciences from Bogaziçi University, Istanbul. He received an MPhil in cultural anthropology at Columbia University, where he is completing his PhD. His research combines ethnography with the philosophy of Friedrich Nietzsche, in order to produce a critique of archaeological knowledge production in Turkey. Erdur was "highly commended" at the third Worldwide Young Sociologists Competition organized in 1998 by the International Sociological Association. He is founding academic director of Platform for Social Archaeology (www.arkeoloji.org), an independent initiative in Turkey that aims to facilitate awareness and discussion about archaeological knowledge and heritage. His publications include *Archaeology: Why? How? What For?* (in Turkish), which he coedited in 2003.

Denise Maria Cavalcante Gomes has a PhD in archaeology from the Museu de Arqueologia e Etnologia, University of São Paulo, Brazil. She has conducted archaeological fieldwork alongside a traditional community called the Parauá, excavating archaeological sites related to the development of formative societies in the Santarém area of Amazonia. Her study of an important collection of ceramics from that region was published as a book entitled *Cerâmica Arqueológica da Amazônia: Vasilhas da Coleção Tapajônica* (2002). Her research interests include Amazonian archaeology, complex and formative precolonial societies in Amazonia, patterns of ceramic use, iconography, gender, the study of museum collections, and archaeological theory.

Charles Goodwin is professor of applied linguistics at the University of California, Los Angeles. His interests include the study of the discursive practices used by hearers and speakers to construct utterances, stories, and other forms of talk; language in the professions (for example, analysis of the courtroom arguments used to free the policemen who beat Rodney King); the ethnography of science (including studies of archaeological field excavations and oceanographers working in the mouth of the Amazon); cognition in the workplace (he spent two years as a member of the Workplace Project at Xerox PARC); and aphasia in discourse.

Anders Gustafsson is a part-time specialist with responsibility for research and development at the National Heritage Board in Stockholm and part-time lecturer in the Department of Archaeology, Gothenburg University. His main research interest is archaeological knowledge production, often from a historical angle. Current research topics are the ideology, theory, and history of archaeological heritage management and the archaeology of the contemporary past. Since 2002 he has been associate editor of the journal *Current Swedish Archaeology*.

Cornelius Holtorf is assistant professor of archaeology at the University of Lund in Sweden. His current research interests are the portrayal of archaeology in contemporary popular culture, the archaeology of zoos, and excavations of a multiperiod site in southern Portugal. His books include *Archaeology and Folklore* (coedited with A. Gazin-Schwartz, 1999), *Philosophy and Archaeological Practice* (coedited with H. Karlsson, 2000), *Monumental Past* (2000), and *From Stonehenge to Las Vegas: Archaeology as Popular Culture* (2005).

Dirk Jacobs is associate professor in sociology at the Université Libre de Bruxelles (Francophone university in Brussels, Belgium). He also teaches at the Katholieke Universiteit Brussel (Flemish university in Brussels, Belgium). Jacobs studied sociology at Ghent University (Belgium) and obtained his PhD in social sciences at Utrecht University (the Netherlands). His research interests include ethnic minorities and political sociology. He teaches courses on sociology, history of sociology, methodology, and quantitative analysis.

Håkan Karlsson is lecturer and director of studies in the Department of Archaeology, Göteborg University, Sweden. He received his doctorate at the department in Gothenburg in 1998. He has written books and articles on topics such as the past in the present, the relationship between archaeology and its public, archaeology's political dimensions, and the epistemology and ontology of archaeology, and he has also coedited several books dealing with these themes. His current research is primarily based on the projects "Cultural Heritage as Societal Dialogue" and "The Contemporary Past in Antiquarian Theory and Practice," which analyze communicative relationships between archaeology/heritage management and the public.

Angela McClanahan has a PhD in archaeology from the University of Manchester, UK, and teaches at the University of Glasgow Crichton Campus in Dumfries, Scotland. Her research interests include the significance and politics of the archaeological past as it is perceived and constructed in the present (especially in

Scotland and the U.S. Southwest) and the role of heritage management in mediating people's experience of archaeological monuments and objects.

Timoteo Rodriguez studied for a BA and MA in anthropology at the University of California, Berkeley. As an undergraduate he was a McNair Scholar and a Haas Scholar. These research scholarships facilitated the three field visits to Yucatán, Mexico, from which the ethnographic data for his chapter was collected. In Yucatán he worked as an archaeological apprentice and an independent ethnographer. His overarching inquiry: what is the relationship of a Yucatecan farming community to the ancient remains embedded in their communal land, and to the foreigners who conduct research on that land? Rodriguez is currently pursuing a PhD as a Chancellor's Fellow at University of California, Berkeley.

Blythe E. Roveland received a BA in anthropology and German from Binghamton University, New York, an MA and PhD in anthropology from the University of Massachusetts, Amherst, and an MLS from St. John's University. She has been the university archivist at St. John's University in New York since 2000. Her research interests include Paleolithic archaeology, the history of archaeology, children in the archaeological record, and juvenile literature with prehistoric themes. Among her publications are articles in *Children and Anthropology: Perspectives for the 21st century* (edited by Helen Schwartzman, 2001), and *Children and Material Culture* (edited by Joanna Sofaer Derevenski, 2000).

David Van Reybrouck is a postdoctoral research fellow of the Fund for Scientific Research, Flanders, who is affiliated with the Department of History of the Katholieke Universiteit Leuven, the Netherlands. He was trained as an archaeologist in Leuven, Cambridge, and Leiden. His research interests include history, theory, and ethnography of (prehistoric) archaeology; history of primatology; and the archaeology of zoos. He has been associate editor of the journal *Archaeological Dialogues* since 1994 and founded, together with Cornelius Holtorf, the British Academy network "The Archaeology of Zoos." In his native language (Dutch) he is equally active as a novelist, a poet, and a playwright.

Michael Wilmore is lecturer at the University of Adelaide, South Australia, where he teaches anthropology. He holds degrees in both archaeology and anthropology and has taught at University College London and for the Open University in the United Kingdom. He has conducted research into the development of media in Nepal and worked as part of the research team of the Leskernick Project. His work explores theoretical and methodological connections between disciplines, particularly media studies and anthropology.

Thomas Yarrow is a doctoral student in the Department of Social Anthropology, University of Cambridge, UK. He has recently returned from Ghana where he spent a year doing participant observation among nongovernmental organizations. Current theoretical interests include the production and circulation of "development" knowledge and the nature of interpersonal relationships among Ghanaian "elites." Previously he worked in developer-funded archaeology, where he became interested in issues of knowledge production and the practice of excavation.